Taking Flight

Number Twenty-one

CENTENNIAL OF FLIGHT

ROGER D. LAUNIUS, GENERAL EDITOR

Taking Flight

The Foundations of American Commercial Aviation, 1918–1938

M. Houston Johnson V

TEXAS A&M UNIVERSITY PRESS
COLLEGE STATION

First edition

This paper meets the requirements of ANSI/NISO Z39.48–1992
(Permanence of Paper).
Binding materials have been chosen for durability.
Manufactured in the United States of America

Library of Congress Cataloging-in-Publication Data

Names: Johnson, M. Houston, V, author.
Title: Taking flight: the foundations of American commercial aviation, 1918–1938 / M. Houston Johnson V.
Description: First edition. | College Station: Texas A&M University Press, [2019] | Series: Centennial of flight; number twenty-one |
Identifiers: LCCN 2018032360 (print) | LCCN 2018043501 (ebook) | ISBN 9781623497224 (ebook) | ISBN 9781623497217 | ISBN 9781623497217 (hardcover: alk. paper)
Subjects: LCSH: Aeronautics, Commercial—United States—History—20th century. | Aeronautics and state—United States—History—20th century. | Aeronautics, Commercial—Government policy—United States—History—20th century.
Classification: LCC HE9803.A3 (ebook) | LCC HE9803.A3 J65 2019 (print) | DDC 387.70973/09041—dc23
LC record available at https://lccn.loc.gov/2018032360

For Kachina

Contents

Acknowledgments

A host of individuals and institutions offered me invaluable support in the research, writing, and editing of this manuscript. Archivists at the National Archives in Washington, DC, and College Park, Maryland; the University of Miami Special Collections; the American Heritage Center at the University of Wyoming; the Smithsonian Institution; Columbia University; the East Tennessee History Center; the Herbert Hoover Presidential Library; and the Franklin D. Roosevelt Presidential Library facilitated my research and helped me locate a plethora of sources. The University of Tennessee, Virginia Military Institute, American Heritage Center, Pan American Airways Historical Foundation, Gilder Lehrman Institute of American History, and Herbert Hoover Presidential Library Association offered generous financial support to fund that research agenda. Colleagues including Mark Wilson, Jason Scott Smith, Jenifer Van Vleck, and members of the Department of History at the Virginia Military Institute read part or all of the manuscript and offered valuable feedback and advice. Jay Dew, my editor, and the entire staff at Texas A&M University Press could not have been more supportive; my deepest thanks to them for their assistance.

Special thanks must go to my dissertation director, G. Kurt Piehler, who helped with every step of the process. He led me to embrace aviation history during my time at the University of Tennessee, provided ongoing support and guidance as I researched and wrote my dissertation, and continued to offer wise counsel as I revised the dissertation into the monograph before you and sought a publisher. His mentorship and friendship have been wonderful influences; I am continually thankful for our relationship.

Finally, I never could have undertaken this project without the support of my family. My mother and father, and most significantly my wife,

Kachina, were always there to provide a ready ear, a critical reading, and a source of sympathy. Kachina's willingness to help me organize my research and endure my absence on research trips, countless hours hunched in front of the computer, and endless conversations about aviation policy and technology made this book possible—I cannot thank her enough.

Taking Flight

Introduction

Between the world wars American aeronautics experienced a radical transformation. These years witnessed the most dynamic developmental period in the nation's aeronautical history as aviation grew from infancy to maturity in less than twenty years. In 1918 a fledgling US Army airmail service struggled to move a tiny amount of mail from Washington, DC, to New York in unreliable open-cockpit biplanes barely faster than contemporary trains; by 1938 passengers could fly coast-to-coast in relative comfort, and airlines were preparing to inaugurate regular commercial service across both the Atlantic and the Pacific. This remarkable period thrust the United States to the forefront of aeronautical development, set the stage for the Army Air Force's wartime success, and laid the foundation for the postwar emergence of the country's modern air transport network.

Federal engagement with American flying played an essential role in facilitating aviation's dramatic interwar growth. During that era policy makers, including Herbert Hoover, William MacCracken, Walter Brown, Hugo Black, Franklin Roosevelt, and Harry Hopkins, played foundational roles in fostering American aeronautics' maturation. Their efforts to create and sustain a coherent federal aviation policy made commercial development possible, in the process laying the foundations of the modern US air transport network. Federal aviation policy during this period serves as an important example of activist government's ability to positively affect the commercial sector. More specifically, it offers a largely unexplored arena in which to examine concrete gains wrought by Hoover's associationalist ideology and Roosevelt's New Deal. Those gains are even more intriguing when considering that aviation achieved financial viability during the Great Depression, an unlikely time for commercial growth and a time of fundamental redefinition of government's proper role. That period thus provides the opportunity to examine the connections between federal aviation policy and larger conceptions of government's proper relationship to the economy and to elucidate aviation's significance within the larger narrative of American economic development.

Within that context, several themes stand out. First, federal efforts to promote the development of commercial aviation demonstrated surprising coherence during the era. In spite of the distinctions many historians have drawn between Herbert Hoover's associationalist economic philosophy and the activism of Franklin Roosevelt's New Deal, their administrations embraced remarkable consistency in their support for commercial flying. Beginning with Hoover's confirmation as commerce secretary in 1921 and continuing through that decade and the next, policy makers focused on creating a regulatory structure to promote safe, efficient commercial operations, promoting commercial flying to the American people, using federal resources to support the creation of infrastructure, and subsidizing nascent airlines through Post Office airmail contracts. This federal activism reflected policy makers' belief that a mature commercial aviation industry would benefit US economics and national defense; in many cases it also reflected the private sector's desire for federal guidance and support. Both public and private actors recognized that the federal government was the only entity with the power and reach to usher the fragile airline industry to maturity. This is particularly remarkable considering policy makers and business leaders remained committed to that vision before and after the onset of the Great Depression and through the transition from Republican to Democratic dominance in Congress and the White House.

Hoover and Roosevelt, however, did not exhibit total coherence in their efforts. While Hoover's commitment to associationalism resulted in a focus on using existing regulatory structures, such as the Commerce Department, to facilitate commercial development, Roosevelt eschewed such limitations. His willingness to create new bureaucratic structures like the Civil Aeronautics Administration and his embrace of public works agencies' ability to fund the creation of aviation infrastructure signaled Roosevelt's commitment to expanding federal responsibilities toward the industry. These distinctions, however, represent differences in degree rather than in kind. Though Roosevelt clearly embraced a more aggressive vision for federal support, that vision remained grounded in Hoover's foundational paradigm.

Second, policy makers' commitment to providing airlines financial support through "informal" subsidies—in the form of Post Office airmail contracts—sharply differentiates the American narrative from that of other developed countries. US policy makers were united in the belief that airmail subsidies represented a way to protect the fledgling airline industry from the perils of the free market while offering an alternative to more direct forms of governmental control. This policy stood in contrast to the contemporary path traveled by European nations, which overwhelmingly embraced nationalization. US airline development therefore represents a global outlier, a fact further emphasizing the significance of federal actions.

Finally, policy makers' fundamental agreement regarding the need to support commercial development and the consistent effort expended to achieve that goal by politicians, federal officials, business leaders, and a wide range of aviation advocates highlights Americans' engagement with aeronautics. While it would be too simplistic to draw a direct line between Americans' ongoing fascination with flying—what historian Joseph Corn dubs "air mindedness"—and federal policy, it is clear that the larger context of enthusiasm created an environment facilitating federal actions and commercial growth. That enthusiasm helps to explain how figures as diverse as Herbert Hoover and Franklin Roosevelt, Walter Brown and Hugo Black, could embrace a fundamentally similar perspective on federal policy—policy that successfully ushered US commercial flying into a position of global leadership.

Although manned powered flight originated in the United States, American aeronautics developed haltingly in the years after the Wright brothers' ascent in 1903. In those early years flying almost exclusively served as a form of entertainment. Few observers believed that aviation would ever amount to anything more than a spectacle; during that period flying remained the domain of wealthy sportsman, daredevils, adrenaline junkies, and military servicemen. Planes were fragile and slow, with limited load capacity and dubious reliability. Flying was dangerous, as scores of early "birdmen" found out too late. In their efforts to entertain crowds, reach new heights and speeds, or simply loose themselves from the bonds of earth, pilots fell from the skies in shocking numbers. Virtually all of the noteworthy pilots of the prewar era, including Lincoln Beachey, Archibald Hoxey, Ralph Johnstone, and Harriet Quimby, ultimately plunged to their deaths. While the American public demonstrated an almost universal fascination with flying, attending air shows and aerial "circuses" by the tens of thousands, Americans overwhelmingly viewed aviation as a dangerous form of entertainment—exciting, but hardly the basis for a stable form of commercial transportation.

Early long-distance flights highlighted the challenges commercial operators would have to overcome to inaugurate safe and reliable air transport service. Perhaps the most famous example occurred in 1911, when Calbraith Perry Rodgers attempted to claim a fifty-thousand-dollar prize offered by William Randolph Hearst to the first pilot to cross the country by air in thirty days or less. Rodgers piloted his Wright Model EX biplane from New York to the West Coast but fell short of winning Hearst's prize, ultimately taking forty-nine days to complete the transit. During this first "successful" cross-country flight, Rodgers stopped sixty-nine times, crashed as many as thirty-nine times—estimates vary, as the distinction between a hard landing and a crash was murky, at best—and replaced almost every piece of his aircraft. When he landed in Pasadena, one of his plane's two rudders and a single wing strut were all that remained from the craft that took to the skies in New York. Rodgers also suffered a broken leg, shrapnel wounds from an exploding cylinder, and numerous cuts and bruises during his transit.

In spite of these daunting obstacles, some aerial pioneers did attempt to make the business of flying work. Only three years after Rodgers's cross-country odyssey a group of Florida investors inaugurated the United States'—and the world's—first scheduled airline service, the short-lived St. Petersburg–Tampa Airboat Line. The airline operated for only three months, between January and March of 1914, but it did achieve some notable successes. Flying during peak tourist season, the airboat line offered a short thirty-minute flight across Tampa Bay, saving its passengers a three-hour boat passage or twelve hours by train. During its tenure the airline transported hundreds of passengers without suffering a fatality. As the tourist season wound down, however, high overhead, waning public enthusiasm, and dwindling passenger numbers doomed the operation.[1] This episode suggested that aviation might have a commercial future, but the airboat line's ultimate failure in the face of almost ideal circumstances—a committed group of backers; good weather; tremendous local enthusiasm; a short, easy, attractive route; and its seaplanes' lack of need for runways or other land-based infrastructure—highlighted just how difficult it would be to establish stable commercial service.

Though the failed Saint Petersburg to Tampa effort effectively ended forays into commercial flying for the next four years, by the spring of 1918 momentum had begun to build for a much larger endeavor: a government-funded airmail service. The federal government had demonstrated a limited interest in aeronautical development as early as 1915 with the establishment of the National Advisory Committee for Aeronautics (NACA), but support for commercial flying remained virtually unknown until aviation found an energetic new supporter in the Post Office Department. Following his appointment as second assistant postmaster in the fall of 1916, Otto Praeger spearheaded an effort to develop a regularly scheduled airmail service. Recognizing aviation's potential to revolutionize commercial transportation, Praeger identified a number of potential test routes, finally settling on a short run from Washington, DC, to New York with a stop in Philadelphia. Lacking any infrastructure, including pilots, planes, or mechanics, Praeger turned to the army to supply the needed manpower and material. Somewhat grudgingly, the army acquiesced, inaugurating service on May 15, 1918. The military ran the service for a year before turning operations over to the Post Office, which by that time had hired pilots, purchased aircraft, and initiated plans to expand operations. During the next six years the Post Office extended the airmail map across the country, inaugurating coast-to-coast service and creating a truly national network before handing over routes to private contractors starting in 1925.

In the spring of 1918, however, there was little evidence to suggest that the army effort would amount to anything more than a stunt. As Praeger and his allies prepared to initiate the United States' first scheduled airmail operation, they had to overcome serious challenges before they could even consider launching the service. Most significantly, New York, Philadelphia, and Washington, DC, lacked suitable airports. There was literally no ground-based infrastructure from which to operate the airmail service. Under Praeger's direction the Post Office and the army worked together to identify suitable landing fields. In Washington they settled on the Polo Grounds—not an airport in any formal sense, but a flat, grassy field large enough to allow aircraft to take off and land. In Philadelphia officials chose a small field near Bustleton, northeast of the city. Although the venue lacked any formal infrastructure, it did provide a well-sited landing area with easy road access to downtown. New York offered the greatest challenge, and there officials embraced the most creative solution. After rejecting a number of possible sites, including public parks and gardens, officials turned to the Belmont Park horse racing circuit. Belmont housed one of the most active racetracks in the country, which on its face made it an odd choice for an airmail terminal. The racetrack, however, had a large, flat infield section that would allow safe aircraft operation. Additionally, the complex had improved road access and was close enough to the city to make operations viable. Remarkably, airmail planes often took off and landed during races, biplanes racing thoroughbreds down the backstretch.[2]

Praeger and army officials also struggled to field qualified pilots and aircraft. Although the United States was at war in Europe in the spring of 1918, the army had a pitifully small number of trained pilots, the majority of whom were deployed overseas. As a result, the pilots assigned to airmail operations lacked adequate training and experience. Of the six pilots initially assigned to fly the mail, two lacked practice flying cross-country and three had been flying for fewer than four months. Only one pilot, Lieutenant Paul Culver, had what any informed observer would term adequate training for the job.[3]

The airmail service's aircraft exhibited analogous limitations. Praeger identified the Curtis JN-4—an army training aircraft known as the Jenny—as a viable plane for the job. The Jenny was arguably the most important American aircraft of the First World War. A two-seat biplane trainer, the Jenny was robust, easy to fly, and readily available. During the war 95 percent of American and Canadian pilots received instruction in a Jenny, and with more than six thousand ultimately produced, it was the most numerous American aircraft of the era. Unfortunately, the Jenny was also slow and possessed a limited cargo capacity.

Attempting to make the most of the available hardware, Praeger contracted with the Curtis Aeroplane Company to modify a fleet of Jennies for airmail use. The Post Office requested that the manufacturer retrofit their aircraft with a mail compartment, replacing the craft's second cockpit. Praeger also mandated that the airmail service's Jennies receive more powerful engines than their standard ninety-horsepower OX-5 units. Although the new Hispano-Suiza engines produced 50 percent more power than the OX-5, the Jenny's cargo capacity remained limited to the weight of a flight trainee: 160 pounds. The planes were also saddled with numerous other limitations—a lack of instrumentation, leaking fuel tanks, and unreliable engines—all of which represented the norm rather than the exception for the day.[4]

In spite of these challenges, the inaugural airmail flight from Washington, DC, on May 15 aroused widespread excitement. President Woodrow Wilson attended the event along with his wife and, notably, Assistant Secretary of the Navy Franklin Roosevelt. According to the *Washington Post*, the flight represented "one of the epoch making events in the [history of] the United States postal service," a sentiment echoed by the *New York Times*. The *Times* reported that airmail service would "go down in history" as inaugurating a new era, "the forerunner of a network of aerial mail lines which will cover the entire world." This official recognition boded well for the new service, and army and Post Office officials did their best not to disappoint.[5]

Despite some initial problems starting the plane's engine—it later emerged that the ground crew had forgotten to fuel it—the flight departed to great fanfare. The pilot, Lieutenant George Boyle, took off smoothly and proceeded on his way—in the wrong direction. Boyle, lacking experience in cross-country navigation, used a road map to guide his way to Philadelphia. Apparently he also lacked a strong sense of direction and followed his chosen railroad-line guide south from the city rather than north. Failing to realize his error, Boyle flew for almost an hour before landing in Waldorf, Maryland, some twenty-five miles southeast of the capital.

Boyle's tribulations were far from finished. Two days later he again lost his way trying to reach Philadelphia. Hoping to forestall the directional difficulties that undermined his earlier flight, Boyle's superiors carefully briefed him to fly east to the Chesapeake Bay, turn left—north—and then follow the bay's shoreline toward Philadelphia. Unfortunately, Boyle interpreted these instructions a bit too literally, as he continued to follow the shoreline, even after crossing the mouth of the Susquehanna River, and traveled south down Maryland's Eastern Shore. After more than three hours Boyle reached the end of his fuel supply and the end of the shoreline as he came face-to-face with the Atlantic Ocean.[6]

Boyle's blunders notwithstanding, for the most part the service experienced success during its first months of service. These early days of operations, however, only further served to demonstrate the primitive conditions facing air transport operations. Pilots had to deal with notoriously unreliable compasses—one of the contributing factors in Boyle's misadventures. Incongruously, the compass represented the only instrument in these early aircraft, yet pilots found that it would often spin aimlessly or provide demonstrably false readings. Captain Benjamin Lipsner, the operations officer for the service, identified the Jenny's control stick as a contributing factor in these problems. Apparently the stick, made of metal, would cause the compass "to go into a crazy little spin" when pilots pushed their controls forward toward the instrument panel. Even after mechanics switched the metal control stick for a wooden one, Lipsner reported that pilots could seldom rely on their compasses. Instead, "smoking chimneys, railroad tracks, creeks, rivers, and similarly outstanding landmarks" offered the most reliable navigational aids.[7]

These problems persisted as airmail service expanded. As late as 1925 pilots found themselves saddled with inferior or nonexistent instrumentation. Flying the mail from New York to Boston, Leroy Ponce de Arce reported that he and his fellow pilots struggled with piloting their craft in poor weather. Their Fokker Universals—high-winged, single-engined metal monoplanes—had a compass, airspeed indicator, and tachometer but no instruments to relay information about the craft's attitude or altitude. As a result, these fliers had no way of determining their plane's orientation when flying in overcast or clouds. Without visual references pilots quickly experience vertigo, losing any sense of up and down in the three-dimensional world aloft. In this environment planes can stall or spin, making flying blind extremely dangerous, particularly at low altitude. Necessity serving as the handmaid of invention, however, Arce and his fellow pilots responded to the danger by purchasing small carpenter levels and fixing them to the side of their planes' fuselage. Preparing for bad weather, the fliers would practice climbing in clear air, increasing the attitude of their climb while looking at the level until the aircraft stalled. Then they created their own makeshift instrument by marking the level with red paint at the point where the aircraft stalled, yellow where it was about to stall, and green where it continued to fly well.[8] This ingenious method allowed airmail pilots to climb through overcast in relative safety, though it was far from an ideal solution. Not until the early 1930s did altimeters and proper turn and bank indicators become standard in the industry.

Poor weather conditions often forced pilots to make difficult choices. In cloudy conditions, or when a solid overcast presented itself, pilots could—like Arce and his fellows—attempt to climb above the offending obstructions to (hopefully) conclude their trip in clear air above. This strategy carried risk, however, as there was no guarantee that the pilots would be able to descend safely at their destination, if they could find it at all. Without radar or radio, pilots had to rely on dead reckoning to determine their position above the clouds; unknown wind patterns, poor compasses, and a lack of visual references could conspire to make this extremely difficult at best. If they were lucky the weather would be clear over their destination, but in winter months in the Northeast, clouds often extended along the entire Eastern Seaboard. Regardless of whether they knew exactly where they were, pilots flying above the weather had to descend eventually. When they did, they let down into the unknown. Clouds and fog could extend all the way to the ground, and in mountainous areas the bottom of the cloud layer often extended below the tops of local peaks. In these conditions an unfortunate pilot's first inkling that he had reached the bottom of the cloud layer could be a hill or tree looming out of the fog. Adding insult to injury, a lack of proper turn and bank indicators meant that pilots risked losing control of their aircraft when flying in clouds for any length of time.

Pilots had to contend with myriad navigational problems as well. In the post–World War I era there were no aerial navigation maps, so pilots used ordinary road maps—hardly the most reliable when operating cross-country. Navigation aids such as radios and beacon lights were nonexistent. In 1921, as the Post Office attempted to prove the viability of cross-country airmail service, officials were forced to employ a veritable army of volunteers across the western half of the country to light bonfires at regular intervals to help guide airmail pilots flying at night.

Responding to these prevailing conditions, pilots quickly found the most effective strategy to be to memorize all aspects of their specific airmail route and never lose sight of the ground. Pilots frequently created detailed notebooks containing prominent landmarks, areas with tricky wind conditions, and potential emergency landing fields. This often led to harrowing tales as pilots flew just above—and at times below—the treetops to escape low clouds. During the early years of airmail service several pilots reported almost colliding with trains while following railroad tracks at extremely low altitude in bad weather; others landed with branches and leaves in their wings and undercarriage.

The primitive nature of these early operations, however, offered pilots options that would have been unthinkable even a few short years later. Pilots who lost their way or ran out of gas often resorted to landing in convenient fields, walking to the nearest house, and asking the owner for aid. Major Reuben Fleet, the air officer in charge of the army's airmail service, resorted to just this tactic while attempting to deliver an aircraft to Philadelphia during the inaugural airmail flight. Fleet lost his way on the flight south from New York and landed to ask directions from a farmer. Resuming his journey, Fleet again became confused and set down on a golf course to ask for directions, damaging his aircraft in the process. After making the necessary repairs and turning the aircraft over to a more experienced pilot, darkness set in, causing Fleet to ask passing motorists for assistance in helping his fellow aviator take off. After persuading several to stop and light the "runway" with their headlights, the aircraft took off and made it safely to the airmail field at Bustleton.[9]

Circumstances like these defined the primitive nature of early air transport operations. Pilots had to fly by the proverbial seat of their pants, trusting instinct and experience to get them through difficult situations. Unreliable equipment and unproven operating procedures combined to make flying regularly scheduled routes an iffy proposition at best. Adding to these difficulties, until 1926 the government had no power to license pilots, inspect aircraft, and assure that aircraft manufacturers conformed to basic safety standards.

In these conditions, comfortable, safe, and reliable passenger service was only a dream. In the late 1920s government airmail subsidies made mail far more valuable to carriers than to passengers, with the result that many passengers were unceremoniously denied their ticketed seat when mail volume proved too great to allow both correspondence and passenger in the plane. When early airmail carriers did consent to carry passengers, the hapless travelers often found themselves sitting atop mail sacks in open-cockpit biplanes. Even if passengers were lucky enough to fly in an enclosed passenger compartment, they had to deal with rough air, poor ventilation, and airsickness. The last was so pervasive that airmail pilot Ben Odell Howard believed the industry had ushered in a new era when only 75 percent of passengers experienced airsickness—and Howard made it clear that he and his peers measured airsickness "by actual evidence," not merely the way that someone felt. Conditions remained so uncomfortable that as late as 1930, Ellen Church, the first female flight attendant and a registered nurse, questioned "why anyone rode at all."[10]

By 1939, however, the industry had experienced fundamental changes. Federal regulation, technological development, and commercial growth combined to create a mature air transport network. Passengers could choose to fly a number of established airlines, many of which are still in operation today. Those airlines used modern terminal buildings—at least in large cities—with regular ticketing and baggage procedures. The Douglas DC-3, a twin-engined aircraft that could comfortably seat more than twenty passengers, ruled the skies. The DC-3 had engine cowlings, retractable landing gear, deicing equipment in its wings, a full slate of navigational and communication equipment, and the ability to cruise at more than twice the top speed of the early airmail craft. Passengers could travel from coast to coast in less than thirty-six hours on regularly scheduled passenger routes. Those routes included radio communications with ground-based dispatchers, radio-based navigational aids, and emergency landing fields if something should go wrong. A national air traffic control system guided aircraft in the skies, maintaining spacing between flights and directing aircraft to crowded airports in bad weather. If money and time allowed, Americans could board a Pan American Airways Clipper flying boat and fly to Europe, Hawaii, or even Hong Kong while enjoying gourmet food, the attentions of a highly trained cabin crew, and comfortable sleeping berths.

Americans who took to the air could rest assured in the knowledge that the government policed the aviation industry through the auspices of a dedicated organization, the Civil Aeronautics Authority. Federal officials licensed all pilots for private, multiengine, instrument, and commercial flying. They inspected manufacturers and awarded airworthiness certificates for all new or significantly modified airframes. Federal employees operated the air traffic control system, and the government consistently funded technological research into new communication, engine, and airframe technologies. Additionally, the federal government continued to support a massive program for the creation of aviation-related infrastructure. Hundreds of millions of federal dollars paid for airport improvements, new fields, and air marking campaigns around the country. As a result, the majority of American population centers with more than five thousand residents had a modern airport complete with lighting, radio communication, a control tower, and multiple concrete or asphalt runways.

Federal efforts to regulate and promote aviation did not emerge in a vacuum. In fact, they reflected a logical—though still significant—development of preexisting American transportation policy stretching back more than 150 years. Although the federal government played a minimal role in crafting transportation policy until the middle of the nineteenth century, almost from the moment of the United States' founding, state and local governments began aggressively to promote transportation infrastructure. Often haphazard, these efforts aided the creation of toll roads, turnpikes, canals, wagon roads, and ferries. As Americans pushed west, state and local efforts to promote infrastructure became increasingly important to economic growth, particularly after the invention of steam-powered boats. As these powered craft came to dominate America's waterways in the nineteenth century, state governments contributed approximately 70 percent of the $125 million spent on canal construction nationally. Communities desiring to play an active role in emerging commercial networks worked diligently to create sufficient infrastructure and make themselves attractive to commercial interests.[11]

The federal government, however, generally proved loath to involve itself with transportation, at least until the midpoint of the nineteenth century. Although early in the century Henry Clay's promotion of the "American System" of internal improvements provided modest support for infrastructure development, according to Robert Dilger, "prior to 1850, the national government's involvement in transportation policy is best characterized as indirect and limited."[12]

Federal reluctance began to diminish as railroads came to play an increasingly important role in American commerce. By the middle of the nineteenth century the federal government embraced several policies focused specifically on promoting the growth of American railways. First, in 1838 the government designated all railroads as postal routes, offering the possibility of subsidy through mail carriage. At the same time, a growing federal consensus that railroads offered an effective means of promoting interstate commerce resulted in efforts to subsidize expansion. Constitutional limitations forbade direct federal subsidies, but lawmakers effectively circumvented these constraints by donating nationally owned land to states. States then sold that land at auction and gave the proceeds to railways. By the turn of the twentieth century the federal government had provided more than 130 million acres of land for railroad improvements, with states contributing almost 50 million more.[13]

At the beginning of the twentieth century the federal government turned its attention to roads. Throughout the nineteenth century state and local governments supported road development on a limited basis, but by the early 1900s the increasing prevalence of the automobile signaled an ever-increasing need for additional infrastructure. Responding to that need, in 1916 the federal government passed the Federal Road Act, approving an expenditure of seventy-five million dollars to improve rural postal roads. The government dispersed these funds to states over a period of five years with the mandate that states provide matching funds on a fifty-fifty basis. At the same time, states began to increase their regulation of highways. In 1913 New Jersey became the first state to mandate a driver's license for anyone operating a motor vehicle, a requirement gradually adopted by other states in following years.[14]

At the same time, the federal government began to play a more active role in regulating transportation, largely through the auspices of the Constitution's Interstate Commerce Clause. Following the creation of the Interstate Commerce Commission (ICC) in 1887, the government embraced newfound responsibilities for American transportation systems. Largely a reaction to the perceived growth of unhealthy monopolies in the railroad industry, the ICC's activism signaled a new federal willingness to referee commercial growth and regulate commercial activity.[15]

By the early years of the twentieth century, then, the federal government embraced an ever-expanding role in the regulation and promotion of American transportation. Federal funds—indirect though they may have been—played a crucial role in promoting railroad growth, and federal regulation of both railroads and vehicular travel suggested a growing consensus that lawmakers saw themselves as having at least some measure of responsibility over these commercial interests. Significantly, it appears that in many cases this federal activity emerged out of a broad consensus shared by lawmakers and businessmen to regulate for business and encourage growth, a pattern echoed in early federal efforts to regulate aeronautics.[16]

Commercial aviation, therefore, emerged during a period of growing federal activism in the transportation arena. In this context federal efforts to regulate the nascent airline industry and promote commercial development through informal subsidization reflect the ongoing emergence of a political consensus. At the same time, however, aviation's fragile nature, its relative danger, and its association with daring and glamour meant that federal efforts to shape the industry's growth differed in significant respects from those for other forms of transportation. Most significantly, those factors suggest that policy makers such as Herbert Hoover, Walter Brown, and William MacCracken were remarkably prescient in their recognition of aviation's potential for future growth, safety, and profitability. These men's vision emerged very early in aviation's commercial development—far earlier than comparable federal engagement with railroads or automobiles—and highlights their particular focus on an exciting but unproven technology.

The relative commercial positions of railroads and aviation during the interwar era underscore the prescience of emerging federal policies. The early 1900s represented the zenith of America's railroad age. As late as 1932 there were more than twenty thousand locomotives in service across the country, railroad stations dominated the American urban landscape, and the train remained synonymous with long-distance transportation of people and cargo. In contrast, Washington Airport, one of the busiest in the country at the time, saw only about 250 passengers a day walk through its terminal. In fact, according to historians Mark Rose, Bruce Seely, and Paul Barrett, "even in 1940, airplanes presented no serious challenge to long-distance railroads, or even buses." This disparity goes a long way toward explaining why railroads offered virtually no opposition to federal efforts to support aeronautical growth. Aviation remained so fragile in the years before World War II, and passenger numbers and cargo volumes so small, that airlines presented little or no direct competition for railroads during the period. In this environment, policy makers' identification of aviation's potential appears even more farsighted.[17]

Historians' treatment of this pivotal era in American aeronautical development has been surprisingly sparse. While the public enjoys ready access to books focused on myriad aspects of aviation—from popular histories of specific planes and famous pilots to thematic works detailing subjects such as barnstorming and air racing—scholarly interest in commercial aviation has not witnessed the same proliferation.[18] The development of federal policy, in particular, has been largely overlooked until relatively recently. This dearth highlights the need for a comprehensive analysis of the development of federal aviation policy between the world wars.

Scholars' engagement with interwar commercial aviation evinces several themes. First, a number of historians provide narrative histories of aeronautical development. Henry Ladd Smith's *Airways: The History of Commercial Aviation in the United States* offers the foundational work in this genre. Originally published in 1942, Smith's work provides a comprehensive overview of the interwar period but relies almost entirely on interviews and media sources, as he lacked access to both public and private archival documents. Additionally, Smith's ambivalent take on Hoover's policies—particularly Walter Brown's actions—reflects the prevailing influence of New Deal politics and assumptions that the preceding Republican administrations had mismanaged the economy. Those limitations notwithstanding, Smith's research colored several generations of subsequent scholarship, including works from R. E. G. Davies and Carl Solberg. More recent works—most notably Roger Bilstein's *Flight in America: From the Wrights to the Astronauts* and T. A. Heppenheimer's *Turbulent Skies: The History of Commercial Aviation*—offer a range of perspectives on aeronautical development while touching only briefly on federal policy.[19]

The relationship between aviation and American culture forms a second prominent theme. All works in this genre reflect the influence of Joseph Corn's seminal work, *The Winged Gospel: America's Romance with Aviation, 1900–1950*. Connecting aviation to Americans' focus on technological prowess and national development, Corn contends that the United States enjoyed a unique relationship with aeronautics, embracing it as a "gospel" that held untold promises for the country's future. Subsequent cultural studies have built upon Corn's foundational thesis, most significantly David Courtwright's *Sky As Frontier: Adventure, Aviation and Empire*. Courtwright employs the metaphor of a frontier to contextualize a narrative history of American aviation, suggesting that like other frontiers, the sky gradually became more densely settled, safer, and filled with populations more representative of the general American populace. Although Courtwright considers the development of federal policy only briefly, his thesis suggests that governmental regulation played a key role in this transformation.[20]

In recent years a growing number of historians have focused attention on specific aspects of federal policy. In this genre two monographs deserve particular mention: Nick Komons's *Bonfires to Beacons: Federal Aviation Policy under the Air Commerce Act, 1926–1938* and F. Robert van der Linden's *Airlines and Airmail: The Post Office and the Birth of the Commercial Aviation Industry*. Komons's work offers a comprehensive history of the complex political machinations that led to the creation of the 1926 Air Commerce Act and the Commerce Department's efforts to promote both safety and regulation as it oversaw the creation of a national air transport network. *Bonfires to Beacons* evidences impressive archival research, and Komons's efforts result in a detailed and comprehensive treatment of the history surrounding the Air Commerce Act; that focus, however, also limits the work's larger value, as it adheres tightly to the premise embodied in its title. Focusing on Post Office airmail policy, van der Linden offers a different perspective, persuasively arguing that informal airmail subsidies formed the core of a range of federal initiatives that created the foundations for American commercial aviation during the 1920s. Leading this charge, he relates, were Progressive Republicans such as Clyde Kelly, Herbert Hoover, and Walter Brown, who applied Theodore Roosevelt's concept of New Nationalism to use the power of the federal government to support the creation of a group of "good" aviation "trusts." Van der Linden argues that this Progressive Republican vision held sway until 1934, when Hugo Black and Franklin Roosevelt—adherents of Woodrow Wilson's New Freedom and thus the idea that any form of economic concentration was harmful—undid the prevailing policies and ushered in a new era of federal oversight. Ultimately, *Airlines and Airmail* makes a compelling case for the Post Office's central role in creating American commercial aviation. Unfortunately, van der Linden's focus on the distinctions between Republican and Democratic progressive attitudes toward business at times obscures and oversimplifies the larger political and economic context.[21]

Surprisingly, historians detailing Hoover's and Roosevelt's political histories pay scant attention to aviation policy. Joan Hoff Wilson's influential biography *Herbert Hoover, Forgotten Progressive* briefly touches upon aviation as she connects Hoover's interest in promoting aeronautical development to his larger associationalist economic philosophy. Ellis Hawley's scholarship also addresses aeronautics, albeit briefly. Several of his essays—most significantly, "Three Facets of the Hooverian Associationalism: Lumber, Aviation, and Movies, 1921–1930," published in Thomas McGraw's *Regulation in Perspective*—offer limited insight into Hoover's aviation policy. Hawley focuses primarily on Hoover's efforts to promote safety regulation through the Commerce Department, again highlighting the central role Hoover's associationalist philosophy played in guiding his actions. In his seminal work *The New Deal and The Problem of Monopoly*, Hawley highlights industry leaders' attempts to define aviation as a special case warranting federal assistance. Aviation's pioneering status, these lawmakers held, mandated federal support, resulting in the passage of legislation such as the Kelly and Air Commence Acts. Hawley argues that Democratic efforts to modify this system were largely unsuccessful, leading to the passage of the Civil Aeronautics Act and confirming aviation's status as a "natural monopoly" warranting continued governmental support. These brief treatments hint at aviation policy's relationship to the larger political and economic context but ultimately raise more questions than they answer. Most glaringly, these works do not adequately account for the extent to which federal actions successfully promoted aviation's commercial development. Scholars of the New Deal, in particular, fail to recognize the concrete gains brought about by public works agencies—the notable exceptions being Robert Leighninger and Jason Scott Smith. New Deal public works created one of the most significant commercial success stories emerging from the period, the almost total revamping of American aviation infrastructure by agencies such as the PWA and WPA.[22]

Those shortcomings notwithstanding, historians have done valuable work examining the multifaceted history of commercial aviation. There remains, however, the need for a comprehensive treatment of federal policy during the interwar era. In a very real sense, the United States' contemporary air transport system traces its origins to the federal government's engagement with aviation during a brief period between the world wars. Decisions made during the Coolidge, Hoover, and Roosevelt administrations revolutionized air transport and contained long-lasting implications for the continued development of the industry. Federal promotion of commercial flying combined with increased regulation, informal subsidization through airmail contracts, and support for infrastructure such as airports, lighted airways, and radio transmitters to facilitate aviation's growth into a dominant force in the transportation of both people and cargo. These governmental actions underlay the growth of the airlines—Pan Am, United, American, and TWA, in particular—that dominated commercial aviation until deregulation in the 1970s and beyond. The organization, structure, and prevalence of modern commercial aviation, then, reflects the effects of prescient policy decisions made between the early 1920s and World War II.

That fact necessitates a reevaluation of federal aviation policy during the interwar years. Only by examining the development of federal policy in its larger cultural and economic context can we fully appreciate the origins of today's air transport network. Federal actions moved beyond airmail subsidies and regulation to encompass a broad-based and comprehensive project specifically designed to foster the growth and development of commercial flying. Policy makers such as Herbert Hoover, William MacCracken, Walter Brown, Franklin Roosevelt, and Harry Hopkins consistently supported the development of American aeronautics, evidencing noteworthy continuity through both Republican and Democratic administrations. Although historians have suggested that the airmail scandal of 1934 and subsequent passage of Democrat-sponsored legislation ushered in a sharp break with Hoover's associationalist policies—at least until the passage of the Civil Aeronautics Act in 1938—in fact, Roosevelt, Hugo Black, and other Democrats shared with Hoover many of the same foundational assumptions about aviation's value to the nation. Indeed, Roosevelt expanded federal engagement with aviation through his commitment to using public works agencies to support development of aviation infrastructure. Collectively, these federal policies created the foundation for today's air transportation network and played a significant role in shaping the contours of modern America.

An investigation of interwar aviation policy also suggests the ongoing necessity of reexamining both Herbert Hoover's and Franklin Roosevelt's legacies. Hoover's foundational contributions to American aeronautical development emphasize the need to acknowledge the ability of his associationalist philosophy to successfully foster commercial growth. With regard to aviation, Hoover must appear as a visionary reformer who played a pivotal role in supporting economic development. This analysis looks beyond Hoover's Depression-era leadership and instead seeks to assess Hoover through a broader lens.

Similarly, Roosevelt's engagement with American aeronautics signifies the continuing need to reconsider the New Deal's legacy. FDR's connections to American flying—particularly though New Deal public works agencies—confirm the necessity of moving beyond discussions of the New Deal's ability to pull the United States out of the Depression. Roosevelt's aviation-related actions demonstrate important elements of continuity between his economic policies and those of his predecessor. Simultaneously, they highlight FDR's willingness to expand federal responsibility over aeronautics in the interests of both the industry and the larger American economy, in the process emphasizing the New Deal's productive capacity—its ability to create infrastructure with the potential to radically alter the American landscape. The New Deal certainly put Americans to work, but with regard to aviation it also promoted the creation of airways and airports that endured far beyond the New Deal era.

By the eve of World War II aviation advocates could proudly point to a mature air transportation network as concrete evidence of their policies' success. Taking place in a larger context of dynamic technological development and public fascination with flying, federal policies undertaken by Hoover, Roosevelt, and others facilitated the creation of the world's largest and most efficient commercial aviation industry. Although the airlines we fly today may appear quite different from their fledgling progenitors, they owe their origins to the interwar period. That era holds the key to unlocking the narrative of American aeronautical development—development that resulted in the domination of the skies by American planes, pilots, and airlines.

1

The Coming Air Age

Herbert Hoover and the Origins of Federal Aviation Policy, 1921–1925

In July 1921, only a few months after assuming the post of commerce secretary, Herbert Hoover organized an informal conference on aviation. Calling representatives from the Society of Automotive Engineers, the Aero Club of America, the National Aircraft Underwriters Association, and the Manufacturers Aircraft Association to his office in Washington, DC, Hoover endeavored to clarify the Commerce Department's relationship with the embryonic air transport industry and lay the foundations for a coherent federal aviation policy. Hoover hoped that the conference would promote an ongoing dialogue between his department and air industry leaders, but even more importantly, he sought to use the meeting to draft a national aviation policy specifically designed to foster the advancement of American aeronautics.[1]

Hoover's notes for the meeting reveal his already firm grasp of the central issues facing aeronautical development in the United States. Building on his well-established correspondence with leading members of the aviation industry, his notes articulate the pressing need for uniform federal oversight, specifically the desire to establish a "governmental agency which shall immediately codify and present rules for interstate flying and map out air lines." Hoover also recognized the need for uniform federal licensing standards, as no authority existed to determine pilots' competence in the air. The commerce secretary understood, however, that these efforts would struggle to bear fruit without public willingness to embrace commercial flying. If Americans saw flying as a stunt or perceived operators to be incompetent or dangerous, then air transport would struggle to get off the ground. In the effort to redress these shortcomings, industry leaders looked to the Commerce Department to exert leadership in defining a program of development that would establish a sound basis for commercial growth—leadership that Hoover readily embraced.[2]

This early glimpse of Hoover's efforts to promote American aeronautical development highlights his commitment to establishing commercial aviation as a safe and viable form of transport. From the earliest days of his tenure as commerce secretary Hoover fostered relationships with parties interested in the advancement of American aviation. Working closely with airline executives, aircraft manufacturers, Post Office and Commerce Department officials, and members of Congress, Hoover used his time in the Commerce Department, and later the White House, to encourage the rational growth of a self-sustaining national air transport network. That work yielded long-lasting success; Hoover's vision for aeronautical development underlay the growth of the industry until deregulation in the late 1970s. That legacy underscores the fact that the creation of a mature commercial aviation network must stand as one of the most significant yet overlooked achievements of Hoover's political career.

The manner in which Hoover strove to promote commercial flying reflected the influence of his unique economic philosophy—associationalism. This ideology emerged from Hoover's faith in a pragmatic, progressive utopianism most clearly defined as a type of liberal corporatism. His efforts at both the Commerce Department and in the White House manifested a dedication to administrative reorganization and decentralization and the desire for voluntary cooperation between government and business. Hoover believed that the government's proper role was to provide information, coordinate activities, and supply guidance to industry, but not to act as a coercive force or involve itself in production or distribution. Ideally, the government would serve as a facilitator, helping Americans pursue their own self-interest in a cooperative and productive manner. Hoover's commitment to making government the ally of business was particularly strong in the field of emerging technologies—most notably radio and aviation. For these young industries, federal support for research, cooperative organization, and regulation had the utmost potential to help stimulate growth.[3]

Aviation represents the most significant—and successful—example of Hoover's implementation of associationalist ideology. Associationalism provided Hoover the means through which to support the development of the fledgling industry, protecting it from the harsh realities of the free market while avoiding the specter of nationalization. Politically, the latter path would have been untenable in the United States, but economically, the creation of a national air carrier represented a sensible option at the time. Nationalization, in fact, represented the avenue through which European commercial aviation developed during the era; by the early 1930s virtually every European nation had a state airline. In the European context—embracing myriad international routes and direct competition from other nations' carriers—industry leaders and governmental officials quickly realized that airlines could not compete without direct governmental subsidies for technological development, manufacturing, and operations. The American context differed in important respects, but it remains significant that Hoover eschewed any push for nationalization in his efforts to promote aeronautical development. In the 1920s American commercial aviation had little hope of surviving without some form of federal support, and Hoover's policies offered financial assistance in a politically tenable package. As both commerce secretary and president, Hoover consistently strove to use federal power to facilitate rational, structured growth without resort to public ownership.

In that effort Hoover embraced several specific policies. He focused on creating legislation to regulate the industry and improve safety, pushed to use federal funds to create and improve infrastructure such as navigational aids and radio communications, and authorized federal support for research into new technologies. Hoover also worked diligently to publicize aviation to the American people. Finally, he worked with the Post Office to establish a system of informal subsidies to help fund the emerging airmail network—in so doing creating the potential for private air carriers to become solvent.

By 1925 Hoover's tireless support for commercial flying resulted in building momentum for federal action. Working with allies such as Postmaster General Harry S. New and Second Assistant Postmaster General Paul Henderson, as well as legislators and members of the budding aviation industry, Hoover framed the debate surrounding air transport and played a key role in legitimizing aviation's commercial appeal. Ultimately, the commerce secretary's efforts facilitated the passage of a key piece of legislation: the 1925 Contract Air Mail Act. That bill provided for private carriage of national airmail for the first time, confirming the need for the federal government to take the lead in regulating the emerging industry. Its passage and the resulting move toward expanded governmental authority highlighted Hoover's success in selling his vision to the aviation industry and the American people. Much work remained to be done; in many ways the Air Mail Act raised more questions than it answered and confirmed the infancy of American commercial flying. Nonetheless, the legislative foundation allowed for the eventual maturation of the industry, firmly establishing Hoover's foundational role in shaping its evolution. His template persevered through Franklin Roosevelt's Democratic administrations and ultimately served as the basis for the 1938 Civil Aeronautics Act, legislation that guided the continuing expansion of commercial aviation for more than forty years.

As they worked to place American aviation on a solid foundation, Hoover and his allies found themselves operating in an environment contextualized by two interrelating factors: aviation's contemporary cultural prevalence and the industry's emergent status. In the early 1920s, aviation formed an increasingly significant presence in American lives, largely through the activities of barnstormers, air shows, and pilots' establishment of ever-increasing speed, altitude, and endurance records. These activities led to a widespread fascination with flying but created divergent perceptions of aviation's larger significance.[4] As aviation drew the attention of more and more Americans, the public overwhelmingly viewed flying as an exciting but dangerous form of entertainment. This association facilitated increasing enthusiasm for aeronautics, even inspiring utopian hopes for some, while simultaneously serving to marginalize flying's commercial potential.

Barnstormers in particular played a key role in undermining the appeal of air transport. These aerial performers introduced tens of thousands of Americans to flying, in the process inspiring widespread admiration for these glamorous and independent pilots. Barnstormers took thousands of Americans for their first ride aloft and perfected myriad stunts such as wing-walking, aerobatics, and in-flight transitions from plane to plane.

Operating in an environment free from governmental regulation and control, barnstormers were free to embrace ever more daring exploits in their efforts to win over crowds and fill their own pockets. Unfortunately, this often resulted in disaster. Barnstormers' planes—most commonly cheap war-surplus Curtis JN-4 Jennies—were underpowered and unreliable and often exhibited hasty and shoddy repairs. Many pilots lacked suitable flying experience, endangering both themselves and their passengers. Even experienced pilots often found themselves falling from the sky. Dean Smith, a former military flier, remembers that he and his partner suffered two crashes almost immediately after taking their Jenny on the road. The Jenny, Smith relates, "was so marginal in taking off that . . . on a hot day [it was] a question of whether it would fly or not." Even in normal operations, and particularly when carrying a passenger, "with any loss of power, why, you were sinking."[5] While barnstormers continued to draw large crowds well into the 1920s, frequent crashes and their activities' association with danger and risk served to reinforce stereotypes of flying as an entertaining but hazardous sideshow.

Those perceptions, moreover, were magnified by the media's obsession with spectacle and disaster. In 1930 *The Nation* used their cover to ask Americans, "Is It Safe to Fly?" and as late as 1934 *Reader's Digest* unequivocally titled a prominent article "Flying Is Still Dangerous." The latter piece urged readers to look beyond the dramatic gains in speed brought about by air travel and "look at the price [flying exacted] . . . in human lives." Numerous movies—such as the famous 1927 film *Wings*—focused on the violence and death associated with military flying, further undermining faith in the viability of commercial flight.[6]

Simultaneously, however, the possibilities that aviation offered inspired utopian hopes. According to historian Joseph Corn, as the rapid advance of aeronautical technology in the early decades of the twentieth century led to ever greater aerial feats, Americans dreamed that the airplane could help cure society's ills and usher in a new air age. This emerging "gospel of aviation" held out hope for a new era in human affairs promising the end of poverty, world peace, and even hopes for immortality. Utopian visions "were both an expression and a cause of the great popular enthusiasm shown for aviation," suggesting that at least some Americans embraced dreams that aviation would quickly become a foundational element of everyday life.[7]

These divergent visions, it appears, coexisted uneasily during the interwar era. While virtually all Americans embraced the excitement aviation embodied, there remained a sharp cultural divide between hopeful and fearful visions of aviation's social and economic possibilities. This context profoundly shaped federal efforts to promote aviation and helps explain policy makers' emphasis on safety and reliability. As flying became safer, aircraft more reliable, and federal regulation stricter, Americans increasingly moved to accept aviation's commercial possibilities. Simultaneously, however, prominent deaths at air races, the disappearance of pilots like Amelia Earhart on long-distance flights, and airline crashes—such as the one resulting in the death of Notre Dame football coach Knute Rockne—continued to highlight aviation's danger. While the pendulum steadily swung in the direction of aviation's positive associations as the era progressed, policy makers remained cognizant of the need to focus on issues related to safety.

While Americans' enthusiasm for aviation formed a powerful context grounding federal efforts to promote commercial growth, the industry's nascent status reinforced perceptions of flying as an entertaining but dangerous sideshow. Indeed, even to refer to it as an industry during the early 1920s is a bit of a misnomer. Although numerous airframe manufacturers and fledgling commercial operations existed in the years following World War I, these disparate corporate entities had little direction and experienced minimal financial success. While flying clearly captured Americans' imaginations, in the absence of federal oversight, adequate ground-based infrastructure, and public demand for air travel, aviation's commercial possibilities remained distinctly limited.

Adding to the industry's challenges, postwar American aviation exhibited a dismal safety record. The prevalence of cheap war surplus aircraft combined with irregular maintenance, little or no pilot training, and a dearth of regulatory oversight made flying exceedingly dangerous. Crashes were common, often injuring or killing pilots as well as their passengers and even spectators on the ground. By the mid-1920s many localities began prohibiting barnstormers and flying circuses from performing within city or town limits to protect citizens against death and injury. Adding to aviators' difficulties, aircraft lacked instruments to allow flight in bad weather; in practice this mattered little, however, as virtually all pilots lacked any training in instrument flying. There were no formal airways, and pilots often struggled to navigate across the country using road maps or following railroad tracks. Air traffic control was nonexistent even where municipalities or the military had established primitive airports, and in any event, pilots did not have the ability to communicate with the ground, because suitable radio transmitters did not exist. Finally, there were no mechanisms to assess the safety and quality of new aircraft, resulting in a trial-and-error approach that often didn't reveal flaws in design or manufacturing until after the planes took to the skies in the hands of consumers.

In spite of these difficulties, in the years immediately after World War I both public and private interests engaged in limited attempts to organize commercial flying ventures. The army's inaugural airmail line from Washington, DC, to New York offers the most significant example, achieving modest success. The operation demonstrated the ability of aircraft to perform a commercial function on a regular schedule with minimal delays, though from a commercial standpoint the experiment proved a failure. Waning enthusiasm for the service steadily reduced the volume of airmail, while the relatively short route offered little time saving over surface transportation routes. In spite of those challenges, in August 1918 the army turned the airmail route over to the Post Office Department, which immediately began to expand the airmail network west from New York, establishing stops in Cleveland and Chicago in 1919 and completing a transcontinental line to San Francisco by September 1920.[8]

The same period also witnessed several private corporations' inauguration of commercial ventures. In 1919 Edward Hubbard organized a mail service from Seattle to Vancouver. Hubbard began daily flights in October 1920 with limited commercial success. Aeromarine West Indies Airways operated a similar service between Miami and Nassau beginning in November 1919. The latter carrier catered to wealthy vacationers, but also carried thirsty passengers eager to escape Prohibition.[9] These private ventures saw limited financial success; neither was able to attract significant numbers of passengers. In addition, both Hubbard and Aeromarine employed the use of seaplanes, avoiding the problems associated with a lack of airport infrastructure but limiting their operations to coastal areas. They also eschewed flying at night or in bad weather—a realistic acknowledgment of their planes' and pilots' limitations, but a policy that sharply limited their operations' commercial potential. In light of these challenges prospective airline operators were forced to accept that flying passengers was simply not profitable. Hubbard's and Aeromarine's postwar efforts were kept afloat only by securing experimental, small-scale government airmail contracts for international routes. In subsequent years dozens of attempts to inaugurate passenger service in the United States ended in commercial failure.

Aircraft manufacturers also struggled during these early years. Although firms such as Curtis had rapidly expanded their operations during the war to fill military contracts, the vast majority of manufacturers were small, informal operations. Boeing, which ultimately grew to become the largest manufacturer of commercial aircraft in the world, used a barn as their production center during the early 1920s. William Boeing, the company's founder, headed a total staff of fewer than a dozen employees, who designed, built, and tested airframes entirely by hand. During that period aircraft were constructed primarily of wooden frames covered with fabric, making the design and production process more akin to carpentry than to industrial design. Aerodynamics was a trial-and-error process, governed by the slide rule and knowledge gained through limited test flights. Corporations such as Boeing, Douglas, and Beechcraft struggled to find buyers for their products; large orders were still measured in the single digits until well into the latter half of the decade. Early airlines often operated with a total inventory of four or five aircraft, hardly enough demand to stimulate the expansion of production facilities.

These prevailing cultural, economic, and developmental factors highlight the remarkable foresight Hoover embraced with regard to American commercial aviation. During an era when both airlines and aircraft manufacturers struggled to become solvent and most Americans associated flying with dangerous entertainment, the commerce secretary envisioned a stable and profitable air transport industry that would bring material benefit to the entire nation. He was, moreover, able to translate that foresight into action, successfully facilitating the growth of commercial carriers and aircraft manufacturers while laying the regulatory foundation for future development. Significantly, Hoover's push for federal oversight predated the development of much of the modern regulatory state. In the 1920s the federal government had little authority to police public safety in particular industries nor willingness to intervene actively in the commercial sphere. Even state governments moved slowly to assume authority over transportation. Although automobiles had begun to travel public roads in the final decade of the nineteenth century, it was not until 1913 that New Jersey became the first state to require a license to operate a motor vehicle, a mandate many other states adopted during the teens and twenties.[10] Though the Progressive Era created a new appreciation for government's ability to safeguard the lives of its citizens, that realization sparked little in the way of formal legislation. The 1906 Pure Food and Drug Act stands as the most significant regulatory bill of that period but in many ways represents the exception that proves the rule. In that light, Hoover's actions are even more noteworthy, particularly with regard to a small and relatively underdeveloped transportation technology.

Hoover's engagement with American aeronautics began almost as soon as President Warren Harding appointed him commerce secretary in March 1921. In April, Hoover helped organize the Committee on Air Navigation, bringing together representatives from the Smithsonian Institution, army, navy, Commerce Department, and Post Office. The committee, headed by National Advisory Committee for Aeronautics (NACA) chairman Dr. Charles Walcott, worked to draft a national aviation policy consistent with military, commercial, and private interests. Representatives proposed a program of development that focused primarily on national defense but also addressed issues of legislation, oversight, aerial navigation, and promotion. The committee concluded that commercial flying would not mature sufficiently to play an important role in American aeronautics for some years, highlighting the need for the military to shoulder the developmental burden in the near term. Nonetheless, Walcott and the other committee members did envisage a future for commercial flying, foreseeing a time when air transport would "secure civilian control" as it became more established.[11]

In spite of their pessimistic assessment of contemporary commercial aviation, the committee did make a number of specific recommendations designed to promote commercial growth. Arguing that progress depended on the establishment of federal legislation and appropriations, representatives agreed on four specific recommendations: the continuation of separate War Department, navy, and Post Office air services; the creation of a Department of Aeronautics in the Department of Commerce to regulate air navigation and "carry out policies which may be adopted to encourage civil and commercial aviation"; an extension of War Department efforts to establish air routes; and continued support for scientific research carried out by the NACA. While these recommendations emphasized the military's role in promoting American aeronautical development, representatives nonetheless exhibited prescient insight regarding the current state of

US civil aeronautics. They correctly identified an urgent need for legislative oversight, highlighted the value of formal airways, and focused on the necessity for further research. In addition, the committee displayed a ready willingness to use the power of the federal government to support the growth of civil and commercial aviation. Hoover readily adopted these recommendations, embracing them in his own efforts moving forward.

Hoover also established contacts with prominent members of the emerging aviation industry in the wake of assuming his post as commerce secretary. In March 1921 Hoover corresponded with Dr. Charles Walcott regarding the NACA's annual report and the potential for short-term congressional legislation pursuant to aeronautics. The NACA report, like Hoover's subsequent Committee on Air Navigation, argued for the necessity of federal legislation to regulate the emerging aviation industry. NACA officials worried that in the absence of federal legislation, "independent and generally conflicting legislation by the various states will be enacted which will greatly hamper the development of aviation." The report went on to suggest that governmental support for commercial aviation would offer a twofold benefit to the nation. First, Walcott wrote that supporting aeronautical development as "the backbone of military preparedness" would save significant costs when compared to those that would accrue from unprepared entry into a future conflict. Second, the NACA report argued that support for commercial aviation would yield immediate returns during peacetime by "promoting and strengthening our means of transportation, advancing the progress of civilization, and increasing the national wealth." Admittedly, the NACA was explicitly tasked with fostering aviation, but that committee's recommendations echoed a growing consensus regarding aviation's place in America's future. The connection between commercial development and military preparedness in particular would come to dominate discussions of federal policy in years to come.[12]

Hoover's interest in commercial aviation quickly drew the attention of industry leaders. As early as June 1921, C. F. Ridden, the president of Aeromarine Airways, wrote the secretary to note his gratitude that Hoover was taking "an active interest in the development of civilian aviation and the Federal Regulation of Aerial Routes."[13] This correspondence inaugurated an ongoing dialogue between Hoover and airline executives, manufacturers, and members of leading aviation organizations. Manufacturers and airlines, in fact, played a key role in pushing for greater federal oversight over aviation, correctly indentifying the need for federal leadership in promoting safety and standardizing licensing. Hoover's decision to appoint an Aviation Consulting Commission in June 1921 emerged in large part from industry efforts. More than fifty executives representing the young airlines, aircraft and engine manufacturers, and pilots petitioned the president for greater federal leadership in aeronautical development. Hoover worked closely with these executives, eventually calling many of them to Washington for an informal conference in July.

Emerging connections between Hoover and members of the aviation industry established the basis for a continuing relationship between governmental officials and industry executives that would prove foundational to aviation's commercial development. Cooperation between government and business was nothing new for Hoover; his support for emerging industries formed a key aspect of his associationalist ideology. Hoover's focus on information gathering, cooperative planning, and, ultimately, the creation of business friendly regulation continued to inform his actions as he worked with policy makers and members of the emergent industry.

Even Hoover, however, was at times surprised by the extent to which industry officials desired federal action. In a 1921 letter to New York congressman Frederick Hicks, Hoover remarked that aviation was "the only industry that favors having itself regulated by the federal government."[14] While unusual, particularly during the Republican-dominated 1920s, the industry's desire for federal regulation represented a rational response to the conditions aircraft manufacturers and airlines faced early in the decade. As historian Nick Komons relates, during that era commercial aviation suffered from the "chaos of laissez faire." Air carriers were widely dispersed and overwhelmingly small; airframe and engine builders often worked from barns and sheds. Little competition existed between these companies, which operated with virtually no regulatory oversight. This environment afforded commercial operators tremendous freedom. That freedom, however, served to limit, rather than encourage, the expansion of air transport.

A dearth of federal engagement presented the industry with several distinct challenges. First, industry executives remained acutely aware that commercial flying would need to overcome aviation's association with recklessness in order to attract passengers. The lack of basic standards for airworthiness, licensing, and navigation allowed virtually anyone with a plane to label him- or herself a qualified pilot and undertake passenger-carrying operations—circumstances that led to many poorly trained and inexperienced pilots taking passengers aloft, often in aircraft held together by bailing wire and twine. Conscientious industry leaders understood that these conditions undermined public confidence, and they hoped that federal establishment of airworthiness certificates would weed out unsafe designs and instill public trust in certified aircraft while federal licensing standards would promote confidence in airline pilots' skill. Second, industry leaders worried that the absence of federal regulation over licensing, operations, navigation, and airports would drive states and localities to take the lead in crafting legislation, resulting in a hodgepodge of conflicting statutes that would complicate operations and hinder expansion.[15] Finally, commercial interests desired that the federal government shoulder the burden of establishing a national network of airways—a necessary precondition for scheduled airline operations. The military and the Post Office had already begun constructing a limited number of airfields and experimenting with signing and lighting air routes, but much work remained to be done to realize a viable national system. These conditions pushed aviation executives to lobby forcefully for federal intervention. They believed that only the power of the federal government could rescue the industry from chaos and provide the necessary leadership to see commercial aviation to maturity.

Few individuals were better placed to confirm the necessity of federal action than Gill Robb Wilson. A former fraternity brother of Calvin Coolidge and a confidant of Hoover, Dwight Morrow, Hiram Bingham, and other prominent policy makers, Wilson flew for the French during World War I, presided over the National Aeronautics Association for four terms, edited *Flying* magazine, and served as director of aeronautics for New Jersey. Reflecting on the state of commercial aviation in the early 1920s, Wilson highlighted the divergence between aviation's lofty goals and the treacherous economic realities of the day. Citing the lack of any law or regulation governing air transport, Wilson related that if the business of aviation "was going to amount to anything," he and like-minded entrepreneurs "recognized that there would have to be some order brought out of the chaos." In an era when "half-baked, half-trained pilots were putting together pieces of junk and killing people all over," Wilson fervently hoped that government oversight would create order and lay the foundation for commercial flying. Tellingly, Wilson looked to Hoover and the Commerce Department for leadership. While trips to Washington before 1926 yielded little in the way of results, Wilson cited the close relationships among the small fraternity of aviation proponents as vital to their eventual success.[16]

Unfortunately, while Hoover's actions in the early 1920s emphasize his desire to enact a wide-ranging federal aviation policy, at that time there existed insufficient congressional support for federal action. Legislators—including Representatives Norman Gould (R-NY), Frederick Hicks (R-NY), Murray Hulbert (D-NY), and Samuel Winslow (R-MA) and Senators Harry New (R-IN), Morris Sheppard (D-TX), and James Wadsworth (R-NY)—introduced bills favoring some level of federal involvement with aviation in the first half of the decade, but none gained traction.[17] Hoover's difficulty in developing congressional support stemmed from the multifaceted nature of commercial aviation's needs. In addition to federal promotion efforts, at least two distinct aspects of federal engagement would be necessary to create a viable private commercial air transport industry. First, airlines' ability to achieve solvency increasingly appeared to necessitate fiscal assistance. Most obviously, this could be facilitated through airmail subsidies—in many ways the same policy that helped underwrite railroad expansion in the previous century. Second, federal officials and airline executives alike recognized the need for overarching federal regulation to promote safety and normalize industry practices.

Before 1925, however, Americans remained unconvinced that commercial flying justified that type of support. Most worrying, the public remained skeptical of aviation's commercial prospects. In light of the available evidence, that skepticism was perfectly reasonable. In the early 1920s Post Office airmail service represented the most visible example of air transport operations. Taking over from and enlarging upon the army's experimental service beginning in the fall of 1918, Post Office officials steadily expanded the airmail map in subsequent years. Moving west from the original Washington-Philadelphia-New York route, Post Office pilots inaugurated service to Chicago in September 1919 and Omaha in May 1920. Only four months later, airmail reached the West Coast, terminating the first transcontinental line in San Francisco on September 8.

As impressive as those efforts were, they remained sharply limited by the available technology and infrastructure. Airmail pilots took to the skies in modified de Havilland DH-4 aircraft—planes that had earned the sobriquet "flying coffin" during the Great War in response to their fuel tanks' propensity to explode in flight. Modified from a light bomber design, these single-engine biplanes represented only a small improvement upon the army's Jennies. The DH-4s were larger, faster, and had more load capacity than the Jennies, but they were similarly limited to only the most basic instruments. Post Office pilots complained that their craft were drafty and lacked any heating system, a particular problem when flying at altitude in the winter. Dean Smith recalls that cockpit temperatures routinely dropped below zero during winter months, creating miserable conditions that impeded pilots' judgment.[18]

Adding to pilots' difficulties, the Post Office struggled to create adequate ground-based infrastructure to support airmail operations. Post Office officials were aware of the pressing need for logistical support and worked diligently to ensure that their pilots could count on reliable aircraft and safe, well-lighted landing fields. Plans called for the installation of powerful beacon lights at thirty-mile intervals along airmail routes, with an emergency landing field located at each beacon. The department also strove to establish rough emergency landing areas between each signal in hope of providing its pilots with some measure of safety in the event of equipment malfunction. As the airmail map extended west, however, the speed of advance often outpaced that infrastructure as the Post Office struggled to fund airmail-related expansion. Famously, pilots attempting to complete the first nonstop transcontinental airmail flight in 1921 found themselves following the lights from a string of bonfires lit by volunteers along the Midwestern nighttime section of the route.

Weather—or more precisely, weather reporting—also presented airmail pilots with significant challenges. Accurate, up-to-date forecasts were crucial to safe operations, particularly in mountainous areas, yet no official reporting system existed. Pilots quickly learned the most dangerous parts of their routes and often asked local farmers to provide regular reports for those particular areas. At times those reports could be as specific as relating whether clouds obscured a specific ridge or peak. Ingenious though this system was, it encompassed serious flaws. Farmers' weather-related concerns differed greatly from those of pilots, often leading to misunderstanding. Airmail pilot Dean Smith relates that farmers would often give pilots strange and inaccurate information—for example, reporting that they could see for a mile or more in foggy conditions. Eventually, the Post Office began employing observers along airmail routes to provide more accurate information. Even the latter system, however, often left much to be desired. In one extreme case, pilots noticed that an observer in the Allegheny Mountains—one of the most dangerous sections of the eastern airmail route—regularly provided inaccurate information. Upon further investigation, officials discovered that he was filing his reports weeks in advance, collecting his salary, and leaving his home to go hunting and fishing.[19]

These conditions made flying the mail one of the most dangerous jobs in the country. Of the forty pilots initially hired by the Post Office in 1918, only eight lived to see the end of the service eight years later. In 1920 alone, one in six airmail pilots perished in the line of duty. Even pilots who survived flying the mail often suffered numerous crashes. Charles Lindbergh parachuted from his de Havilland shortly after he began carrying airmail, and Dean Smith demolished several aircraft during his service, in one incident crashing directly into a cow, which forced him to send the following telegram to the second assistant postmaster general: "Flying [airmail route] four westbound. Engine quit. Only place to land, on cow. Killed cow, wrecked plane, scared me."[20]

Deaths and crashes reinforced public skepticism about commercial service, while logistical barriers limited airmail's potential value to Americans. In the absence of lighted airways, instrument training for pilots, and adequate instrumentation in their planes, Post Office pilots could fly only during daylight hours. This offered some time saving over ground-based transportation—in the early twenties airmail crossed the country in about ninety hours, saving almost a day over rail transport—but did not fully capitalize on the speed advantage aircraft enjoyed. While many in the industry and government saw great potential in the Post Office's ongoing efforts, those supporters struggled to gain wider support.

As a result, although the Post Office's early efforts played a crucial role in pointing the way forward for future air transport operations, they did little to create public demand for passenger service. Airmail remained something of a sideshow, and air transport proponents found themselves unable to create sufficient momentum behind legislative action. As Nick Komons argues, in the absence of public pressure, Congress had no popular mandate to act. Impetus for federal engagement came from a special interest group—the aviation industry itself—that did not carry the weight of the American people. Although pressure for federal action built steadily within that group, it had little effect in the early years of the decade.[21]

By 1924, however, circumstances began to change as improvements to the airmail network and strong advocacy by Hoover and Post Office officials built momentum for federal action. The previous year the Post Office completed an ongoing effort to light the airmail route between Chicago and Cheyenne, Wyoming, the section over which pilots would need to fly at night in order to realize continuous cross-country service. That effort encompassed the construction of 289 rotating beacon lights, five lighted primary landing fields, thirty-four lighted secondary fields, and modifications to seventeen DH-4s to enable nighttime operations.[22] After a number of successful test flights, Post Office officials began regular overnight service in July 1924. These developments allowed the department to shorten transcontinental transit time by two-thirds to only thirty hours, underlining the growing speed advantage aircraft enjoyed over trucks and trains.

By the beginning of 1925, Post Office airmail service had achieved some measure of maturity. Accident rates fell sharply as pilots gained skill and experience, aircraft received upgraded heating systems and better instrumentation, and a cross-country system of beacon lights and emergency landing fields helped guide airmail carriers from coast to coast—a far cry from conditions only six years earlier. The department's success in establishing regularly scheduled cross-country service began to point to a viable commercial future for aviation. Post Office officials did their best to publicize their achievements, hoping to build public support for air commerce in the government and with the American people.

From the outset, government officials understood army and Post Office activities as tests designed to demonstrate the viability of an airmail service. Believing they had made their case, after 1924 Postmaster General Paul Henderson and his allies increasingly turned their attention to facilitating the transfer of airmail routes to private companies. That goal meshed well with Hoover's larger vision for commercial flying and offered commercial air carriers the possibility of stable profits in the form of airmail subsidies. Fledgling airlines would also benefit from the infrastructure the Post Office had worked so diligently to construct across the country and the experience that pilots, dispatchers, and ground crews gained flying the mail. Post Office efforts had clearly accomplished their goal: offering concrete evidence that air transport could work and beginning to build public confidence in commercial flying.

By 1925, then, both legislators and commercial interests looked forward to the end of government-run airmail operations. Interested parties understood, however, that bringing about that end necessitated a new level of federal guidance. As yet, there existed no legislation providing for federal payments to airmail carriers, and the government still had no regulatory authority over aviation. Post Office operations suggested that a commercial future was achievable, but possibilities remained distinctly limited without federal support and oversight. Momentum was building for congressional action, but many questions remained unanswered: What form would airmail subsidies take? How would air carriers qualify for airmail routes? Would the federal government regulate licensing and airworthiness? If so, how? What role would the government play in regulating the commercial aspects of the industry? Would the government continue to play a leading role in promoting aviation?

In an effort to answer these questions and point the way forward for American aeronautics, Herbert Hoover and key allies such as Henderson and Postmaster General Harry S. New worked to define and publicize a comprehensive vision for American air commerce. Their actions built support for congressional action and shaped the discourse surrounding federal aviation policy. Hoover took the lead in this endeavor, working closely with airline executives, engine and airframe manufacturers, aviation interest groups, federal officials, and the military in his efforts to define the federal government's relationship with the aviation industry with regard to regulation, infrastructure, oversight, and research. Hoover also strove to delineate the relationship between civil and military aviation and worked to create a politically viable system of financial support for aeronautical development. Those efforts, according to Robert van der Linden, ultimately allowed Hoover to "forge a new consensus concerning his vision of the role that aviation might play in the future."[23]

Hoover's efforts reflected his commitment to a core set of priorities. First, the commerce secretary continued to emphasize aviation's need for federal assistance and oversight. Hoover believed that commercial growth needed to take place in a structured environment. In his mind, federal control over licensing and safety were necessary preconditions for commercial growth. In addition, he stressed that the government had an obligation to provide lighted airways, emergency fields, and navigation aids for commercial networks. Second, Hoover worked to craft an aviation policy that provided some level of fiscal support for air transport operators while steering clear of direct subsidies or overt nationalization. Finally, Hoover emphasized the connections between civil and military aviation. For him, the development of commercial aviation represented a positive end in itself, but he also believed that a mature aviation industry would help aid military preparedness. Beginning in 1925, Hoover fleshed out those priorities, refining his vision for the future of aviation while attempting to sell it to both Congress and the American people.

Hoover prefaced his message by emphasizing aviation's pressing need for federal assistance. While he proudly drew attention to the strides aviation had made in recent years, suggesting that flying was coming close to achieving "self supporting application," those gains did not allay Hoover's conviction "that we can not have the successful development of commercial aviation until . . . government services are provided." To achieve that goal, the commerce secretary advocated creating within his department a Bureau of Civil Aviation tasked with responsibility over all aspects of regulation and oversight. Hoover marshaled several powerful arguments in support of federal supervision. First, he claimed that government safety regulation was vital for commercial growth. In his opinion the ongoing prevalence of aviation accidents highlighted the crucial need for federal standards, and he contended that such standards were, in fact, a necessary precondition for aeronautical development. Speaking to the San Francisco Chamber of Commerce, he related his conviction that passenger service would not and could not develop without "the rigorous inspection of planes and the licensing of pilots, based on competency, by some central authority." In light of the interstate nature of air commerce, Hoover went on to argue, "that authority must be the Federal Government."[24]

Hoover buttressed his push for federal regulation by stressing that such oversight was necessary in order to protect human life. Not surprisingly, Hoover's commitment to safety reflected a rational desire to protect his fellow countrymen. A second line of argument, however, was much more enlightening. Looking once more to aviation's commercial future, Hoover maintained that clear safety standards were crucial to "establishing public confidence in aviation as a method of passenger transport." Hoover made this same point even more strongly a year later, arguing that "public confidence in aerial navigation can only be established by the assurance that there is rigorous inspection of planes and competent personnel." Here Hoover moved beyond a push for safety on its own merits, revealing an awareness of aviation's limited contemporary appeal. A strong focus on safety reflected the commerce secretary's efforts to move aviation from the margins of American commerce to the center, the success of which depended in large part on establishing public confidence in commercial flying.[25]

In making his case for federal action, Hoover drew heavily on the government's relationship with the shipping industry. Historically, the federal government oversaw maritime safety and navigation; provided buoys, lighthouses, and similar infrastructure; and undertook scientific research related to ocean currents, meteorology, and other relevant matters. Hoover argued that there existed a "complete analogy" between federal maritime policies and the contemporary state of aviation. As such, the federal government had a responsibility to "provide for charting the airways; for lighting and marking them; for warnings of weather disturbances. . . . We must provide a body of law comparable to our merchant marine law." Without those services, Hoover believed that aviation would "only develop in a primitive way."[26]

Hoover frequently returned to this analogy when promoting his aviation policy. In 1926 he responded to suggestions that private corporations should be responsible for establishing airways and constructing ground-based infrastructure as the railways did. This line of argument exemplifies much of the criticism levied against Hoover's policies—specifically that they encouraged the creation of a damaging concentration of wealth. Congressional progressives such as Congressman John Nelson (R-WI) went so far as to charge that a pernicious "aircraft trust" was behind Hoover's efforts to support aeronautical development.[27]

Hoover's response was instructive. He countered by arguing that aviation had much more in common with shipping than with railroads. For him, federal support for infrastructure merely paralleled more than a century of governmental activity on the nation's waterways. More importantly, Hoover argued that railroad infrastructure differed from that of both aviation and shipping in critical ways. Hoover believed it was unrealistic to expect that any one private company would undertake construction of emergency landings fields, beacon lights, and the like, "because the moment they are provided they would be open to all competitors without payment."[28] In other words, railways owned their specific transportation routes, and thus directly benefited from any outlay for infrastructure. Air and waterways, in contrast, were open to all, and therefore the government had a responsibility to make passage safe without unduly burdening any individual commercial operator.

Guided by federal regulation and support for infrastructure development, Hoover believed that air transport had the potential to revolutionize American commerce. In his opinion the development of a viable air transport network had numerous economic advantages. Most significantly, Hoover emphasized the time savings aviation offered. Contending that "the economic importance of higher speed . . . is considerable," Hoover argued that many industries would be willing to pay a premium for the speed aviation enjoyed. In the long term, speedy transport options would provide revenues for the young air transport industry, while at the same time promoting more general economic advantage. In fact, Hoover explicitly linked the growth of air transport to national economic development. In 1926 he tied aviation's progress to America's, suggesting that "through economics in time and motion" aviation had the potential to "add effectively to national productivity and wealth." In this context, aviation represented much more than a new and exciting technology; air transport had the potential to fundamentally alter the American commercial landscape.[29]

While Hoover placed great emphasis on the government's role in bringing about that commercial future, he argued that federal investment need not be excessive. In 1925 Hoover suggested that providing aviation with the same level of services—airways, safety regulation, and so on—as the government provided for shipping would not require "an extravagant sum." In fact, he articulated two interrelated points regarding federal expenditures on aviation. First, he asserted that federal oversight of regulation and infrastructure development represented "a most constructive drive for immediate economy." In Hoover's mind, supporting aviation's growth at worst would be revenue neutral and at best, it was to be hoped, would enrich the government's coffers. He based this judgment on several related factors. Promoting commercial development would result in significant savings on military expenditures, as private industry would be given new motives for technological development. Additionally, the transfer of airmail from public—Post Office—to private responsibility would result in significant savings. Thus, even with increased federal responsibility for licensing, safety, and infrastructure, in the end Hoover believed his policy would offer a "relief, not an additional burden" to American taxpayers. In fact, he went so far as to claim that enacting his proposals "should in fact result in actual saving to the Government."[30]

Second, Hoover argued that placing responsibility for aviation oversight under the auspices of the Commerce Department presented possibilities for further savings. Citing the department's history of maritime regulation, he suggested savings could be realized "because we are simply extending our already established navigation bureaus further inland, and with comparatively little addition to staff and equipment."[31] Hoover's statements oversimplified the issue, but the commerce secretary was fundamentally correct to state that Commerce Department oversight would involve comparatively little new infrastructure within the department itself.

All of Hoover's financial arguments, however, must be seen in the larger context of his efforts to promote commercial aviation without resort to either a direct subsidy or nationalization. Hoover's support for close cooperation between the government and private interests, and federal support for research, infrastructure, and regulation, emerged naturally from his progressive economic ideology. He drew the line, however, at explicitly subsidizing industrial growth. That type of governmental action ran counter to Hoover's associationalist philosophy, and the conservative economic environment of the 1920s militated against any direct federal intervention in the economy. Instead, Hoover believed that fiscal support in the form of airmail contracts—what he and his supporters termed "informal subsidies"—represented a productive middle ground between the harsh realities of the free market and the political specter of government-owned airlines. "We should contract out the carriage of the mail," Hoover asserted; doing so would provide embryonic airlines with fiscal stability and induce them to begin carrying passengers.[32]

The final element of Hoover's aviation policy tied commercial development to national defense. In his mind commercial and military goals were complementary; in fact, Hoover argued that increased preparedness would emerge as a natural by-product of commercial expansion. To that end Hoover stressed that the development of air transport would provide three concrete benefits to American security. The growth in aviation-related manufacturing, airway development, and the aeronautical gains to be derived from commercial expansion would provide material contributions "to the defense arms of the government."[33] Hoover's support for private airlines would, in his mind, naturally result in the manufacture of more aircraft. This would in turn provide more capacity that could, in the event of war, be converted to military production. Additionally, the development of commercial airlines would push the private sector to develop larger and more efficient aircraft as airlines competed for passengers and profits; these advances in aeronautical technology would serve as an additional source of research and development for the military. Hoover also saw federal efforts to construct a lighted airway network across the country as performing an important military function. Much as later policy makers saw the Interstate Highway System as promoting both commercial and military goals, Hoover foresaw national airways providing crucial infrastructure in times of war. Finally, increased aircraft production would result in more efficient manufacturing techniques that would benefit both private industry and the government.

Hoover also highlighted the cost savings that could be realized from the confluence of commercial and military goals. He based this claim primarily on the fact that his policies would "relieve the government of the indirect expenditure necessary to maintain a reserve of manufacturing equipment for defense purposes." In the next few years Hoover would also argue that the expansion of commercial aviation would absolve the military of expenses associated with constructing emergency landing fields around the country and provide supplemental infrastructure in the form of municipal airports and lighted airways. While the government would still foot the bill for much of that construction, Hoover remained adamant that savings would ultimately result. By 1927 he confidently concluded that his aviation policy would "save huge sums which otherwise would have to be appropriated for a purely military or naval service."[34]

Hoover's efforts to tie aviation's commercial development to military preparedness appear to have served him well, as his consistent focus on national defense made his policy palatable to a wider audience. In fact, Hoover demonstrated a remarkable ability to construct a visionary aviation policy while still appealing to moderate and conservative policy makers. His support for military preparedness and focus on establishing American commercial aviation without a direct subsidy expanded the appeal of his policies and, in many ways, created the conditions for the possibility of their success.

Hoover, however, was not alone in his efforts to promote aeronautical development and build support for congressional action. As Robert van der Linden has shown, Hoover's views were instrumental in building a constituency behind federal action. Perhaps not surprisingly, Hoover's influence was particularly strong in the Post Office, the government agency with the most immediate connection to commercial flying. During the early 1920s Postmaster General Harry S. New and Second Assistant Postmaster General Paul Henderson emerged as vocal proponents of Hoover's policies. By the middle of the decade, New consistently articulated a hopeful vision for the future of US commercial aviation, grounding that vision in calls for federal regulation, infrastructure development, and the promotion of commercial activity without resort to formal subsidies. Although his perspective was understandably shaped by his position in the Post Office, New's position on these issues came to echo Hoover's almost exactly.

An examination of New's testimony before the Congressional Air Service Board in 1925 offers a comprehensive summary of his views. The board was created to ascertain why the US aviation industry found itself almost totally unprepared for entry into World War I and to offer recommendations for future policy. Called before the board to explain what the federal government should do to regulate air navigation and promote the industry, New proceeded to outline his hopes for aviation's commercial future. Arguing that the country's primary need was "a continuing national program for the promotion of aeronautics," New suggested that such a program take a holistic view of American aviation in order to promote both military and civilian goals. Commercial aviation, for the postmaster general, represented the cornerstone of that endeavor.[35]

New expressed disappointment that the government had failed to embrace any such program to date. Readily admitting that he didn't know what the future would hold for commercial flying, he suggested a greater rather than a lesser need for focused federal action in light of that uncertainty. Aviation had such promise, he related, "that it becomes a matter of first national importance" to explore the possibilities flying offered. New identified numerous avenues for federal action that represented "absolute prerequisites to the success of commercial aeronautics," none of which were receiving attention. The lack of a responsible federal regulatory agency was particularly worrying. New reported that the Post Office was inundated with requests from business and public officials for federal aid in constructing airfields, beacon lights, and other infrastructure. These activities, however, were beyond Post Office purview when they did not directly relate to the airmail network. New lamented the fact that there existed no authority to which to forward these requests, emphasizing that the Post Office's role in serving airmail routes ill prepared the department for questions of aviation policy. Bearing those limitations in mind, he pushed for the creation of a separate regulatory body, identifying the Commerce Department as the natural place for such an agency.[36]

New's support for Commerce Department oversight, and his push for regulatory legislation, underline the uniformity of opinion between the postmaster general and the commerce secretary, uniformity that extended to the issue of subsidy. Although New had overseen the creation of an airmail network run explicitly by the US government as a service to the nation, he fervently denied the need for subsidization of private commercial carriers. New told the board that for commercial aviation "to be successful it must pay its own way." Limited federal support, however, was appropriate, primarily through airmail payments and government-funded technological research.[37]

Like Hoover, New hoped that the government would take the lead in creating aviation infrastructure. Focusing specifically on airways construction, New argued that the Commerce Department should be given the authority "to provide for lighted airways for the use of companies engaged in aerial transportation." In his mind this represented the extension of existing policy; aviation would receive no more assistance than had other transportation forms. New drew the sharpest comparison between aviation and shipping, seeing a natural correlation between the government's role in creating and maintaining shipping channels and the potential for federal responsibility over airways. His oversight of the federal airmail network left him with an appreciation for the importance airway construction held for commercial flying, and he stridently supported governmental appropriations for that purpose.[38]

Finally, New argued that promoting commercial aviation would also serve military ends. Believing "successful commercial aviation and national security go hand in hand," he echoed Hoover's faith in the informal role commercial aeronautics would play in aiding military preparedness. Like Hoover, New did not believe that civil aviation should form an explicit reserve force for the military. Instead, the development of commercial flying would promote increased manufacturing, infrastructure development, pilot training, and technological research that would benefit both civil and military flying.

While this testimony represents only a snapshot of New's views on aviation, it is nonetheless instructive to note the striking similarities with Hoover's policy pronouncements. As postmaster general, New understood the challenges of operating an air commerce network. His focus on federal guidance, airways construction, the need for a federal bureau, the connections between civil and military aviation, and opposition to a direct subsidy demonstrate a remarkable coherence with the positions the commerce secretary staked out. Specifically, it suggests that Hoover's continued focus on developing a coherent aviation policy was well founded. Ultimately, New's support was more theoretical than practical—he had little direct engagement with the efforts to transform the Post Office airmail service into a viable private industry—but his willingness to nurture the airmail service and his public support for wider government action made him one of Hoover's key allies.

New also aided aviation's cause through his encouragement of Paul Henderson, the second assistant postmaster general and the man tasked with overseeing the Post Office's airmail service. Henderson ardently supported privatizing airmail routes, while his competence in overseeing the Post Office's service provided evidence that commercial flying could achieve success. Henderson was the driving force behind departmental efforts to establish nighttime operations, using the army's experimental lighted airway between Dayton and Columbus, Ohio, as a model for future expansion. Henderson viewed continuous service—and the associated time savings it brought—as a necessary precondition for privatization and a demonstration that aircraft could successfully engage in a stable, worthwhile commercial activity. Beyond that, however, Henderson understood the Post Office's efforts as a crucial step in aviation's development, offering the opportunity to prove to business leaders that flying was worth their investment. In a 1925 article for *Aero Digest*, Henderson addressed this issue explicitly, arguing that the "general theory upon which the Air Mail Service is operated is that of demonstrating the practicability of aviation and thereby stimulating its commercial development."[39]

By 1925 Henderson believed that the service had achieved that goal, creating the necessary foundation for privatization. He understood, however, that the Post Office example alone was not sufficient to draw private capital into the industry. Clearly, the absence of federal regulation presented a barrier to private investment, a situation Henderson well understood. Speaking to Congress about the issue, Henderson emphasized that few would consider investing a significant sum in aviation without "some basic law" to define the rights and responsibilities of the aviator.[40] During this period Henderson worked diligently to establish relationships with leading investors, trying to sell them on the financial possibilities aviation would offer moving forward. That work ultimately bore fruit, attracting interest from Henry Ford, William Rockefeller, Cornelius Vanderbilt Whitney, and other business leaders. Dollars would not be forthcoming, however, until Congress acted to define federal responsibility over the airways.

By 1925, Hoover and his allies were able to marshal a compelling set of arguments in support of the federal government's establishment of regulatory authority over the skies. Hoover's core vision—informal subsidization, federal responsibility over airways to promote safety and commercial growth, and an economical focus on using existing government agencies to provide a home for regulators—found wide support in both government and business circles. As yet, though, there existed insufficient backing for translating that vision into legislative action. Despite the Post Office's successful airmail service, private commercial aviation remained a marginal enterprise at best, providing little impetus for federal engagement.

In February, however, Congressman Clyde Kelly of Pennsylvania introduced a bill that threw the lack of federal regulation into sharp relief and hastened the push for Congress to act. Kelly, chairman of the House Post Office Committee, crafted legislation providing for the transfer of airmail routes from the Post Office to private contractors. The bill authorized a special ten-cent-per-ounce airmail rate and promised airmail carriers 80 percent of operating revenues. These provisions opened new financial possibilities for commercial aviation, offering consistent income and federal support for the continued expansion of the airmail network. Not surprisingly, Kelly's model for airmail payments also aligned with Hoover's push for informal subsidization of the industry.

Ironically, Kelly, a Republican and a staunch ally of railroad interests, crafted the bill at least in large part to limit the expansion of government-funded mail carriage. Kelly hoped to get the government out of the airmail business as soon as possible to prevent direct competition between Post Office planes and his railroad constituents. So eager was Kelly to bring about an end to Post Office airmail service that Paul Henderson had entreated Kelly to delay introducing his bill the previous year. Henderson hoped to delay legislative action until the Post Office was able to undertake successful nighttime operations, making airmail contracts more palatable to Congress and the public while, he hoped, making them more attractive to commercial interests. In the interim, Henderson used the promise of coming legislation to whip up support with potential financiers.[41]

The delay served Kelly well on the legislative front; the Contract Airmail Act sailed through Congress, and in February 1925 President Calvin Coolidge signed it into law. The bill's passage signaled a new era for American commercial aviation, but its general popularity obscured the need for further clarification of the government's responsibility to commercial aeronautics. The so-called Kelly Act allayed financial fears by providing a stable basis for growth in the form of government contracts. It also circumvented congressional worries about governmental subsidization by guaranteeing that airmail carriers would receive revenues from postal receipts rather than from general tax revenues.[42] The bill's passage, however, ultimately served as the beginning, rather than the end, of the debate concerning the federal government's proper relationship to this emerging commercial concern.

Kelly's bill made no mention of federal regulation; its focus was purely the privatization of airmail contracts. As such, its passage focused congressional attention on the need for a federally enforced regulatory framework, in effect mandating some form of federal oversight lest private airmail carriers operate in an environment totally free from supervision. In that sense the Kelly Act hastened additional federal engagement; its passage represented a tacit admission that Hoover's desire for federal safety and licensing guidelines necessitated immediate legislative action, as private carriers would now be entrusted with the safety of the US mail.

By the summer of 1925 virtually all interested parties agreed on the government's need to codify regulatory policy, but uncertainty remained regarding proper extent of federal power. Some members of Congress, state governors, and local and municipal officials pushed to allow individual states and municipalities to license pilots and develop air traffic rules—a situation that flew in the face of Hoover's efforts to promote a national basis for stable growth.[43] Other aviation advocates, most vocally Brigadier General William "Billy" Mitchell, stridently argued that the government needed to create an independent Department of the Air with responsibility over all aspects of military and civilian flying. Further muddying the waters, uncertainty reigned over how the government would create and enforce licensing and airworthiness standards, foundational aspects of any regulatory effort. Despite its easy passage, therefore, the Kelly Act served to encourage, rather than close, debate on these issues as bidding for airmail contracts loomed. Moving forward, it was clear that much work remained to be done; nonetheless, Hoover and his allies had done yeoman's work in framing the conversation. In less than a year their efforts would bear fruit and launch commercial aviation onto the national stage.

2

Regulating the Skies

The Air Commerce Act of 1926

As Herbert Hoover and his allies labored to create a coherent federal aviation policy, they could take pride in the rapid development of American aeronautics. In 1923 the United States, for the first time, captured the prestigious Schneider Trophy, an international seaplane race first held in 1913 and hotly contested by the United States, Britain, France, and Italy. Over land, contestants in the national Pulitzer Trophy air races were reaching speeds approaching 250 miles per hour, almost 100 miles per hour more than they had achieved only five years earlier. In June of 1924, army pilot Russell Maughan became the first person to cross the country in less than a day, flying from Long Island to San Francisco in a shade less than twenty-two hours.

That same year, the Army Air Service initiated plans to embark upon the first aerial circumnavigation of the globe. The army effort was driven in large part by a desire to demonstrate the Air Service's relevance to a skeptical Army General Staff and an increasingly tight-fisted Congress. Like the rest of the army and navy, military aviators found themselves understaffed and saddled with obsolete equipment, conditions that were growing worse every year. Aviation advocates believed that their circumstances reflected military and civilian leaders' lack of appreciation for aviation's unique value to national defense. Brigadier General William "Billy" Mitchell, assistant chief of the Army Air Service, represented the loudest voice in that camp. Mitchell had sponsored aerial exhibitions for military and civilian leaders in 1921 and 1923, the most famous of which resulted in the sinking of the captured German dreadnaught *Ostfriesland* by US Army bombers in only twenty-two minutes. In the wake of the bombers' spectacular success, Mitchell argued that the Air Service should supplant the navy as the foremost guardian of US shores. With aircraft achieving sufficient range to protect American coasts at distances approaching two hundred miles, Mitchell and his supporters pushed for military and congressional leaders to place their trust—and their appropriations—in the hands of the Air Service.

Unfortunately for Mitchell, the Air Service had few supporters in the General Staff or in Congress. Americans' disenchantment with the Versailles Treaty combined with rising isolationist sentiment to make national defense a low priority. With the United States enjoying allies on its borders and oceans separating it from potential enemies, the country's strategic position appeared secure. The prospects of an enemy air attack seemed far-fetched at best in an era when transoceanic flight largely remained a dream. In this context the most likely challenge the US military would face was a naval invasion—a challenge most military and civilian leaders agreed would best be met by seaborne forces. Despite Mitchell's vociferous efforts to challenge this perceived wisdom, Air Service requests for additional funding fell on deaf ears.

With frustration building, Air Service leaders hoped that a successful around-the-world flight would draw attention to their growing capabilities and raise the service's profile. Preparations began in 1923 with two officers embarking on an information-gathering trip to chart a route for the proposed endeavor. The Air Service contracted the Douglas Aircraft Company to construct five planes—a prototype and four for the flight itself—for the undertaking, specifying that the craft had to be rugged and reliable and have the capability to use wheels or pontoons for takeoff and landing. The resulting Douglas World Cruisers were large, single-engined, two-seat biplanes developed from an existing navy bomber. Major General Mason M. Patrick, chief of the Air Service, oversaw the selection of four of the army's top pilots for the flight and ensured that army personnel completed extensive preparations for fueling and repairs along the route. Following exhaustive training and flight testing, the crews piloted their aircraft from the Douglas factory in southern California to Seattle to begin their journey officially. On April 6, 1924, the *Seattle*, *Boston*, *Chicago*, and *New Orleans* took to the skies to great fanfare, destined for Alaska, Japan, China, Thailand, Burma, India, Iran, the Balkans, France, England, Canada, and a return to the west coast of the United States. Only two of the original aircraft completed the trip: the *Seattle* crashed into a mountain in Alaska, and the *Boston* suffered engine failure in the North Atlantic, rendering the plane inoperable. Fortunately, though, none of the crewmen were badly injured. The surviving World Cruisers landed in Seattle on September 28, having flown 27,553 miles in 175 days, with a flight time of just over 371 hours.[1]

The triumphal return of the army planes and pilots to the United States prefaced an emerging boom in American commercial flying. The passage of the Kelly Act heralded a new era of economic stability and emphasized the pressing need for the federal government to establish regulatory authority over the skies. The emerging consensus behind federal regulation, however, obscured disagreement over how to translate that vision into reality. Hoover and his allies had been largely successful in their efforts to frame the public debate surrounding the need for federal action, but through 1925 they remained unable to secure legislation. While the passage of the Kelly Act spurred efforts to formalize federal oversight, a number of issues stood in the way of congressional action, including a lack of presidential engagement; ongoing calls for the government to consolidate all military and civilian aviation-related activities in a single, independent department; political infighting in Congress; constitutional concerns regarding the federal government's ability to regulate air commerce; and disagreement over the proper balance of state and federal regulatory power.

By 1926 Hoover and a cast of supporters would overcome these obstacles and realize their goal of formalizing federal control over air commerce. Making the most of the rapidly changing aeronautical and legislative landscape, aviation advocates such as William MacCracken would join forces with industry leaders and lawmakers to craft American air commerce's legislative cornerstone, the Air Commerce Act of 1926. That bill codified the federal government's commitment to supporting the development of commercial aviation and created the conditions for the possibility of stable, solvent airline operations. In so doing the act represented the culmination of Hoover's efforts as commerce secretary, finally realizing his vision of a sound, government-guided commercial aviation industry.

While the army's dramatic around-the-world flight demonstrated the dramatic gains aviation continued to make, its completion had unintended repercussions for US aviation policy, helping to set in motion a series of events leading to congressional passage of the 1926 Air Commerce Act. Mitchell, though not directly involved in the effort, used the flight as an impetus to expand his lobbying activities. Citing the circumnavigation as evidence that the United States could no longer count on ocean barriers to protect the country from air attack, Mitchell renewed his calls for greater appropriations for military aviation while petitioning Congress to create a Department of the Air encompassing all aspects of civil and military aviation. For Mitchell, aviation's revolutionary nature held tremendous promise, promise that was hamstrung by shortsighted military and civilian leaders. Only a separate department free from such meddling would allow aeronautics to achieve its full potential. Mitchell's outspoken efforts quickly aroused opposition in both military and governmental circles, but the maverick general soon found a new platform from which to trumpet his views.[2]

While the Air Service was engaged in preparations for its round-the-world flight, progressive Republicans in Congress began launching increasingly pointed attacks on the Coolidge administration's aviation policy. Led by Congressman John M. Nelson of Wisconsin, these legislators charged Hoover and others with overseeing policies that facilitated collusion in the aircraft industry. Progressives argued that Commerce Department activities were creating monopolies, and that leaders of an emerging aircraft trust were behind Hoover's calls for a Bureau of Aeronautics. Nelson also charged the army and navy with improperly letting out contracts for military aircraft. These attacks eventually coalesced during the Sixty-Eighth Congress when Republican insurgents created the House of Representatives Select Committee on Inquiry into Operations of the United States Air Service, more commonly known as the Lampert committee after its chair, Florian Lampert (R-WI).[3]

Lampert quickly indicated that the committee would not limit its activities to questions surrounding military contracts; it would engage in a thoroughgoing investigation of American aeronautics. Doing just that, the committee heard testimony from numerous industry leaders in 1924 and early 1925. Significantly, one of the committee members, Frank L. Reid (R-IL), was a Mitchell supporter and facilitated Mitchell's testimony before the group. Making the most of his platform, Mitchell engaged in a scathing attack on army leadership, arguing that the General Staff was engaged in a deliberate effort to obstruct aeronautical development. Mitchell's outspoken testimony drew significant attention, most of it negative. His public willingness to castigate his superiors resulted in his being stripped of his post as assistant chief of the Air Service. He resigned from the Army soon afterward.[4]

As the Lampert committee concluded its hearing in early 1925 and its members began the arduous task of synthesizing its findings, President Coolidge grew increasingly worried about the impending publication of the committee's report. The influence of Mitchell's strident calls for a Department of the Air and insurgent Republican concerns about collusion in the industry suggested that the committee's recommendations would oppose the model Hoover had worked so hard to define. The passage of the Kelly Act in February, moreover, highlighted the impending need for federal action vis-à-vis commercial flying. Those concerns, combined with the political challenge Coolidge perceived in the committee's activities, spurred the president to action. Knowing that Lampert's report would not be finalized until the end of the year, Coolidge sought to preempt the House committee by establishing his own investigatory body.

Before the president could act, two intervening incidents hastened Coolidge's efforts. First, in late August two navy flying boats attempted a nonstop flight from California to Hawaii. One had engine trouble soon after taking off, and the second aircraft ran out of fuel and was forced to land in the central Pacific about four hundred miles from Oahu, at which point the navy lost contact with it. Three days later, while Americans remained caught up in the search for the missing seaplane, the *Shenandoah*, a Navy dirigible, crashed during a storm in Ohio, resulting in the deaths of thirteen servicemen. Nine days later, after the search for it had been ended, the flying boat, navigating on the surface with an improvised sail made of wing cloth, arrived at the island of Kauai. These two incidents, a disaster and a near-disaster, provided administration opponents with new ammunition for their attacks against the president, his advisors, and the military. Not surprisingly, Billy Mitchell responded with the loudest criticism. In a widely released statement to the press, Mitchell, now a colonel, charged the military leadership with deliberately obstructing aeronautical development. This "criminal neglect" represented an "almost treasonable offense" in Mitchell's opinion and heightened his calls for a Department of the Air. While the navy subsequently located the lost seaplane, its crew none the worse for wear, the damage had been done. Mitchell's vitriolic opposition to the administration resulted in his court-martial, but Coolidge could not dismiss the public challenge to his administration so easily. Worried that the recent uproar would provide the Lampert committee with greater momentum, Coolidge acted swiftly to regain control of the debate.[5]

The result was the President's Aircraft Board, led by Dwight Morrow, a partner in J. P Morgan and a close confidant of the president since their college days at Amherst. Coolidge hand-picked the committee members, who included William Durand of the NACA, Senator Hiram Bingham, a former army pilot and sponsor of aviation regulatory legislation supported by Hoover, and Howard Coffin, first president of the National Aeronautics Association (NAA) and president of National Air Transport. Most immediately, Coolidge tasked the board with determining "the best means of developing and applying aircraft in the national defense," but in reality the board's purview was much wider. Coolidge hoped that his working group would engage all aspects of American aeronautics and return with a comprehensive set of recommendations. Concurrently, Coolidge evidenced a growing personal interest in commercial flying. The same day that he extended invitations to members of the proposed board, the president met with a "group interested in commercial air transportation" for three-quarters of an hour, asking many questions and taking an active role in the discussion.[6]

Coolidge and Morrow knew they had little time to waste. With the Lampert committee's report due in mid-December, the President's Aircraft Board had less than three months to complete its activities. Working diligently, the board interviewed nearly one hundred witnesses in less than a month. Their testimony broke little new ground, as virtually all had appeared before the Lampert committee during the latter's five-month-long series of hearings. Nonetheless, upon completing the investigatory portion of their activities, Morrow and his colleagues retired from the public eye to engage in four weeks of internal conferences, striving for unanimity in their recommendations to the president. By the end of November they achieved that goal and formally submitted their report to Coolidge on December 2, almost two weeks before the Lampert committee publicized its findings.[7]

Coolidge could hardly have been happier with the results. Breaking little new ground, the Morrow board report primarily served to summarize the prevailing wisdom concerning the federal government's role in aeronautical development. With regard to military aviation, Morrow and his colleagues advised against the creation of a separate air branch. Emphasizing that both the army and the navy should continue to evolve their respective air arms, the board recommended that those arms receive additional autonomy and fall under the leadership of experienced airmen. In line with Hoover's vision, the report strongly supported a continued separation between civil and military aviation, additional federal aid for aeronautical development, federal establishment and maintenance of air navigation facilities, federal regulation over air transport, federal inspection and regulation of airframes and engines, and the creation of a Bureau of Civil Aeronautics in the Department of Commerce. While hardly revelatory, the board's proposals provided Coolidge with powerful ammunition in favor of the administration's prevailing aviation policy and a foil for any challenges from the Lampert committee.[8]

Coolidge found more support in the conclusions of an additional investigatory body that completed its activities at virtually the same time. Dating its origins to the spring of 1925, the Joint Committee on Civil Aviation represented yet another effort by Herbert Hoover to define the proper nature of federal engagement with commercial flying. Leaning on his background as an engineer, Hoover authorized a comprehensive study of transportation networks, to be performed in concert with leading figures in the private sector. The commerce secretary brought together members of the American Engineering Council, the aviation industry, technical experts, and representatives from the Commerce Department to create a voluntary technical commission to consider the state of aviation both in America and abroad. The committee's brief was to determine the possibility of "lifting a sufficient amount of the existing traffic into the air to make it self-supporting."[9]

Unsurprisingly, the joint committee's recommendations cohered almost exactly with those of the Morrow board, most significantly in the call for the creation of an aviation regulatory agency within the Department of Commerce. Hoover's group, did, however, accumulate prodigious amounts of research that gave additional weight to the joint committee's proposals; those proposals also moved beyond those of the Morrow board in several important aspects. The joint committee counseled that the government work actively to encourage civilian flying, conduct competitions to encourage the development of improved commercial aircraft, work to lower insurance rates for airline passengers, and encourage localities to develop airfields to help extend air transport service. These recommendations prefaced the expanding role the Department of Commerce would embrace in coming years and furthered the ongoing relationships Hoover had nurtured with leading members of the aeronautics industry.[10]

Ironically, when the Lampert committee released its findings on December 14, the results were far less radical than Mitchell and his supporters had hoped and Coolidge and Hoover had feared. While Lampert did recommend that the government create a Department of Defense overseeing the army, the navy, and a separate air branch, each with equal standing, the group's findings with regard to commercial aviation were almost indistinguishable from Morrow's. Most importantly, Lampert pushed for a separation between civil and military aviation, much to Mitchell's chagrin; federal regulation of the airways; federal responsibility for air navigation; and the creation of a regulatory bureau in the Commerce Department. Far from representing a challenge to Coolidge administration policy, the report largely confirmed the widespread agreement on the proper course of federal action moving forward.[11]

By the end of 1925, then, conditions augured well for the federal government to act. Following his review of the Morrow board's report, Coolidge forwarded it to Congress with his full support, encouraging lawmakers to translate the board's recommendations into legislative action. With the Lampert committee's conclusions supporting, rather than opposing, administration wishes and the additional evidence provided by Hoover's joint committee, Coolidge occupied a position of strength. The clear presidential mandate to act, moreover, represented an unambiguous message to uninterested and uninformed legislators. These conditions, combined with the looming implications of the Kelly Act and continued success of Post Office operations suggested that commercial aviation advocates had achieved an important tipping point. In an address to the Law Club that December, William MacCracken—a lawyer and pivotal figure in the crafting and implementation of subsequent legislation—spoke for many like-minded supporters, stating, "We have reached the point where investigations should cease." For MacCracken, Hoover, Henderson, and others, the time was overdue for "constructive accomplishment [to] begin."[12]

By the new year Coolidge's mandate bore fruit as "legislators scurried to get in on the act." Lawmakers introduced a flurry of aviation-related bills that spring, ultimately more than twenty during the first session of the Sixty-Ninth Congress.[13] The path to a new law would not be entirely smooth, however. Significant obstacles remained to be overcome, the majority of which reflected long-standing disagreements about the legal and constitutional implications of federal control over the skies.

The origins of legislative discord emerged well before Coolidge encouraged Congress to act. In the years after World War I a number of lawmakers had introduced legislation providing for some measure of federal jurisdiction over civil aviation. Senator James Wadsworth (R-NY) and Congressman Samuel Winslow (R-MA) sponsored two of the most influential bills, both of which enjoyed support from the Commerce Department and powerful members of the aviation community. Wadsworth's bill, first introduced in 1921, offered a broad outline for federal control over interstate air commerce. Seeking to keep his bill simple, Wadsworth's proposal granted the secretary of commerce the power to organize, implement, and enforce a regulatory structure for civil aviation; it did not delve into the specifics of that oversight. Winslow's bill, in contrast, was much more detailed. Introduced in 1923, it granted the government power to regulate both interstate and intrastate air commerce and laid out a comprehensive set of regulations designed to govern all aspects of civil flying.[14] In spite of their popularity with aviation supporters, neither bill found sufficient support in Congress for passage. The narrative of these failed efforts sheds light on the congressional barriers aviation advocates faced in their efforts to secure federal regulation and the strategies they employed as they attempted to build a coalition for legislative action; it also prefaces the challenges facing legislators in the wake of Coolidge's mandate to act.

Wadsworth's proposal grew out of Hoover's July 1921 conference with the Aero Club of America, Society of Automotive Engineers, National Aircraft Underwriters Association, and Manufacturers Aircraft Association. At that meeting industry leaders pushed the Commerce Department to take the lead in defining a path forward for commercial flying, preferably one that included federal oversight. Hoover concurred, encouraging the delegation to draft appropriate legislation. The ensuing bill, in modified form, found its way to Wadsworth's office by the end of 1921. Wadsworth submitted it to Congress in December and would continue to do so in each session for the next five years.[15]

The Winslow bill evidenced a more complicated history. Primarily the work of Chicago lawyer William MacCracken, the House bill's gestation reflected the ongoing effects of legal and organizational changes in the larger aeronautical context. MacCracken, like many other aviation advocates, had flown for the US Air Service during the war, sparking a long-lasting affinity for aviation. After the war he embraced a law career and soon found himself delving into the legal dictates of flying. Surprisingly for MacCracken, virtually no such law existed. In 1920 it was not even clear whether aircraft overflying private property were engaged in criminal trespass. Attending a 1920 American Bar Association (ABA) session on aviation law, MacCracken was dismayed to discover that not only was engagement with aeronautics sorely lacking, little impetus existed to formulate guidelines moving forward. MacCracken took it upon himself to do so, assuming leadership of a committee tasked to study the subject. The group's conclusions highlighted the legal vacuum in which aviation then operated and stressed the need for the federal government to assume leadership by establishing comprehensive regulatory legislation. Unfortunately for MacCracken, his conclusions rubbed many in the ABA the wrong way, and he found himself forced to begin work anew with a reconstituted group.[16]

MacCracken's subsequent work with the Committee on the Law of Aeronautics immersed him in the most pressing legal issue of the period: the tension between state and federal power with regard to aviation. MacCracken firmly supported federal preeminence, arguing "regulation by the several states is bound to be costly, lead to confusion, and once established will be difficult to dislodge." He, like Hoover, worried that a patchwork of state laws would establish overlapping and conflicting regulations, creating a complicated and costly legal framework hindering the expansion of air commerce. MacCracken quickly found, however, that support for that view was not unanimous. George Bogert, another member of the group, was simultaneously chairing a committee to draft a uniform state aviation law, action that flew in the face of MacCracken's desire to see overarching federal control over the skies. Neither man wished their respective committees to create mutually exclusive recommendations, so Bogert and MacCracken agreed to a conference to iron out the thorny issue. They met in Washington in February 1922, where MacCracken's view prevailed. He and Bogert agreed that federal rather than state law should govern flying; they also believed that the current legal vacuum cried out for comprehensive legislation. The participants left the capital satisfied with their progress, but as they would discover, their agreement did not extend to Congress.[17]

As MacCracken immersed himself in aviation law, he simultaneously found himself engaged in an effort to create a new aviation advocacy organization. MacCracken's involvement coincided with a transitional period for aviation supporters in the private sector. As interested parties increasingly pushed for federal action and found themselves working ever more closely with officials in the Commerce Department, industry leaders sought greater unity in their lobbying efforts. Existing organizations such as the Manufacturers Aircraft Association (MAA) and Aeronautical Chamber of Commerce (ACC) were too parochial, unequal to the task of promoting broad-based support, raising money, and developing lasting influence with policy makers. The MAA, in particular, functioned primarily as a trade organization and had ties to the controversy surrounding wartime production contracts, a significant mark against it in many eyes. Industry leaders saw the need for a broad-based organization that would bring together all aviation supporters under a single umbrella. Since 1905 the Aero Club of America—the oldest private aviation promotion organization in the United States—had nominally served in that role, but in the early 1920s the Aero Club was in turmoil. Originally established as a gentlemen's club for aviation enthusiasts, the Aero Club was little prepared to embrace national marketing and lobbying efforts. Worse, new Aero Club leadership had embarked on a war of words against aircraft manufacturers and financiers linked to wartime production scandals. Many of those men were Aero Club members, and the ensuing uproar rent the organization apart.

The collapse of the Aero Club of America opened the door for the creation of a new advocacy group better positioned to promote industry interests to the government and American people. Led by Howard Coffin, a group of industry leaders set out to organize a national home for all parties interested in American aeronautical development. Herbert Hoover proved a key supporter of that effort, writing that he "would welcome such an association," particularly if federal aviation oversight found a home in the Commerce Department.[18] Coffin and his allies initiated a coup in the Aero Club, assuming leadership of that organization and transferring its assets and the majority of its membership to the new group—the National Aeronautics Association (NAA). The creation of the NAA marked a milestone for aviation advocates. For the first time they could rely on a national organization specifically tasked with promoting American flying. From the outset the NAA leadership focused on fundraising, marketing, and lobbying efforts designed to promote all aspects of US aeronautics.

MacCracken played a central role in the NAA from the very beginning. Primarily responsible for the legal work necessary to incorporate the new group, he also presided at the October 1922 conference that created the NAA. Subsequently, he assumed leadership of the NAA's Legislative Committee, unifying the ABA's and NAA's legal agendas and legislative goals. For the time being, MacCracken had found a home, allowing him the time and financial security to expand his support for American flying. First on his agenda was the passage of federal regulatory legislation, a goal that now had the full support of the nation's largest aviation lobbying group.[19]

MacCracken went to work immediately. Unsatisfied with the Wadsworth bill, which he believed lacked the specificity necessary to assert positive control over commercial flying, MacCracken leaned on a relationship he had established during his earlier Washington conference. In February, while he was in the capital attempting to reconcile his legal agenda with Bogert's, MacCracken met with Representative Winslow regarding the congressman's willingness to sponsor an aviation bill. For MacCracken, Winslow, the chairman of the House Committee on Interstate and Foreign Commerce, was the ideal candidate to introduce legislation. The representative assented, granting MacCracken broad latitude to craft a bill as the latter saw fit. Through the spring and summer of 1922, as Coffin and his allies organized the NAA, MacCracken worked to draft a bill embracing his and the new group's desires for comprehensive federal oversight. In that effort MacCracken worked closely with the Commerce Department, as both sides recognized that implementation would fall to Hoover and his subordinates. To that end Hoover tasked the Commerce Department solicitor, William Lamb, to aid in crafting the legislation. As the proposal developed, MacCracken also benefited from ongoing input from Hoover and Frederick Lee, a lawyer working for Winslow via the House Legislative Drafting Service. By the following January, MacCracken was finished, and Winslow introduced the bill in the closing weeks of the congressional term. The finished product was far more detailed than Wadsworth's, reflecting an effort to both establish a basis for federal oversight and articulate a set of regulations defining the nature and extent of federal responsibilities.[20]

By the spring of 1923 supporters of aviation legislation had reason for optimism as the two influential bills sat before Congress. Unfortunately, in spite of their best efforts, neither garnered sufficient support for passage. Wadsworth's bill was more successful, clearing the Senate on several occasions. Its popularity stemmed from its limited nature; the proposal made no mention of specific regulations, and it applied only to interstate commerce. Its lack of specificity, however, also gained less support with the aviation lobby, many of whom felt that the bill failed to provide for sufficient federal engagement. Winslow's bill, in contrast, drew criticism from states' rights supporters objecting to federal control over intrastate commerce and private fliers who believed the proposed regulations would be so rigorous as to inhibit their airborne activities. The states' rights issue was a particular thorny one, as many Southern congressmen argued that the bill was unconstitutional in light of the limitations the Interstate Commerce Act placed on federal control within the separate states. These issues, combined with the larger cultural and economic atmosphere, doomed efforts to pass either bill—at least before outside events intervened.

Those concerns notwithstanding, both the Wadsworth and Winslow bills drew tremendous interest from the aviation community. Correspondence flourished between members of the ACC, MAA, and NAA expressing a desire for Congress to pass new legislation; many of these same figures also spoke with Commerce Department officials and members of Congress in support of federal action. In the fall of 1922 Godfrey Cabot, a member of the board of governors of the newly formed NAA, wrote to MacCracken to express his belief that the NAA's "most important duty" was to support regulatory legislation. Samuel Bradley, a leading figure in the MAA and ACC, looked to the Wadsworth bill to fulfill that goal, emphasizing the need to "impress upon President Harding, Secretary Hoover [and] Senators and Congressman generally" the need to pass the Wadsworth bill "without further delay." The following June, NAA president Howard Coffin confirmed the NAA's focus on securing the passage of a new law, writing that "obtaining the obviously necessary congressional action for the proper control of aviation" remained at the heart of association goals.[21]

MacCracken stood at the center of those efforts. In addition to his work crafting the Winslow bill, MacCracken engaged in ongoing lobbying efforts on behalf of his new employer. Writing to Samuel Bradley in response to a request to help "get some prompt action" on pending aviation legislation, MacCracken responded with assurances that he would "scare up some activity" in Washington to "impress upon Congressman Winslow the desire for action."[22] Winslow, however, demonstrated a maddening lack of focus. Initially content to sponsor MacCracken's creation, he subsequently became enamored with the idea of an independent Department of the Air. Though MacCracken and Hoover were able to bring the congressman back around to the initial proposal, Winslow displayed an inconsistent interest in the measure, failing to lobby for its passage with the vigor aviation advocates desired.

As the months dragged on without much apparent progress, frustrations grew. Ongoing efforts to modify the Winslow bill drew particular concern from Howard Coffin. In the summer of 1923, several months after Winslow first introduced the bill, Coffin wrote NAA vice president B. H. Mulvihill expressing his worry that "if we continue making changes in the Winslow Bill there will be no possible chance of getting it enacted." While Coffin admitted that the current bill was not perfect, he emphasized that it was a clear step forward and "nearly enough right" to serve as the basis for future provisions. Shortly thereafter MacCracken emphasized to Coffin the need to "present a united front" in order to push the legislative proposal forward. Responding to Coffin's concerns about ongoing modifications to the bill, MacCracken also assured the NAA president that "any suggested changes will be carefully scrutinized by [Fred Lee] as well as myself." MacCracken's assurances, however, did not calm the NAA president; by the fall Coffin vigorously emphasizing that "the Winslow . . . or similar bills [*sic*] must be passed." While MacCracken continued to press Winslow to act, writing to him on several occasions, the bill made little progress during the Sixty-Eighth Congress.[23]

As Coffin, MacCracken, and others pushed Congress to act, they found themselves embroiled in an ongoing struggle to preempt independent state action. George Bogert had left his 1922 meeting with MacCracken believing that federal law should govern commercial flying, but the lack of federal action perpetuated a worrying legal vacuum. With Congress's failure to take action, the Commission on Uniform State Laws had approved an aviation statute, which subsequently received the ABA's endorsement. Bogert remained a supporter of federal authority, but as time passed, more and more states began exploring independent legislative action. By the spring of 1923 Massachusetts had passed an aviation law, and forty other states were considering such a measure.

Aviation supporters immediately expressed concern about the situation and worked to forestall state action. In March, Samuel Bradley wrote to B. H. Mulvihill regarding the "premature and perhaps obstructive legislation by the separate states." Bradley hoped that the NAA vice president would push the association's legislative committee to "give immediate concern to this situation." Bradley suggested that the NAA sponsor a national publicity campaign in favor of federal action, supported by a vigorous lobbying effort in the capital. MacCracken, chair of the legislative committee, was clearly on Bradley's side and on numerous occasions emphasized his preference for national over state legislation. In April the situation appeared worrying enough to the NAA leadership that Mulvihill wrote MacCracken suggesting that the NAA sponsor a conference to address all aspects of aviation law and reconcile state and federal efforts. MacCracken vehemently opposed such action, arguing that the NAA should maintain its focus on passing the Winslow bill, which would supersede any state-level activity. MacCracken's argument swayed Howard Coffin, and the NAA leadership agreed to postpone any engagement with state laws.[24]

As the fall dragged on without any movement from Winslow, MacCracken reluctantly modified his view on state-level action. While he remained focused on securing federal legislation, MacCracken moved to mitigate the potential confusion state laws could create by giving tepid support to the uniform statute Bogert backed. In December, MacCracken wrote to Bogert urging "everyone who is interested in aviation legislation . . . to oppose all measures except the uniform law." MacCracken also made clear his opposition to any modifications to that statute, hoping to maintain at least some measure of consistency in the legal realm.[25]

As MacCracken and his allies sought to forestall state action, they maintained their focus on pushing Congress to act. Although Winslow demonstrated inconsistent interest in the aviation bill, aviation advocates continued to express faith in their ability to secure its passage. "A vast amount of work lies ahead," wrote Howard Coffin in September, reflecting on the goals put forward at the NAA's national convention in September, but he maintained the organization's focus on the legislative push. MacCracken maintained periodic correspondence with Winslow, which he invariably used to prod the congressman to action. Winslow would not be hurried, and his committee did not begin hearings on the aviation statute until December 1924.[26]

Winslow's bill cleared the committee in January 1925, though not without difficulty. MacCracken's proposal drew significant criticism from many members, largely in light of its comprehensive approach to federal control. Detailed as it was, congressmen found themselves examining not merely a proposal for federal regulation, but also the regulatory structure itself. As such, the bill encompassed myriad points with which committee members could take issue, and take issue they did. Most prominently, Southerners objected to the proposal's call for federal regulation of intrastate commerce. Many felt that this provision extended beyond the constitutional boundaries established by the Commerce Clause and worried about the future implications for federal control over other forms of transportation. With Winslow's blessing, MacCracken appeared before the committee and provided an eloquent defense of the legislation's constitutional foundation. Though he was not able to quell all committee members' concerns, MacCracken's advocacy was sufficient to move the bill out of committee, where it languished for the remainder of the Sixty-Eighth Congress.[27]

By the spring of 1925, then, aviation advocates could look hopefully to either the Wadsworth or the Winslow bill for the promise of federal action. Unfortunately, neither bill made any headway in Congress, frustrating advocates' desires finally to formalize federal control over the skies. Behind the scenes, however, conditions augured well for congressional action in the coming year. Herbert Hoover's tireless work to create a consensus regarding the need for and proper scope of federal action increasingly bore fruit, and the passage of the Kelly Act focused attention on the pressing need for federal regulation. It was in this environment that the Lampert committee, the Morrow board, and the Joint Committee on Civil Aviation undertook their respective activities. Their findings, combined with a clear mandate to act from the president, provided the impetus necessary finally to secure legislation.

The bill that ultimately became the Civil Aeronautics Act emerged directly from Hoover's and Coolidge's advocacy. Crafted by Stephen Davis—successor to William Lamb as Commerce Department solicitor—and introduced by Senator Hiram Bingham (R-CT) on December 8, 1925, the proposed legislation adhered to the recommendations of the Morrow board in almost every way. This was no surprise, as Bingham had served with that group and had helped to craft its recommendations. In effect, Bingham's bill served as a new version of the Wadsworth bill, though one that more explicitly reflected Hoover's vision. Bingham's proposal provided for federal regulation of interstate air commerce, placed responsibility for that oversight in the Commerce Department, and allowed for federal authorities to create and maintain airways and air navigation facilities. Hoover's influence showed also in the fact that Bingham proposed using existing bureaus to facilitate oversight and regulation of the skies—for example, the Bureau of Lighthouses would oversee airway development and lighting. This model fit well with Hoover's drive for economy while still providing for expanded federal authority.

Bingham's bill fared well in the Senate. Its focus on interstate flying avoided the controversy that dogged Winslow's bill, and clear support from the president and commerce secretary helped facilitate its passage. In one area, however, Bingham experienced significant pushback. Seeking to unify federal responsibilities over aeronautics, the senator proposed placing the National Advisory Committee for Aeronautics (NACA) under Commerce Department control—a proposal that originated with Hoover's desire to streamline federal oversight and center federal engagement with civil aviation under the Commerce Department umbrella. This did not sit well with NACA leadership and quickly drew a strong response from NACA chairman Charles Walcott. Only four days after Bingham introduced his bill, Walcott wrote the senator, stating that "the War and Navy Departments and the Advisory Committee are much concerned with the provision." Walcott went on to emphasize that the Morrow board report failed to endorse such a move, and that Coolidge had recently highlighted the NACA's independent status as integral to its mission and success. In subsequent days Walcott followed his letter with a series of phone calls entreating Bingham to strike the provision from his bill, requests echoed by army and navy leaders. Although Hoover opposed such a move—going so far as to object to a request from the secretary of war to bow to pressure from Walcott—on December 16 Bingham's bill, minus the NACA provision, cleared the Senate with minimal opposition.[28]

On the House side, James Parker (R-NY) led the charge, introducing a bill identical to Bingham's on December 10. There, Davis's bill encountered rougher waters. Almost immediately supporters of Winslow's old bill objected to the lack of specificity and strength in the proposed law. Notably, William MacCracken led a charge to revise the legislation by extending federal regulatory authority to some aspects of intrastate flying—most significantly by mandating that all aircraft receive federal registration and certification, not only those engaged in interstate commerce, and that the federal government take responsibility for establishing airports. While MacCracken's revisions did not encompass the level of specificity that Winslow's bill had, they nonetheless revived worries that Southern opponents would block the passage of the newly strengthened proposal. Several Southern congressmen did wave the states' rights banner during the House debate, but ultimately their opposition was no match for the momentum pushing the bill forward. Parker's legislation cleared the House on April 12, 1926, and within the week the House-Senate conference began ironing out the differences between the bills.[29]

As the conference began, Bingham turned to the NACA for support in unifying the two bills. On April 15 Bingham asked Charles Walcott to convene a subcommittee to draft a report with recommendations to that effect.[30] Not surprisingly, the NACA, one of the Senate conferees and a consistently conservative voice in the aviation advocacy community, returned a series of recommendations that resolved the disparities between the House and Senate bills overwhelmingly in the Senate bill's favor.

Crucially, the subcommittee provided unequivocal guidance on the two most significant points of disagreement between the two bills: federal responsibility for airports and federal regulation of intrastate commerce. On the former issue the NACA echoed Hoover's opinion—and followed the recommendations of the Morrow board—almost exactly. Writing in their report that federal policy "regarding airports . . . should be analogous to its policy regarding seaports," the subcommittee highlighted the fact that government control over waterways ended at the dock, leaving to local authorities control over port facilities. In addition to citing this existing precedent, the subcommittee noted two negative ramifications that would emerge from federal control over airports. First, federal responsibility for airports would be expensive; it would mandate large congressional appropriations to allow the secretary of commerce to purchase land in cities and towns throughout the nation and prepare that real estate for use as airports. Citing the tremendous burden on the treasury, the NACA expressed doubt that such a policy would allow for the adequate expansion of aviation-related infrastructure. In fact, the NACA report went so far as to suggest that the resulting failure to establish airports "as needed" would result in "the primary object of the bill—the encouragement of commercial aviation"—being defeated. In a related vein, the subcommittee suggested the expanded federal authority would destroy local initiative, removing the motivation to establish local airports and hindering the development of air commerce.[31]

NACA leaders also opposed extending federal regulatory authority to intrastate commerce and private flying. While acknowledging the existence of both constitutional and practical concerns with such an extension, the advisory committee restricted its commentary to the practical ramifications of the provision, leaving the constitutional issue to Congress. On the practical side, the subcommittee began by highlighting the purpose of the proposed legislation: to encourage commercial aviation by providing "reasonable and needful regulations." Extending those regulations to intrastate and private efforts was not necessary and in fact represented an unnecessary complication that detracted from the bill's core agenda. Further, NACA leaders believed that if the federal government's authority extended to private flying, the effect would be "to drive out of the air a major portion of the privately owned aircraft and private flyers" due to "the nuisance and inconvenience of unnecessary regulation."[32] Therefore, the NACA strongly recommended striking the relevant provisions from the bill for the benefit of commercial and private aviators alike.

On April 22 the subcommittee submitted their report to Walcott, who approved it and sent it on to Bingham the next day. The report then informed the discussions of the House-Senate conference, shaping the debate as Bingham had hoped. Ultimately, the conference concurred with the subcommittee on the airport issue, clearly establishing airports as private concerns. On the regulatory issue, however, MacCracken and his supporters were able to force a compromise. Senate and House conferees agreed that federal licensing and certification would only apply to aircraft and aviators engaged in interstate commerce. All pilots, however, would have to accede to federal air traffic rules while aloft. This compromise helped mollify Southern opponents of expanded federal control and cohered with the NACA's desire that federal regulations not present a barrier to private pilots, while still pushing forward federal responsibility for safety and commercial growth. Both houses of Congress agreed to the conference report on May 13, and President Coolidge signed the Air Commerce Act (ACA) into law only a week later.

Coolidge's signature signaled a new era for American commercial aviation. After a decade of at times hesitant progress, air transport seemed poised for dramatic gains. The Post Office's persistent efforts to pioneer scheduled airmail service, the Kelly Act's transfer of those routes to private contractors, and the newly signed ACA's codification of federal authority over regulation, infrastructure development, and promotion created a stable foundation and new commercial opportunities for airlines. These developments owed much to Hoover's vision and his persistent efforts to champion the nascent air transport industry. His model for federal engagement, shaped by William MacCracken's desire for expanded federal authority over commercial flying, now held sway, providing both financial and regulatory foundations for pioneering air carriers.

Important questions remained to be answered, however. Most important: Who would serve as the new assistant secretary for aeronautics? This question created an unexpected challenge for Hoover. The commerce secretary first turned to Paul Henderson, a natural fit in the wake of his activities overseeing the Post Office airmail service. Henderson, however, had transitioned out of government service and had found employment with the newly created National Air Transport. His position provided him the opportunity to build an airline from the ground up and, perhaps even more importantly, receive far better compensation than the government could offer. Henderson passed on the nomination, leading Hoover to turn to Hollinshead N. Taylor, a Philadelphia businessman with long-standing connections to the aviation community. Taylor too refused, like Henderson preferring to remain in the private sector. At this juncture Hoover tapped none other than William MacCracken, perhaps the most logical choice in light of his activities concerning the ACA and his legal training but also a controversial one. While MacCracken had support from Hoover and many leading members of the aviation community—whose interest he had served so well in the legislative battles of the mid-1920s—Hiram Bingham strenuously objected to his nomination. Bingham viewed MacCracken as one of the leading opponents of the senator's legislative efforts; the latter's nomination appeared to fly in the face of Bingham's efforts to rein in MacCracken's desires for more federal control over commercial flying. Eventually, however, Hoover was able to overcome Bingham's objections—in part by promising to keep MacCracken and the Aeronautics Branch on a short leash—and MacCracken soon found himself confirmed as the assistant secretary of aeronautics.

MacCracken immediately found himself faced with a host of challenges as he worked to determine how the Commerce Department would implement the dictates of the Air Commerce Act. Although MacCracken's lobbying served to clarify and expand federal responsibilities under the new law, the legislation provided little information regarding how federal officials would actually go about the business of exercising their new responsibilities. Narrowly, the ACA charged the commerce secretary and the assistant secretary for aeronautics with fostering air commerce by encouraging the establishment of airports, airways, and air navigation facilities; studying and encouraging the development of air transport and trade; establishing and maintaining civil airways, including emergency landing fields and navigation aids; charting airways and publishing air maps; working with the secretary of agriculture to produce meteorological information for pilots; collecting and disseminating "information relative to air commerce and the state of the art"; working with other government agencies to research and develop air navigation facilities; investigating all air accidents; and exchanging information regarding civil aviation with foreign governments. With regard to regulation, the bill established regulatory authority over aircraft registration; airworthiness standards; licensing requirements for pilots, mechanics, and air navigators; ratings for air navigation facilities; and air traffic rules.[33]

While seemingly comprehensive, the ACA's articulation of federal authority raised a host of new questions. How would pilots qualify for a license? Would they need a medical check? If so, would the Commerce Department administer those checks? Would a single type of license serve for all pilots? How would the department define airworthiness standards? Would bureau inspectors approve all new designs? Did individual aircraft require an inspection, or only new aircraft types? What constituted a new type? What rules would govern air traffic? What penalties would the Commerce Department impose for violations of federal regulations? Additionally, specifics regarding Commerce Department responsibilities for promotion activities and creation of infrastructure remained undefined. All of these issues raised questions about staffing and funding above and beyond the regulatory questions at issue.

MacCracken immediately threw himself into the task of answering these questions as he worked to staff the new Aeronautics Branch. His first task was to formalize staffing responsibilities within the Commerce Department. As Hoover had envisioned, the ACA did not create a new bureau within the department, but rather sought—to the extent that it was possible—to use existing bureaucratic structures to oversee aviation-related activities. As such, the Lighthouse Service division oversaw air navigation, the Coast and Geodetic Survey had responsibility for mapping air routes, and the Bureau of Standards oversaw scientific research designed to improve air navigation aids. Some aspects of federal oversight, however, found no ready home within existing department structures. The department had no ready facilities for the examination and licensing of pilots and aircraft, enforcing air traffic laws, or collecting and disseminating aviation-related information. MacCracken thus worked to create two new divisions to coordinate these activities: the Division of Air Regulations and the Division of Air Information.[34]

As MacCracken built the bureaucratic foundation for federal oversight, he maintained an overriding commitment to using his power to promote commercial air transport. Like Hoover, MacCracken believed that the industry needed federal support to grow, and his ultimate goal remained fixed on using federal engagement to place commercial flying on a "sound economic basis." In support of that end, one of MacCracken's first actions was to commission a survey of air transport, "with particular reference to the existing commercial carriers," to determine the commercial possibilities and operating methods necessary to create a solvent industry. Simultaneously, he undertook a departmental review of regulatory responsibilities, aided by conferences with "every expert . . . the aeronautics industry provides." These conferences brought together leading figures from the military, airlines, engine and airframe manufacturers, aeronautical engineers, federal officials, and pilots in an effort to define the clearest and most logical model for a comprehensive set of federal regulations. This intense effort, he hoped, would result in the promulgation of a comprehensive set of regulations by the end of 1926.[35]

With those surveys ongoing, MacCracken began to define the Aeronautics Branch's priorities moving forward. First and foremost, he sought to improve and expand navigation aids to promote safety and efficiency. Noting that aviation's greatest benefit over land- or sea-based transportation methods was speed, MacCracken bemoaned the fact that in early 1926, aside from the Post Office–pioneered route between Cheyenne and New York, virtually all commercial flying took place during daylight hours in the summer months. Observing that "the economical use of the airplane demands flying by night as well as by day, and in all vicissitudes of weather and season," MacCracken created a prioritized list of Commerce Department activities: airway lighting, weather forecasting and a weather communication system for airports, radio beacons, radio markers, and finally, radios to allow air-to-ground and ground-to-air communication. This ambitious list presciently identified commercial carriers' most pressing needs, but MacCracken understood that accomplishing those goals remained far beyond his current capabilities. Repeatedly noting fiscal limits—Congress provided only three hundred thousand dollars in appropriations for the Aeronautics Branch in 1926—the assistant secretary established far more modest goals for the remainder of the year. These included lighting over one thousand miles of airways, constructing a limited number of emergency landing fields, and establishing twenty-two upper air weather stations to provide meteorological information to pilots. During the remainder of the year the Aeronautics Branch worked to achieve these goals while formulating federal regulations slated to go into effect on January 1.[36]

The year 1927 witnessed a significant expansion of Commerce Department activities and the formal implementation of federal regulations. Though the Aeronautics Branch received only $550,000 in appropriations for the year, Congress had approved a much larger budget of almost $3,800,000 for fiscal year 1928; some of those funds were available for expenditure in the latter half of 1927. That looming windfall notwithstanding, fiscal realities placed sharp limits on branch activities; MacCracken and his staff were nonetheless able to make significant progress.[37]

The Division of Air Regulation began implementing new licensing, registration, and air traffic rules on January 1 while working to build a diverse staff. Following the intense conferences of the previous year, which included "representatives from every interested branch of aeronautics," MacCracken and his staff created a tiered system of licenses, from a private license for noncommercial operators to a transport license authorizing pilots to carry passengers for profit. All aircraft had to bear a federal registration number; airworthiness requirements applied only to planes used for interstate or foreign commerce. Those requirements created something of a dilemma for the Aeronautics Branch. MacCracken believed that the most efficient way for the government to certify aircraft was to examine the blueprints for new aircraft types. Technically, the government did not have the authority to require manufacturers to surrender these plans, so MacCracken leaned on his associationalist background and hoped to enlist the manufacturers in the certification process. His staff created a set of minimum engineering standards that manufacturers had to meet. Upon creation of a new aircraft type, the manufacturer would send a copy of the blueprints for the new craft to the Aeronautics Branch. If Commerce Department engineers found the plans satisfactory, a Commerce Department inspector would perform a factory visit and ensure that the physical aircraft conformed to the blueprints. Both a manufacturer and a federal test pilot would then flight test the new craft. Assuming everything went well, the department would issue a type certificate for the plane, allowing the manufacturer to produce a theoretically unlimited number of planes of that specific type. A striking success, the type approval process minimized federal staffing requirements, absolved the government of testing every single plane rolling off factory floors, and enlisted the manufacturers in the regulatory system. This system soon expanded to include aero engines, propellers, and a host of other aviation-related products.[38]

The diverse responsibilities the Division of Air Regulation embraced necessitated a multifaceted staff. MacCracken hired aeronautical engineers and inspectors, technical experts, test pilots, mechanics, and doctors to fulfill these duties. Medical inspectors formed perhaps the most significant challenge, as a federally approved medical inspector had to perform flight physicals for any pilot applying for a federal license and then periodically reaffirm pilots' fitness. To perform these examinations, the department designated more than two hundred physicians and surgeons around the country as official Aeronautics Branch medical examiners, a number that was to increase substantially in coming years. Fiscal limitations sharply limited other staffing considerations, and MacCracken was able to hire only fifteen men as pilots and aircraft and engine inspectors, though he hoped to expand that number to at least fifty by the middle of 1928.[39]

Within the Bureau of Lighthouses, a new Airways Division worked to light the nation's airways, push forward development of radio beacons and weather reporting stations, construct and light intermediate landing fields, provide mileage marking for national airways, and maintain new and existing facilities. During 1927 the division lighted more than thirteen hundred airway miles and made plans to light an equivalent amount the following year. On June 30 the Post Office formally transferred control of the Transcontinental Airway, running from New York to San Francisco, to the Commerce Department. The route encompassed more than two thousand miles of lighted airways, almost doubling the number of beacons and intermediate fields under Commerce Department control. By the end of the year the Airways Division employed thirty-one airways mechanics and 161 caretakers to oversee the nation's airways, while steadily working to improve lighting, signage, and related infrastructure across the country.[40]

As the airway map expanded, the new Airway Mapping Division of the Coast and Geodetic Survey Department worked to produce small-scale (1:500,000) maps of those routes. The division completed only a single map—of the route from Kansas City to Moline—during 1927 as it worked to augment the well-established marine charting functions of the department. Ten additional maps were planned for 1928, however, signaling the division's intention to offer detailed charts to private and commercial pilots alike at a nominal fee.[41]

Collecting data and publicizing Aeronautics Branch activities was the job of the newly created Airways Information Division. Tasked with collecting and disseminating information on civil aeronautics; publishing information about airways, airports, and flying aids; and encouraging the construction of airports and navigation aids, the development of air commerce, and the "general promotion of civil flight," the division formed the most visible element of the new section and the point of contact among the office of the assistant secretary of aeronautics, the industry, and other interested parties. In its first full year of operation, the Air Information Division issued numerous airways bulletins—illustrated sheets describing airports, intermediate fields, airways, air marking, meteorological conditions, and other pieces of air navigation information. These publications emerged from the division's information gathering activities but served to publicize division activities and serve as a record of the Airways Section's ongoing progress. The division also issued a semimonthly newsletter that included "all news of the Aeronautics Branch," including lists of pilots and planes receiving licenses, new airports, industry statistics, and other promotional materials. These efforts represented the heart of MacCracken's desire to use his resources to promote air commerce, and the Air Information Division embraced a rapidly expanding agenda.[42]

By 1927 Herbert Hoover finally witnessed his vision for a comprehensive federal aeronautics policy come to fruition. As the Post Office continued to turn its airmail routes over to private contractors under the dictates of the Kelly Act, and the Aeronautics Branch formalized federal regulatory authority over the skies, commercial aviation finally appeared poised to achieve stability and profitability. By the latter half of 1927 airlines could bid for airmail contracts that promised to provide steady and sustaining revenue, revenue that would fund investments in larger, faster, more reliable aircraft, new safety technologies, increased pilot training, and expanded ground-based infrastructure. Airline pilots, in possession of federally administered commercial pilots' licenses and medical certificates certifying their fitness to perform their duties, took to the skies in planes displaying federal registration numbers and adhering to federally defined airworthiness standards. In the air they had to obey a rigid set of air traffic rules and benefited from a federally funded—and rapidly expanding—system of beacon lights, radio aids, emergency landing fields, and radio navigation beacons. They could check weather conditions and forecasts for their routes courtesy of government-sponsored upper-air weather reporting stations and federally funded forecasters. Pilots, airframe and engine manufacturers, and airlines alike also benefited from a concerted effort by Commerce Department officials to publicize their accomplishments and encourage aeronautical development. Herbert Hoover, William MacCracken, and other officials continued their close relationship with leading members of the aviation industry and leading trade organizations, often requesting guidance and suggestions regarding how ongoing federal efforts could aid the industry. Hoover also worked closely with the NACA to encourage research into technologies that could help commercial flying, such as engine cowlings to reduce drag, deicing equipment to make flying in cold weather safer, and navigation aids to assist pilots flying in the dark or with low visibility.

Collectively, these developments created the potential for budding air carriers to establish stable, fiscally solvent commercial operations. While the industry as a whole remained fragile, forced to address an ongoing lack of public confidence in the safety of its operations, prohibitive insurance rates, engines and airframes of at times dubious reliability, and a frustrating lack of mail and passenger volume, the seeds had been planted for a bright commercial future. While many Americans remained skeptical, investors began to flock to aeronautics corporations, providing financing for ongoing expansion efforts. These circumstances propelled a steady though limited expansion of commercial service in the years after 1927. Soon, however, a series of events would conspire to dramatically shake up commercial aeronautics. The looming stock market crash affected aviation firms as it did virtually all other publically traded corporations, but perhaps even more significantly, a new postmaster general would initiate a series of policy changes with significant ramifications for airlines. Walter Folger Brown, a progressive Republican and a key figure in Herbert Hoover's successful run to the presidency in 1928, was a man few observers believed would initiate a dramatic shakeup of federal airmail policy. Nonetheless, Brown soon demonstrated his commitment to doing just that, in the process creating a looming controversy that threatened to undermine the entire commercial aviation industry.

3

"A Sound Basis" for Air Transport

Walter F. Brown and Commercial Aviation, 1927–1932

As William MacCracken and his colleagues in the Aeronautics Branch of the Department of Commerce labored to implement newly created aeronautics regulations, a showdown loomed 250 miles to the northeast that would prove to have lasting implications for American commercial flying. In the spring of 1927, on Roosevelt Field in Long Island, some of the most well known American pilots were poised to attempt the most publicized long-distance flight of all time. They were attempting to fly nonstop from New York to Paris, hoping to claim the prize of twenty-five thousand dollars put up by hotel magnate Raymond Orteig. Orteig, a French immigrant, first offered the prize in 1919. Though at that time claiming the prize seemed a long shot at best, by 1926 it appeared that Orteig's purse was ready for the taking. Powerful radial engines and new monoplane airframes held the promise of greater speed, range, and reliability than ever before. Nonetheless, tremendous challenges remained for transatlantic contenders—most significantly the need to carry sufficient fuel to stay in the air for more than thirty hours.

Perhaps because of the challenge, or perhaps because of the cachet of flying from one great city to another, the competition for the Orteig Prize captured Americans' imagination and became national news. The participation of many of the United States' leading pilots heightened public interest. Entrants included Admiral Richard Byrd, who won the Medal of Honor in 1926 for being the first man to fly over the North Pole; noted air racer Clarence Chamberlin; and navy pilots Noel Davis and Stanton Wooster, in addition to French World War I heroes René Fonck, Charles Nungesser, and François Coli.[1] The French pilots' participation lent a nationalistic edge to the competition and ensured that observers on both sides of the Atlantic would follow the proceedings with rapt attention.

Among those contenders was a little-known airmail pilot from Minnesota: Charles Lindbergh. Though he lacked the notoriety of his fellow competitors, Lindbergh had compiled an impressive aeronautical résumé that prepared him well for the challenges ahead. Lindbergh had worked as a wing walker, parachutist, and aerial daredevil in a flying circus before scraping together sufficient funds to purchase a war surplus JN-4 Jenny in the summer of 1923 and embark on a short career as a barnstormer. In 1924 Lindbergh entered the US Army Air Service, training for a year before receiving a commission in the Air Service Reserve Corps. Unable to secure an active-duty position, Lindbergh returned to barnstorming and giving flying lessons before securing employment as an airmail pilot with the Robertson Aircraft Corporation in Saint Louis, Missouri. With Robertson, Lindbergh flew the mail on Contract Air Mail Route (CAM) 2 from Saint Louis to Chicago, Illinois. Robertson was one of the first private carriers to bid for an airmail route following the passage of the Kelly bill in 1925 and hired Lindbergh to serve as chief pilot and oversee preparations for inaugurating service in the spring of 1926. Forced to bail out of his DH-4 mail plane twice during the ten months that he flew the mail, Lindbergh nonetheless survived as many of his peers perished in the dangerous business of flying the mail in all weather and all seasons in aircraft with only the most primitive of instruments. Lindbergh's skill at the controls quickly became apparent; Harold Bixby, one of Robertson's owners and the president of the Saint Louis Chamber of Commerce, called Lindbergh "an exceptional pilot," remarking that "even then [during his airmail days] you could see that he was a master."[2]

As he escorted the mail to and from Chicago, Lindbergh began to dream of embarking on a flight to Paris. Though he had little money and lacked the name recognition and résumé that Byrd and Chamberlin possessed, Lindbergh believed that he could triumph through careful planning and painstaking preparation. First, however, Lindbergh had to secure financing for his attempt. Putting up $2,000 he had diligently saved from his barnstorming activities and airmail paychecks, Lindbergh turned to leading Saint Louis businessmen in the hopes they would front the remaining $15,000 he estimated he would need for the flight. Securing $1,000 from Bill Robertson, head of the Robertson Aircraft Corporation, Lindbergh also received pledges from broker Harry Knight, aviation pioneer Albert Lambert, and newspaper publisher E. Lansing Ray. Still short of his total, Knight and Harold Bixby agreed to secure a loan from the State National Bank for the outstanding $10,500. In return, Lindbergh agreed to christen his aircraft the *Spirit of St. Louis* as a nod to the civic pride that in part motivated his backers. Though they remained nervous about Lindbergh's chances—particularly since Lindbergh, a "pretty good talker," in the words of Bixby, had to convince them on several occasions that a single-engine plane was the right choice for the task—his backers expressed unwavering support, driven by a desire to publicize their city and help aviation.[3]

With funding in hand, Lindbergh turned to choosing an aircraft. After being rebuffed in his attempt to purchase a Wright-Bellanca high-wing monoplane, the pilot turned to Ryan Aircraft Corporation in San Diego, a small and relatively unknown manufacturer with a gifted chief engineer, Donald Hall. Hall agreed to design and produce a new aircraft to Lindbergh's specifications in only sixty days, often working around the clock to make good on that promise. The resulting craft embodied Lindbergh's philosophy for the flight and incorporated a number of unique design elements. Lindbergh chose to power his plane with a single Wright J-5 air-cooled radial engine, at that time the most reliable aircraft engine in existence. Hall and Lindbergh's design philosophy for the *Spirit of St. Louis*'s airframe focused on minimizing weight and maximizing fuel capacity. Lindbergh did away with a windscreen in lieu of a small periscope to cut drag. He chose to sit on a wicker chair, and he made the interior height of the cockpit exactly as large as it needed to be to fit his six-foot, three-inch frame—including a small cutout in the roof rib above his head. He fitted the craft with a variable-pitch propeller that could be tailored—on the ground—to maximize efficiency at the expense of thrust. He was also fanatical about his personal effects, cutting unneeded parts off his charts and taking two small flashlights to save weight and provide redundancy.

Following shakedown flights from San Diego to Saint Louis and Saint Louis to New York, Lindbergh arrived on Long Island in the second week of May as anticipation surrounding the Orteig Prize mounted. As late as March the *New York Times* reported that details regarding Lindbergh and his plane were not readily available—in fact inaccurately reporting that Lindbergh would fly with a copilot—but by May the country had come to view the former airmail pilot as a dark-horse contender for the prize.[4] Only a week earlier, Nungesser and Coli had disappeared during a westbound attempt, and Wooster and Davis had been killed while testing their plane. With both Byrd and Chamberlin preparing to depart, Lindbergh's arrival further heightened the drama. A series of bad weather forecasts frustrated Lindbergh, but finally, on May 19 a break in the weather appeared, and Lindbergh departed the following morning.

Though he slept little the night before his departure and needed the assistance of a ground crew to break the *Spirit of St. Louis* free from a muddy field and begin his takeoff roll—barely clearing the trees at the end of the runway—Lindbergh arrived in Paris the following evening, several hours ahead of schedule and with enough fuel remaining in his tanks to fly another thousand miles. Perhaps Lindbergh's biggest challenge lay in finding Le Bourget airfield. He did not have precise directions and was confused by thousands of car headlights converging on the field to welcome him to Europe. Bedlam ensued after his touchdown; Lindbergh—and the *Spirit of St. Louis*—had to be rescued from the crowds, and he found himself whisked off to the American embassy for the remainder of the night.

Although Lindbergh may not have realized it when he woke the next morning, his accomplishment had forever changed both his life and the trajectory of American aeronautics. Lindbergh found himself instantly elevated to the highest rank of American celebrities. According to the *New York Times*, the enthusiasm expressed by fellow aviators and the American public alike "knew no bounds" when word of Lindbergh's success reached the United States. Following a series of appearances in France, Belgium, and England, all attended by tens of thousands, Lindbergh received a personal note of congratulations from President Calvin Coolidge, who dispatched a US Navy cruiser to transport him back across the Atlantic. Upon his arrival, the president awarded him the Distinguished Flying Cross in a flowery ceremony. No less a figure than Orville Wright lauded praise on Lindbergh's accomplishment, stating, "The flight [was] beyond all expectation . . . we hardly dreamed that some day [such a flight] could be accomplished."[5]

Lindbergh next traveled to New York, where he was feted with a ticker-tape parade and hundreds of thousands of well-wishers let out a "frenzied outburst of whole-hearted affection" as they listened to his short speech at

City Hall.[6] Over the following weeks and months the Post Office commissioned a commemorative airmail stamp to celebrate his accomplishment, he embarked on goodwill tours of the United States and Mexico and Central America in the *Spirit of St. Louis*, received the Congressional Medal of Honor, and agreed to positions with both Pan American Airways and Transcontinental Air Transport—which subsequently became known as the Lindbergh Line.

More than any other event, Lindbergh's triumph facilitated a remarkable boom in aviation's fortunes and, combined with the legislative foundation provided by the Kelly bill and Air Commerce Act, jump-started US commercial flying. Lindbergh's accomplishment demonstrated the airplane's ability to span continents and make the world smaller; Americans could now envision a future when travel to Europe would take mere hours and the United States' far-flung holdings—Hawaii, the Philippines—could be reached in less time than it took to travel cross-country by rail. The result, argues Joseph Corn, was "a high-water mark for aviation enthusiasm" in the United States, resulting in "a major stimulus to airmindedness."[7]

Lindbergh's consistent focus on aviation's practical benefits was particularly significant. In an era when most Americans viewed flying as a reckless and exciting form of entertainment, Lindbergh's emphasis on safety and practicality played a key role in changing the narrative of American aeronautics. Remarking on the revolutionary effects Lindbergh's flight had, pilot and noted author Ernest Gann suggests that its "timing was exactly right to light the fuse of a phenomenon. . . . From the very date of his arrival in Paris, aviation graduated from being the bailiwick of adventurers and began to be taken very seriously."[8] As such, Lindbergh's actions facilitated aviation's move into the mainstream as they provided the impetus for Americans to open themselves to its commercial possibilities.

Naturally, airlines reaped the benefits. On the heels of the stability offered by the Kelly Act and the Air Commerce Act, the public's willingness to embrace aviation as a legitimate business endeavor fueled a dramatic increase in airlines' fortunes. Investors flocked to aviation firms, seeing an opportunity to put their money behind a nascent industry poised to explode. Looking back in March 1930, a *Time* magazine article acknowledged this transition, stating, "When Lindbergh got down in Paris (1927), U.S. aviation stocks [went] up." In fact, aviation stocks rose so quickly that one observer noted that "after the Lindbergh flight . . . even charwomen were buying aviation stocks." Wright Aeronautical, the manufacturer of Lindbergh's J-5 engine, enjoyed a $2.5 million increase in value in the immediate wake of the flight. The boom in investment provided crucial funds for research and development while also financing a new fleet of aircraft ready to carry an interested public aloft. At the same time, however, newfound resources also stimulated a wave of consolidation, eventually leading to the creation of four large aviation holding corporations that dominated the industry until 1934.[9]

Lindbergh himself played a central role in facilitating this expansion. Almost immediately after his return to the United States, he began actively to promote commercial flying. He became the public face of Transcontinental Air Transport—the forerunner of Trans World Airlines (TWA)—and worked as a consultant for Pan American Airways. In those capacities Lindbergh helped map out transcontinental air routes, offered technical support to pilots trying to minimize fuel consumption, and oversaw the construction of emergency landing fields. Lindbergh also promoted aviation's commercial potential during goodwill tours through the United States and Latin America. During his US tour he stopped in eighty-eight US cities; thirty million Americans, or more than a quarter of the US population, came to see him. In speeches across the country Lindbergh urged his fellow citizens to embrace air travel and use airmail, and he pushed municipalities to construct more and better airports, beacon lights, and other navigational aids.[10]

Heeding Lindbergh's advice, Americans took to the air in hitherto unseen numbers. In 1926 a total of 5,782 Americans ascended in airliners; by 1929 that number had grown to more than 173,000. In 1928 alone, passenger volume rose more than fourfold, and twenty-three new lines either began or significantly expanded their operations. Airmail volume increased by more than 300 percent over 1927, and the number of commercial operators increased from nineteen in 1926 to more than one hundred by the end of 1928. Nick Komons points to the dramatic increase in applications for pilot licenses following Lindbergh's achievement as concrete evidence of the American public's growing enthusiasm for flying. Between the Aeronautics Branch's creation in May 1926 and December 1928, more than 17,000 Americans applied for licenses; more than 80 percent of those applications occurred in the wake of Lindbergh's flight.[11]

Though Lindbergh's actions alone cannot account for the entirety of these increases, it is clear that his flight fundamentally transformed the field of American aeronautics and ushered in a new era for commercial flying. Combined with the Kelly Act, the Air Commerce Act, and ongoing efforts by the Aeronautics Branch to create a foundation for growth and expansion, Lindbergh's accomplishment pushed air commerce into the mainstream where an increasing number of Americans—particularly businessmen—began to take advantage of its benefits. Public interest and new investment dollars spurred on technological developments that increased speed, comfort, and reliability while the government continued to build beacon lights and emergency landing fields, improve weather reporting, and perfect air-to-ground and ground-to-air communication systems. Together, these advances held the promise of stability, expansion, and profitability for airlines. As commercial flying matured, however, its growth increasingly exposed questions about the course it would chart moving forward. Most pressingly, commercial flying's dramatic expansion in the years following Lindbergh's flight placed new burdens on the federal government as policy makers strove to use their power to facilitate rational growth while maintaining a free market.

Postmaster General Walter Forger Brown would emerge as the key figure in that effort. Though Brown had no previous connection to commercial aviation, after Hoover appointed him to head the Post Office, Brown aggressively moved to use his powers to reshape the airmail map. Using associationalist principles, Brown worked with industry leaders to create a rational system of airways and a subsidy model that would promote the orderly growth of commercial operations. Largely successful in that effort, Brown nonetheless found himself pilloried by Democrats who charged the postmaster general with collusion and fraud. Those charges notwithstanding, Brown's actions brought dramatic gains to US commercial flying and offer the clearest example of Hoover's economic philosophy operating in practice.

In the wake of Lindbergh's successful flight, Herbert Hoover's associationalist vision for American flying continued to hold sway as commercial operators strove to expand their operations. In the latter half of 1927 William MacCracken and the Aeronautics Branch were able to draw upon congressional appropriations for the 1928 fiscal year to push forward efforts to create infrastructure as they continued to focus on publicizing commercial flying to the American people. By the end of the year the Post Office finalized the transfer of all airmail routes to private contractors, making good on the promises of the Kelly Act. Buoyed by an American public eager to embrace all aspects of aeronautics and the ready promise of airmail profits, airlines appeared poised to establish themselves as an integral aspect of the American transportation network. In that effort Hoover continued to foster close relationships between Commerce Department and Post Office officials and industry leaders in his ongoing efforts to use federal power to encourage commercial development. He also maintained his focus on publicizing commercial flying. Speaking to the *New York Times* in June 1927, the commerce secretary reiterated that the government was in the process of "providing the emergency landing fields where needed, surveying and mapping the air routes, licensing pilots . . . supplying air charts to pilots and other air personnel, and producing lighthouses for the air in the same way as it does to safeguard maritime navigation."[12] These activities, he argued, had finally put within reach the goal of placing commercial flying on a solid economic foundation.

Hoover maintained his focus on aeronautics after winning the presidency the following year. By 1929 commercial operations were flying more than sixty-nine thousand miles every day, although airlines without the financial benefit afforded by federal airmail contracts almost universally operated at a loss. Hoover, sensitive to those circumstances, looked to bring increased stability to the industry while also maintaining his relationships with leading figures in American aeronautics. Naturally, as president, Hoover continued to enjoy a close relationship with members of the Commerce Department, which he had so recently headed. In 1930 Hoover requested a summary of the progress commercial aviation had made over the previous eighteen months from Assistant Secretary of Commerce Clarence Young. Desiring a comprehensive overview of commercial activities to date, Hoover was particularly interested in airmail routes and subsidies, infrastructure, technological development, profitability, and suggestions for future growth. Less than a year later, Hoover desired a further update on commercial flying. Following a comprehensive review of a Commerce Department report, the president suggested several updates and additions to the document, instructing his secretary to forward his suggestions to Young.[13]

Hoover also continued to nurture relationships with leading members of the aviation industry. During his term in office Hoover maintained an active correspondence with the ACC, the leading national trade organization of the aircraft industry. Hoover had a personal relationship with the chamber's general manager, Luther K. Bell, and granted Bell and members of the chamber's board of directors several audiences at the White House. In March 1931 a delegation from the ACC called on the president to discuss the contemporary state of commercial and military aviation in the United States. The delegation presented Hoover with a report on the progress of American commercial flying that offered an overview of the industry's current position and a focused discussion of the ACC's hopes for the future. In July, Hoover acquiesced to an ACC request to supply a note of congratulations to Wiley Post and his navigator, Harold Gatty, after their around-the-world flight, and he later received the two fliers at the White House.[14]

Hoover's interest extended to ongoing aeronautical research efforts as well. As commerce secretary, Hoover established an active relationship with the NACA, a body he saw as key to the continued technological development of American aircraft. In the 1920s the NACA played a key role in developing technologies that made flying safer and more efficient. Among their many notable breakthroughs were the development of the so-called NACA cowl to house radial engines, which provided tremendous advances in speed and efficiency, and the perfection of deicing equipment that allowed safer operations in winter weather. As president, Hoover maintained his close relationship with the NACA, going so far as to enlist William MacCracken's help in vetting possible candidates to sit on the NACA board.[15]

While Hoover's ongoing emphasis on fostering aeronautical development may not be surprising in light of his concentrated focus on the industry during his time in the Commerce Department, his presidential activities hold particular significance, considering the burdens Hoover faced while in office. Quickly submerged in the deepening crisis of the Great Depression, Hoover nonetheless expended valuable time and effort on American flying. Reflecting on this tumultuous period, Clarence Young marveled that even during the depths of the financial crisis, Hoover "never raised a question" about his commitment to aeronautical development.[16] This commitment speaks volumes about how central aviation was to Hoover's vision for America's future and what stock he placed in its commercial success. Unfortunately, however, another decision made by the president—the appointment of Walter F. Brown as postmaster general—overshadowed Hoover's accomplishments and led directly to a Senate investigation.

Hoover's decision to appoint Walter Brown as postmaster general initially held little interest for those involved with commercial aviation. Brown had no history of engagement with aeronautics, and before assuming his new position had not indicated any interest in using his power to shape the path of commercial flying. In fact, most observers looked at Brown's appointment primarily as a reward for his long service to Hoover and the Republican Party. While that may have been true, Brown quickly demonstrated a focus on using Post Office airmail payments as a tool to push the industry forward and encourage the development of passenger service. Brown led the charge for new airmail legislation granting the postmaster general broader powers to shape the growth of the industry, and he worked with airline executives to rationalize the US air transport network. Though his actions met with significant success, they also drew the ire of airlines cut out of Brown's vision for the future of commercial flying and, significantly, their Democratic allies in Congress. Growing opposition to Brown's policies ultimately exploded following the Democratic tidal wave in 1932, culminating in one of the greatest upheavals in the history of federal aviation policy.

Although Walter Brown had little connection to aviation before he assumed leadership of the Post Office Department in 1929, he did possess an accomplished political résumé. Brown hailed from Ohio and had strong connections to the progressive politics that dominated that state as he came of age. He campaigned on behalf of William McKinley during the latter's gubernatorial campaign and helped secure the election of Progressive Party reformer Samuel Jones as mayor of Toledo in 1897. An avid supporter of Theodore Roosevelt, Brown broke with the Republican Party to become chairman of the newly created Bull Moose Party in 1912. Following Roosevelt's defeat, Brown worked hard to rejoin the Republican ranks, and by 1920 he found himself in the influential position of helping to secure Warren Harding's nomination to the Republican ticket. Brown served as chairman of a special commission charged with reorganizing the executive branch during Harding's tenure in office, although Harding's unexpected death stymied any hopes for real change. Significantly, during his time in Washington Brown met and formed a close relationship with Herbert Hoover, then serving as secretary of commerce. This relationship led Hoover to bring Brown into the department as assistant secretary in 1927. Brown subsequently served as Hoover's campaign manager in the

1928 presidential election and found himself rewarded with the position of postmaster general following Hoover's successful campaign.[17]

Brown's political education had prepared him well for his new position. His activity in the Ohio Republican Party had made him into a "political animal of great influence," according to Robert van der Linden, and Brown quickly demonstrated his ability to put those skills to work in Washington.[18] His time in the Commerce Department acquainted Brown with Hoover's associationalist ideology and the secretary's strong focus on promoting aviation. After assuming the office of postmaster general, Brown immediately began working to rationalize the air transport industry while maintaining a focus on promoting flying to the American public. While that effort in many ways built on the actions of his predecessor, Harry S. New, financial realities in the form of a massive budget shortfall pushed Brown to embrace a much more aggressive agenda.

Violating expectations from many in the air transport industry who believed that Brown would merely serve as a custodian of existing policy, the postmaster general almost immediately began working to shake up the airmail system. In doing so he demonstrated a firm grasp of the economic and political factors facing commercial aviation in 1929. In the years following the passage of the 1925 Kelly Act, the ever-expanding US airmail route structure supported the development of numerous commercial carriers. These airlines relied almost wholly on Post Office subsidies for survival; competition for new routes and route extensions was fierce. By the end of the decade, this Darwinian process resulted in the creation of three large aviation holding companies: the Aviation Corporation (of Delaware), North American Aviation, and United Aircraft and Transportation Corporation. These three corporations each controlled airlines, airframe manufacturers, engine builders, and financial interests in an effort to secure a maximum of control over the expanding air commerce network. By 1929 these three holding corporations controlled more than 90 percent of airmail revenues.[19]

In spite of these corporations' size and holdings, a growing set of concerns cast doubt on the financial stability of the contemporary air commerce industry. First, airlines, like other publicly traded industries, had become overvalued in the years preceding the stock market crash. This was particularly worrisome for Brown because airlines were almost totally dependent on federal airmail contracts for solvency. In addition, aviation increasingly suffered from overproduction. During the 1920s, as the Post

Office offered numerous new airmail routes up for private bids, airlines and aircraft manufacturing firms had grown quickly to keep up with demand. As the creation of new routes slowed and aircraft became more advanced and expensive, however, production—of both aircraft and airlines themselves—quickly grew beyond demand. Finally, the rapid expansion of airmail routes promoted a haphazard system of growth for airlines, resulting in a number of inefficient and unnecessary routes and great disparities in airmail payments.

The Post Office airmail rate policies and route structure were of particular concern for Brown. In its initial incarnation, the Kelly bill authorized the Post Office to issue airmail payments from the revenue derived from a new ten-cent-per-ounce airmail stamp. Operators could receive up to 80 percent of that revenue, although the Post Office awarded airmail route contracts to the lowest responsible bidder. Local postmasters would tabulate the number of letters and packages and their weight before each airmail run to calculate the specific payments airlines received. Since 1924 the Post Office had separated the country into three airmail zones, roughly east, central, and west. Payments within a zone were fixed without regard to distance, though carriers could receive a bonus for flying routes across multiple zones. In practice this created a system whereby operators benefited from carrying large numbers of letters or packages over a short distance—unless they were lucky enough to secure a route encompassing multiple zones—since their payments related only to the weight of mail they carried regardless of the distance over which they carried it. Considering planes' relative fragility and engines' lack of reliability, not to mention high operating costs, there was little incentive for operators to expand the airmail map and take on longer routes.

These realities flew in the face of aviation advocates' hopes that federal payments would encourage a dramatic expansion of US airways and led to a revision of the Kelly Act only a year after its passage. The 1926 amendment to the Contract Airmail Act created a new system that granted carriers a maximum payment of three dollars per pound for the first one thousand miles and up to thirty cents per pound for every hundred miles thereafter. Further changes in 1927 and 1928 did away with the complex zone system and reduced airmail postage to five cents per ounce. The resulting model provided more inducement for carriers to fly longer routes and increased airmail volume, but it created a host of problems. First, the Post Office's reduction of airmail postage without a concomitant reduction in airmail payments significantly increased the government's financial commitment to airmail—effectively creating a subsidized industry rather than one financed through profits from airmail postage. Second, because the Post Office continued to bid out each contract individually, carriers often received wildly different rates for carrying the mail. For example, in 1929 Colonial Air Transport was receiving three dollars per pound on the lucrative New York to Boston route, while Interstate Airlines received only seventy-eight cents per pound flying the mail from Chicago to Atlanta. Further, even with the rate revisions, airlines lucky enough to secure a short route with high mail volume—as Colonial had with the New York to Boston route—could reap significant profits, while an airline flying a long-distance, low-volume route—say, Chicago to Fort Worth—would struggle to make ends meet. Finally, the 1928 reduction in airmail postage made it possible for airlines receiving relatively high federal rates to profit from sending airmail to themselves. With a three-dollar-per-pound contract, an airline could spend eighty cents to send a pound of its own mail up to one thousand miles and pocket two dollars and twenty cents as profit. As a result, when Brown took over the Post Office in 1929, he found himself faced with a haphazard and problematic system calling out for a comprehensive overhaul.[20]

Beyond financial issues, aviation's rapid technological and commercial development suggested an uncertain future for the industry. Flying was still a dangerous business, requiring skill and experience in order to meet a set schedule safely and reliably. While safety had improved markedly since the first private airmail flights began flying in 1926, much work remained to be done if flying was ever to become a mainstream form of transportation. Aeronautical technology advanced rapidly during the period, with new innovations such as improved instruments, radios, and deicing equipment and newer and faster aircraft constantly raising the bar for performance and safety. These developments held much promise for the future of air transport but required significant investments of time and, more importantly, money before their effects would be felt. Finally, while virtually all airlines depended on airmail contracts to remain solvent, passengers began to form an increasingly important element of air commerce. Flying passengers, however, required different equipment and different skills than did flying mail alone. Most significantly, carrying passengers necessitated larger and more comfortable aircraft, a much more expensive proposition than the small, cheap, and relatively crude planes used to carry mail.

These factors resulted in a rapidly expanding air commerce industry lacking focus and direction. For the most part an airmail contract remained a necessary precondition for commercial success, but securing such a contract at the lowest profitable rate often meant eschewing larger, safer aircraft and the possibility of passenger service. More experienced operators led the way in promoting new safety equipment, pilot training, and the use of larger passenger aircraft, but these same carriers suffered from increased overhead as a result, factors that threatened their ability to remain competitive for airmail contracts. Even airlines controlled by the large aviation holding corporations found themselves struggling to compete for lucrative routes in this uncertain atmosphere. Overproduction of planes and engines and the overvaluation of airline stock only further complicated this picture, and by the eve of the Great Depression aviation—although it had experienced tremendous success since 1927—appeared vulnerable on several fronts.[21]

In spite of these challenges, Brown believed that aviation was poised to reach a new level of maturity and become a central part of the American transportation system. Soon after assuming his new position, Brown asserted that the pioneering era for "air mail is nearly over so far as experimentation is concerned."[22] In his mind, the immediate future held great promise for aviation, but also encompassed significant risk. The key to making good on air transport's promise, Brown believed, lay in using the power of the federal government to encourage rational growth. For him, that meant using airmail payments and route contracts to foster stability and technological development in order to rationalize the airway network and promote passenger-carrying operations—the ultimate goal for Hoover, Brown, and the airlines themselves.

Central to Brown's strategy was a desire to steadily decrease the amount of subsidy paid out to airmail carriers. Brown argued that "there is not, in air mail, the fundamental reason for subsidy that exists in shipping, where foreign competition in ship construction and cost of operation are essential factors." Although domestic airlines did not have to compete in an international arena, the postmaster general still believed that the emergent industry deserved financial support from the government—at least in the short term. Brown emphasized, "We [in the government] want you [the airlines] to prosper and the service to grow. I want to give air mail every encouragement consistent with sound business." As a result, the postmaster was not "disposed to drive a hard bargain" with those "who have put their money and skill into the flying game." Instead, Brown desired to work with the airlines to lower airmail payments in a manner that would facilitate the ongoing development of the industry while maintaining operators' financial health.[23]

Simultaneously, the postmaster general hoped to rationalize the airmail route system to promote orderly, structured growth. Speaking to the House Post Office and Post Roads Committee, Brown lamented that fact that as a result of halting and inconsistent growth, the airmail map, by 1929, had become "entirely illogical." Some routes "had no real excuse for existence and others . . . could be greatly improved with small additions." Brown desired a logical map that would stabilize airmail revenues, support ongoing airline development, and provide a maximum of value to the country. Achieving that end would require a wholesale reorganization of the airmail contract system and policy makers' willingness to play an active role in that effort—a role Brown was willing to embrace.[24]

Brown launched his reform efforts with a public commitment to revise the rate system. In a May 27, 1929, Post Office press release, the postmaster general argued that federal airmail payments "must be reduced and carrying rates readjusted to a sound basis." Brown based his judgment on the "disparity between the amount earned and expended by the government for air mail and also the wide differences in pay to different contractors." In plain terms, Brown abhorred the wide imbalance in contract airmail payments and hoped to create a more rational system that would lower federal expenditures while encouraging airlines to expand the air transport network in a rational manner. The solution, he suggested, was a policy whereby the Post Office would compensate operators strictly on the basis of distance, rather than the prevailing system based on weight.[25]

In support of that end, Brown initiated a series of meetings between Post Office officials and airline executives designed to facilitate the creation of a sensible airmail payment and route system that would support the continued development of American commercial aviation. During the first meeting, on May 27, Brown and airline executives agreed that any change in airmail policy necessitated a thorough investigation of current practices. To that end Post Office officials agreed to prepare a questionnaire the department would send out to current and possible future contractors, designed to provide Brown with "information on operating costs and other factors entering into the business on which to base revisions of pay rates to the operators." On the basis of that survey, the postmaster general hoped to inaugurate wholesale changes to both rate and route policies.[26]

Brown made good on that promise in September, calling airline executives to Washington to discuss the results of the surveys. His foremost concern was to work with the airlines to negotiate contract extensions good for ten years from the date on which each airline began to fly the mail, more than doubling the contracts' initial four-year term. Asserting that he should "be authorized by negotiation with present air mail contractors to extend air mail contracts to a maximum period of ten years from the date of the original award," Brown hoped to be able to reward successful and stable pioneer operators. This policy would allow the postmaster to guide the growth of the industry—at least in the short term—by granting contract extensions without competitive bidding to those operators he felt had demonstrated the ability to promote American air commerce. This policy would significantly reduce open competition, competition Brown believed had the potential to create chaos and threaten the future of American air commerce.[27]

Brown's focus on extending these contracts reflected his desire to promote greater stability in the airmail system and reward so-called pioneer operators with guaranteed revenue that would encourage further development. Arguing that "with the passenger lines, as with the exclusively mail lines, preference . . . should be given to pioneers in the air transport industry of good character and financial responsibility," Brown emphasized that these pioneers—the air transport companies that had inaugurated commercial service by winning the first wave of airmail contracts—were worthy of preferential treatment in light of their trailblazing efforts to inaugurate reliable commercial service.[28] These airlines had undertaken myriad trial-and-error efforts to find suitable aircraft, train pilots, create maintenance schedules, and establish routes at a time when air transport was a marginal industry at best. They built emergency landing fields and erected beacon lights on their routes, perfected pilot training programs, and invested in better aircraft with more instrumentation in an effort to improve their service.

Brown worried that short-term contracts and competitive bidding had the potential to undermine the position of established carriers that had worked long and hard to establish reliable service. Specifically, Brown hoped to prevent new, untested carriers with little experience and limited potential for stable growth from underbidding these pioneers and stunting the growth of the American air transport system. The same attributes that gave pioneer carriers great potential for further development—particularly into passenger service—also raised overhead, opening the door for later air transport operators to reap the benefits of the pioneers' investments. Brown worried that the short-term route contracts mandated by prevailing legislation would give unfair advantage to small and/or unprepared operators not willing or able to invest in the training and safety equipment needed to promote safe operations with the hope of carrying passengers in addition to cargo. As R. E. G. Davies explains, "any private company with a couple of worn-out aircraft could have put in a low tender, aiming only at making a few quick dollars at the expense of the Post Office and then pulling out."[29] Such a company would also be able to take advantage of the infrastructure built by its predecessor and potentially poach its pilots and its maintenance and administrative staff as well.

Brown believed that these circumstances had the potential to cause great harm to American aviation, undermining public confidence in air safety and shutting out the pioneer operators who had worked diligently to promote safe and reliable operations. As he told Congress, "If we throw these matters all open to competitive bidding, you will find promoters coming in and wanting to bid off the contract, having no knowledge of the cost of obsolescence . . . [and] having no knowledge of the bad luck" and logistical challenges involved in operating a regularly scheduled airline. To forestall those circumstances, Brown worked to reward the pioneers for their efforts and make sure they had continuing access to airmail subsidies to protect their investments and support further growth.[30]

As Brown endeavored to craft contract extensions, he also worked with Hoover to establish greater transparency between governmental agencies and commercial interests with the goal of promoting economic growth. In May 1929 the Post Office proudly announced the creation of the Interdepartmental Committee on Airways. The committee—created at Hoover's behest—was tasked to "hear and determine questions relating to the extension of the civil airways system of the United States." Its membership included prominent members of the Post Office and Commerce Departments, including W. Irving Glover, second assistant postmaster general; E. B. Wadsworth, superintendent of the Air Mail Service; William MacCracken, assistant secretary of commerce for aviation; and F. C. Hingsburg, chief of the Commerce Department Airways Division. Brown was delighted, arguing that the committee's creation represented a crucial step in rationalizing American air commerce. "The fast growing business of air transport," he articulated, "with its air mail nucleus, and the consequent vast numbers of applications for extensions of existing routes and the establishment of new ones, have made the organization of a committee to handle the relevant problems a necessary expedient." Brown related that the committee would hold public meetings at regular intervals in order to "entertain suggestions from representatives of commercial organizations . . . for the establishment, extension, or modification of the airways system."[31]

Despite Brown's best efforts, neither his conferences with airline executives nor the work of the new Interdepartmental Committee on Airways was able to secure agreement on airmail contract extensions. The haphazard contemporary system, with its myriad inequalities, militated against any easy solution to the prevailing disparities in airmail payments. Representatives of airlines benefiting from Post Office largesse saw little need for change, putting them at odds with their peers who received smaller payments and creating a barrier to easy agreement on the proper path moving forward. Further, all airline executives worried that Brown's desire to reduce the level of federal subsidy would threaten their long-term stability. Although the postmaster general went so far as to ask industry leaders to submit their own plan for his examination, ongoing disagreements between those executives prevented any real progress.

With negotiations going nowhere, Brown turned to a more comprehensive solution—new legislation. Working with William MacCracken—who had returned to practicing aviation law—Second Assistant Postmaster General Glover, and leading industry lobbyists, Brown sought to craft a wholesale overhaul of Post Office airmail policy.[32] As they set about their work, Brown redoubled his efforts to publicize commercial flying and educate the American people about the government's responsibility to stimulate the development of aeronautics. His clearest expression of that vision came in a January 1930 speech to the Cleveland Chamber of Commerce in which he articulated a sweeping vision for federal policy that emphasized aviation's value to the nation, echoing many aspects of Hoover's core vision in the process.

Brown began by highlighting aviation's dramatic progress since the Wright Brothers' flight in 1903, but he quickly moved to focus on the government's contributions to aeronautical development. Reminding the audience that the government had consistently played a leading role in promoting aviation, Brown emphasized how the Post Office's "pioneering operations with the air mail" were "actuated by a major purpose to encourage the art of flying and the aviation industry." The goal of those efforts, Brown related, was for the United States to "lead the nations of the earth in commercial flying." Achieving that goal was within reach but necessitated ongoing efforts from both the government and the aeronautics industry. With regard to the former, Brown told the audience that the government should "by every reasonable and practical method . . . encourage the development of better airplanes, landing fields, weather reporting services and aids to aerial navigation." The Post Office and Commerce Department had made significant progress in those areas to date, but much work remained to ensure the maturation of the commercial industry.[33]

More worryingly for Brown, the aviation industry was then facing serious challenges. First and foremost, the Depression was wreaking havoc on commercial flying operations. Brown told his audience that virtually all airlines, even those that had been profitable before the economic downturn, had closed 1929 operating at a significant deficit. As a result of those dire financial straits, he contended, "the very life of the . . . industry today is in the balance." Overproduction, a loss of passenger volume, and a reduction in airmail revenue combined to create circumstances that the Postmaster General believed occasioned "the deepest public concern." If the industry continued to struggle, he suggested, government time, money, and effort, not to mention the public investment in the aviation industry, would be lost.[34]

Such a circumstance would be disastrous, Brown argued, in light of the benefits aviation had the potential to bring the country. On the one hand he believed that aeronautical development would bring with it increased commercial efficiency, technological innovation, and the promotion of safer and more effective communication. These positive effects, he emphasized, "will rebound immeasurably to the progress, prosperity, and security of our country." On the other hand he, like others in the Hoover administration, tied the development of commercial aviation to national defense. Brown believed that the creation of a stable air transport industry would result in Americans having "no anxiety about being able to defend ourselves in the air if the occasion should ever arise." Here Brown echoed one of Hoover's most powerful arguments for government support of commercial flying.[35]

In 1927, shortly before resigning his position as commerce secretary to launch his presidential bid, Hoover argued "that the development of commercial aviation will prove a military asset of the first rank" because "it will mean the training of a great source of wonderful aviators whose service will be available in the moment of emergency, the assembling of a great reserve in equipment and the fostering of the manufacturing industry as essential in the hour of need." This argument, reiterated by Paul Henderson, William MacCracken, and others, consistently formed one of the most compelling arguments for government engagement with commercial flying, resonating with members of Congress and the public alike.[36]

Turning to his plans to achieve those goals, Brown offered the Chamber of Commerce a clear vision for federal policy moving forward. Unsurprisingly, Brown began by highlighting the necessity of rationalizing the airmail network by enacting changes to both the rate structure and the route system. In response to the most pressing need, Brown desired to abolish the poundage-based system that perpetuated an unequal payment scale. Brown hoped that a move to a space-based system would alleviate the inequalities and promote even more growth while simultaneously allowing the Post Office to support the development of passenger service. He suggested that such a move "would enable the Post Office Department to give immediate assistance to air passenger carriers on such routes as were deemed essential" by offering them "substantial" financial support through airmail payments. Further clarifying his ideas, Brown continued: "Various factors, of course, should determine the amount of weight-space to be taken, . . . the character and frequency of the service, the volume of mail flowing, and the financial necessities of the carrier." In short, Brown wanted to transition to a space-based system in order to use Post Office contracts to shape the industry according to his vision. Brown believed that these changes, when combined with the freedom to grant mail carriers ten-year contracts, would allow him to encourage airlines to purchase larger, safer, more technologically advanced planes to encourage passenger-carrying operations and extend the airmail map.[37]

By early spring Brown and his allies finished drafting what would ultimately become H.R. 9500, the third amendment to the 1925 Airmail Act. Brown submitted the legislation to representative Laurence Watres (R-PA), a member of the House Post Office Committee, with hopes for its speedy passage. Clearly reflecting Brown's desires, the bill changed the Post Office's payment system to one based on space available rather than poundage (specifically, authorizing the Post Office to pay a fixed amount per cubic foot of available space not to exceed $1.25 per mile), authorized the postmaster general to exchange airlines' original four-year contracts for ten-year route certificates, allowed the postmaster to revise rates for operators receiving a ten-year certificate, and enabled the postmaster to approve route extensions and consolidations in the public interest. Brown initially hoped that the law would allow him to grant new contacts without competitive bidding, but congressional opposition forced a compromise. As a result, the bill restricted bidding on airmail contracts to operators with six months of operating experience on routes of four hundred miles or longer and allowed Brown the freedom to extend and consolidate routes at his discretion. The result was a system that embraced many of Brown's ideas—granting preference to established operators, giving the postmaster the freedom to rationalize airmail routes through extensions and consolidations, promoting the establishment of passenger service, and promoting technological development—while at the same time leaving the door open to new, independent operators.[38]

Brown specifically crafted the bill to promote passenger service by including provisions that encouraged airlines to use larger, more technologically advanced aircraft. Airmail carriers would receive bonuses—added as an increase in payment per mile to the base rate—for carrying radios, flying in the fog or after dark, and using multiengine aircraft. More significantly, Brown explicitly encouraged airlines to carry passengers by offering a sliding scale of increased payment tied to aircraft size. At minimum, planes carrying between two and five passengers received an additional 1.5 cents per mile, while, at the other end of the spectrum, planes carrying more than thirty passengers received an additional 7.5 cents.[39] These provisions created a system that embraced Brown's core philosophy—an effort to create a rational, stable air transport network that promoted the public good through the carriage of cargo and passengers.

Immediately after President Hoover signed the Watres Act into law in April, Brown moved to take advantage of his new powers. True to his belief that the government should work with business interests to promote development, he began by calling representatives from all of the major airlines to Washington, DC, for an informational meeting with the goal of acquainting them with the specifics of the new legislation.[40] This meeting would be the first of a series of operators' conferences during which Brown would grant airmail routes to major airlines using his expanded powers. Independent air transport operators—those without federal airmail contracts—and congressional Democrats would later use these meetings—dubbed "spoils conferences"—as evidence that Brown colluded with airlines and engaged in fraud and corruption at taxpayers' expense. Ultimately, the uproar over these conferences led to Senator Hugo Black's creation of a Senate special investigation.

An examination of Brown's rationale for calling these meetings, and the response from airlines in attendance, however, paints a very different picture. In a May 15, 1930, Post Office memorandum, Irving Glover explained Brown's goals for these meetings. Glover began by expressing the postmaster general's desire to meet with "substantial representatives" from major airlines. Brown, Glover related, hoped to engage in a dialogue focused on the best way for the Post Office to encourage the development of passenger lines. More specifically, Glover wrote that Brown desired the Post Office and the airlines "to come to some understanding so that it [airmail payments] will not all be thrown into the pot and the passenger line operators left entirely outside due to the fact that the air mail operators would have the inside and have the territory covered." In other words, Brown was worried that competitive bidding would allow new and untried operators with low overhead and no potential for carrying passengers to undercut the established airlines and gain access to the bulk of federal airmail subsidies. This would have the effect of stunting the growth of passenger service, a situation Brown hoped to avoid at all costs.[41]

Brown's response was to facilitate a meeting at which the major passenger-carrying airlines would voluntarily split up the airmail map in order to distribute subsidies to the benefit of all attendees. Although Brown was frustrated that the Watres Act had not granted him the freedom he hoped for, the sections of the act providing for certificates in place of contracts and granting the postmaster power to extend and consolidate routes offered Brown significant room to maneuver. He planned to work with the airlines to use his Watres Act–derived powers to grant established carriers routes with the greatest potential to foster passenger service. This was the ultimate purpose of the May 19 conference, a meeting Brown hoped would set a solid foundation for the future of American air transport. The postmaster invited only well-established carriers with a history of passenger service—most prominently United, American, and Transcontinental Air Transport—a fact that left a number of small, independent operators unable even to bid on airmail routes. This situation would later give rise to charges of collusion, as Brown's actions—at least in spirit—violated the Watres Act's mandate for competitive bidding.[42]

Brown, however, believed that his actions represented the best and most logical way to secure the future of American passenger airlines. In a memorandum summarizing the May 19 meeting, Earl Wadsworth wrote that Brown organized the conference in order to discuss "the provisions of the Watres' [*sic*] Bill insofar as it offered aid to the passenger lines." According to the postmaster general, it was common knowledge that "none of the so-called strictly passenger lines are breaking even and it is apparent that they will need some assistance if they are going to continue." Even established airmail operators were struggling during the depths of the Depression, and Brown recognized the necessity of focused federal support to realize any form of solvent passenger service. To address those conditions, "the PMG [postmaster general] expressed the desire to know whether it is going to be possible for the so-called pioneer operators to agree among themselves as to the territory in which they shall have paramount interest."[43] Here Wadsworth confirmed Brown's plan for securing the health of passenger carriers, a plan centered on voluntary cooperation between the government and commercial interests and among the commercial interests themselves.

The airline executives at the meeting approved of Brown's plan. Hainer Hinshaw of Northwest Airways echoed the general consensus that the postmaster general's plan was sound and had merit. Jack Maddux, representing Maddux Airlines and Transcontinental Air Transport, argued that if airlines did "not receive an air mail contract then they could not live"; he hoped that "the [Watres] Bill would take care of this." At the same time, Maddux and his peers seconded Brown's desire for the assembled carriers to come to some agreement without recourse to competitive bidding. Harris Hanshue, the representative from Western Air Express, most clearly articulated the group's thinking on the subject, stating, "We are willing to do anything within reason to work out the plan rather than go into competitive bidding." After asking if there were any objections to his plan—there were none—Brown allowed the assembled airline executives to use the room for negotiations, leaving them with a request "to report back to the PMG when they had reached a conclusion in regard to the suggested plan."[44]

While Brown was content to let the airlines negotiate among themselves to a point, he did have concrete ideas regarding the airway map he wanted to emerge from the operators' conferences. Specifically, the postmaster general desired that a single, powerful airline control each transcontinental "trunk" line stretching from the East Coast to the West Coast. Although only two of these lines existed in the spring of 1930—the north and central routes—throughout the conferences Brown worked to use extensions and consolidations to create a third, southern trunk route. In his mind this model would support the continued development of a number of mature airlines while encouraging technological advances and passenger service by creating long-distance routes between major passenger destinations—New York, Philadelphia, Atlanta, Dallas, Chicago, Denver, San Francisco, and Los Angeles, for example.

Brown was not reticent in making his views known to the assembled representatives. A Northwest Airways representative reported that Brown's "expressed intention" was to develop three "competing trans-continental lines; each line distinctly independent of the other and each controlled by one . . . of the strongest aviation groups." C. E. Woolman of Delta Airlines confirmed that intention, relating, "the Postmaster General had definitely stated that he intended that each of the three transcontinental routes would be operated by a single company." Interestingly, Woolman had not received an invitation to the May 19 meeting, but after consulting with William MacCracken and demonstrating that Delta had the necessary requirements to qualify for the conferences, he gained admittance to subsequent meetings beginning in June. Woolman made several keen observations regarding Brown's growing frustration that the airline executives were struggling to realize his vision. Pointedly, the Delta executive remarked that the postmaster general visited the negotiations on a number of occasions and "expressed some irritation over the fact that the conflicting interests in dividing the air mail routes under consideration could not settle [the airlines'] differences."[45]

Ultimately, the conferences failed to produce unanimity, and Brown stepped in to act as a referee, splitting up the airway map according to what he believed to be the best interests of both the carriers and the country. On June 4 William MacCracken wrote Brown, informing the postmaster general that "the Committee has instructed me to advise you that the representatives of all the parties involved in the controversies desire to submit these controversies to you as arbiter and agree to be bound by your decision." Using his ability to extend and consolidate routes, Brown remade the airmail map as he desired. He approved contract extensions that were in some cases significantly longer than the initial routes, pushed through route consolidations in the interest of airway coherence, and used the leverage provided by the lucrative contracts to secure the merger of airlines—for example, the Aviation Corporation of America, the holding corporation controlling American Airways, purchased a majority stake in Delta at Brown's urging. Technically legal according to the dictates of the Watres Act, Brown's activities certainly violated the spirit of the law, which maintained requirements for competitive bidding.[46] Nonetheless, the result was a much more rational airmail map dominated by large, established carriers poised to expand their passenger-carrying operations using money from larger airmail contracts and the bonus system Brown crafted for the Watres bill.

Before Brown could implement his vision, however, his actions attracted unwanted scrutiny from the US comptroller general, J. R. McCarl. McCarl, who embraced a more conservative view of Brown's powers under the new legislation, "declared unlawful the granting of these routes by extensions as presented to him by the Postmaster General" and limited route extensions to distances no more than half as long as the originally contracted route. According to Woolman, Brown responded to McCarl's actions by announcing that he would entertain bids for uncontracted routes, but only under "specifications which virtually eliminated from bidding any other than" Brown's chosen airlines. Specifically, Brown mandated that prospective bidders post a $250,000 bond to ensure financial stability and establish good faith. Bond posting was not a new requirement for airlines interested in securing a Post Office route, but the new amount was many times greater than that required for previous contracts—generally under $15,000. Further, at the urging of William MacCracken, Brown imposed a night flying requirement, which the former believed would separate the experienced operators from new upstarts. Neither of these new requirements was unreasonable, but they had the effect of radically limiting the number of airlines qualified to bid on airmail contracts. As a result, Brown was largely able to achieve his goals, though in a more convoluted manner than he had initially planned.[47]

These maneuverings ultimately allowed Brown to realize the vast majority of his goals. The new contract requirements disallowed bids from virtually all of the unproven airlines Brown hoped to exclude from Post Office largesse; even paying heed to the limitations McCarl imposed on his freedom, Brown was able to extend and consolidate existing lines to fit his logical plan. By the summer of 1930 Brown had created a map defined by major airlines flying three foundational transcontinental lines, with feeder lines serving the majority of large US population centers. He also worked to eliminate small routes with minimal mail volume and little potential for growth into passenger service. Brown's efforts allowed him to support passenger-carrying operations while simultaneously embarking on a steady reduction in Post Office mail subsidies. Following an additional round of operators' conferences in the spring of 1931, Brown convinced airmail contract operators to accept a payment reduction of between five and fifteen cents per mile; he also continued to fine-tune the airway map through route extensions and cancellations. While many of the leading airlines continued to struggle financially, Brown's actions increased passenger numbers, and the postmaster general hoped that through ongoing efforts he would finally be able to place the air transport industry on a sound footing.[48]

New technological breakthroughs suggested that goal might be within reach. In 1930 the majority of airlines continued to rely on single-engine mail planes, some of which were still biplane designs, and trimotor aircraft from companies such as Boeing, Fokker, and Ford for carrying passengers. The Ford trimotor, probably the most ubiquitous airliner of the era, entered service in 1926 and continued to be produced until 1933. It could carry about ten passengers, depending on the variant; cruised at a little more than one hundred miles per hour; and had a range of less than six hundred miles. The figures would have been impressive in 1920, but by 1930 Brown was frustrated by airlines' inability to carry passengers and cargo with sufficient speed and reliability. He, like Hoover, believed that speed and efficiency were the keys to luring passengers off trains and into the air, and the current aerial fleet was, in his opinion, not adequate to that task. The Watres bill's incentive clauses represented an effort to promote the development of new, faster aircraft, and by the early 1930s that effort began to bear fruit.

In 1931 Boeing began developing the model 247, an outgrowth of their B-9 bomber. The 247 was the first modern airliner, a two-engine, low-wing, all-metal monoplane capable of carrying ten passengers more than 750 miles at a cruising speed approaching 180 miles per hour. These figures represented a quantum leap over contemporary airliners and spurred Boeing's rival, Douglas Aircraft, to embark on an even more ambitious design effort. The resulting DC-2—subsequently developed into the DC-3, the most successful airliner of all time—could carry fourteen passengers 1,000 miles at a cruising speed of 190 miles per hour. The 247 and DC-2 entered service in 1933 and 1934, respectively, ushering in a new age of air transport. By 1936, when Boeing introduced the DC-3, airlines could for the first time achieve profitability from carrying passengers alone, finally freeing them from the necessity of securing airmail payments. To a significant extent, this progress represented an outgrowth of Brown's desire to promote aeronautical development; the ultimate success of these planes and the airlines employing them speaks to the soundness of Brown's basic vision.

Unfortunately, while Brown's ongoing efforts to mold the development of US airlines did bear fruit, they also attracted increasingly scathing criticism from airlines cut out of Brown's vision and congressional Democrats chafing under twelve years of leadership from Republican presidents. Frustration and resentment over Brown's supposedly "dictatorial" control of the airline industry peaked following the Democratic landslide in the 1932 elections, ushering in a tumultuous period defined by Senator Hugo Black's Senate investigation into supposed fraud and collusion between the Post Office and the airlines. Though the investigation sought to discredit both Brown and his policies, to the end Brown maintained that he had acted in the best interest of the Post Office, the air transport industry, and the country.

Brown's defense of his actions during the Senate investigation offers the clearest articulation of the postmaster's views on aviation's significance to the United States and the government's proper role in promoting its growth. Brown began his testimony by explaining the rationale that guided his thinking as he crafted the Watres bill. "The major purpose of the legislation," he stated, "was not to transport the mails at the lowest possible cost to the government, but to foster the . . . aeronautical industr[y]." The wording of the bill itself, he explained, clearly articulated that the legislation's goal was to "'encourage commercial aviation.'" Drawing from that foundational purpose, Brown argued that the ultimate goal of federal policy lay in fostering the development of "an economically independent aeronautical industry." To achieve that end, Brown specifically constructed Post Office airmail subsidies to enable "air transport operators to recoup in the form of mail pay their out-of-pocket losses while they are building up adequate passenger and express revenues from the public and are developing transport airplanes capable under competitive conditions of earning their costs of operation." Here Brown defined aviation as a fledgling industry in need of public aid. Airmail revenue, in this context, served as a kind of grant, enabling air transport operators to remain solvent while encouraging maturation that would eventually wean them off federal payments. Bearing that fact in mind, Brown argued that he undertook all of his actions under the Watres Act to serve the public interest. "Every such action," he argued, "resulted in improved public service and ultimately in lower flying costs which were passed on to the Government in the form of reduced mail pay."[49]

The former postmaster general also emphasized that he worked diligently to craft policies specifically designed to promote passenger-carrying operations. The new powers granted him by the Watres Act, he stated, allowed him to exert "pressure on the air mail carriers, who with minor exceptions had theretofore been confining their operations exclusively to carrying the mail, to transport passengers and express in order to build up revenues from the public and thus lighten the load on the Post Office Department." At the same time, Brown explained that his actions served to rationalize the air transport map by using every power at his disposal "to consolidate the short, detached and failing lines into well financed and well managed systems." Most importantly, he emphasized his success in facilitating the establishment of "three independent intercontinental operations," the core of a stable airways map poised for future expansion. Presciently, the former postmaster general related his belief that his policies would ultimately create a commercial aviation industry with the ability to "attract public patronage, reduce operating costs and develop, if possible, a transport airplane capable . . . of earning enough to pay its own way without subsidy," a reality that would come to pass in only a few short years.[50]

Brown also tied aviation's health to the well-being of the nation. In his work for the Post Office, Brown stated that he "took it for granted that the uninterrupted development of the air transport industry, necessary to keep the aeronautical art in our country abreast of that art throughout the world, was vital to our national security and that the air mail itself was performing an essential service for the business of the country."[51] Aviation, in his view, represented an important and growing factor in the economic health of the nation, while simultaneously benefiting America's security. Maintaining a technological edge, he argued, was a key aspect of protecting American interests at home and abroad.

These statements confirm that Brown saw his role as postmaster general extending far beyond the carriage of the mail. He used the power granted him by the Watres Act to take almost single-handed control of commercial aviation with the goal of shaping it into a fiscally solvent, technologically advanced industry predicated on carrying passengers over a rational network of airways. In that effort he worked closely with members of the industry to promote the growth of airlines he felt had the best potential to realize those goals. As such, his actions represented an effort to apply associative principles to the air transport industry, providing the clearest example of Hoover's economic ideology operating in practice. Though at times Brown's actions demonstrated a heavy-handed approach that suggests the limitations of Hoover's philosophy, the postmaster general's efforts were, for the most part, effective in stimulating the growth of young airlines, promoting safe operations, and beginning to increase airlines' ability and willingness to carry passengers. Brown's specific decisions emerged from a logical analysis of the emerging industry and reflected a genuine desire to benefit both aviation and the United States. For him, these activities did not represent collusion or fraud. Rather, they offered the best way for the government to help promote the rational growth of an embryonic industry while avoiding counterproductive competition.

Senator Hugo Black did not agree. His and Democratic allies' opposition to prevailing Republican policy threw US commercial aviation into turmoil, ushering in one of the most contentious periods in its history. Airmail contracts were canceled, aviation executives found themselves divorced from companies they had built from the ground up, aviation holding corporations were broken up, army pilots fought for their lives flying obsolescent aircraft over rugged terrain in horrid weather, and Charles Lindbergh and Franklin Roosevelt, the two most famous men in the country, found themselves locked in a very public feud. Black's Senate investigation and the surrounding furor, however, ultimately concluded with a most unexpected result.

Calbraith Perry Rodgers poses in front of his plane, 1911. That year Rodgers became the first person to fly from coast to coast, a feat he accomplished in forty-nine days. (Courtesy Library of Congress Prints and Photographs Division, Washington, DC, http://www.loc.gov/pictures/item/2001704121/.)

Army Curtis JN-4 Jenny airmail planes at the Washington, DC, polo grounds, 1918. (Courtesy Library of Congress Prints and Photographs Division, Washington, DC, http://www.loc.gov/pictures/resource/hec.10833/.)

Postmaster General Albert Burleson (*left*) and President Woodrow Wilson at the inauguration of the army's airmail service, May 1918. (Courtesy Library of Congress Prints and Photographs Division, Washington, DC, http://www.loc.gov/pictures/resource/hec.10821/.)

Postmaster General Albert Burleson (*third from left*) poses with members of the army's airmail service on the first anniversary of its inception, May 1919. (Courtesy Library of Congress Prints and Photographs Division, Washington, DC, http://www.loc.gov/pictures/item/npc2007018658/.)

Herbert Hoover. (Courtesy Library of Congress Prints and Photographs Division, Washington, DC, http://www.loc.gov/pictures/item/hec2013001329/.)

An Aeromarine Airways flying boat arrives in Bimini, the Bahamas, 1922. (Courtesy Library of Congress Prints and Photographs Division, Washington, DC, http://www.loc.gov/pictures/item/2002711188/.)

An army DH-4B. The Post Office purchased and modified DH-4Bs, which were originally designed as bombers, for use by its airmail pilots. (Courtesy Library of Congress Prints and Photographs Division, Washington, DC, http://www.loc.gov/pictures/item/ggb2006007373/.)

Third Assistant Postmaster General W. Irving Glover (*left*) and Second Assistant Postmaster General Paul Henderson pose with a model of a Post Office airmail plane, 1925. (Courtesy Library of Congress Prints and Photographs Division, Washington, DC, http://www.loc.gov/pictures/item/npc2008007641/.)

Postmaster General Harry S. New opens the first private bids for federal airmail contracts, September 1925. (Courtesy Library of Congress Prints and Photographs Division, Washington, DC, http://www.loc.gov/pictures/item/npc2007014436/.)

President Calvin Coolidge (fifth from left) poses with members of his aviation board, September 1925. (Courtesy Library of Congress Prints and Photographs Division, Washington, DC, http://www.loc.gov/pictures/item/npc2008007755/.)

Left to right: A. D. Denison, Dwight W. Morrow, and W. F. Durand, members of President Calvin Coolidge's Special Aviation Board, 1925. (Courtesy Library of Congress Prints and Photographs Division, Washington, DC, http://www.loc.gov/pictures/item/npc2007014540/.)

Colonel William “Billy” Mitchell (*center*) testifies before President Calvin Coolidge’s Special Aviation Board, September 1925. (Courtesy Library of Congress Prints and Photographs Division, Washington, DC, http://www.loc.gov/pictures/item/npc2007014546/.)

Secretary of Commerce Herbert Hoover (*second from left*) stands with a group in front of a Fokker trimotor airmail plane. (Courtesy Library of Congress Prints and Photographs Division, Washington, DC, http://www.loc.gov/pictures/item/hec2013004226/.)

President Calvin Coolidge (*left*), with Secretary of Commerce Herbert Hoover, 1928. (Courtesy Library of Congress Prints and Photographs Division, Washington, DC, http://www.loc.gov/pictures/item/hec2013005197/.)

The *Columbus*, a Ford trimotor operated by Transcontinental Air Transport (TAT). TAT inaugurated the first transcontinental passenger service in the United States; Charles Lindbergh was one of the airline's organizers. (Courtesy Library of Congress Prints and Photographs Division, Washington, DC, http://www.loc.gov/pictures/item/hec2013005214/.)

Charles Lindbergh poses in front of his plane, the *Spirit of St. Louis*, May 1927. (Courtesy Library of Congress Prints and Photographs Division, Washington, DC, http://www.loc.gov/pictures/item/2002721494/.)

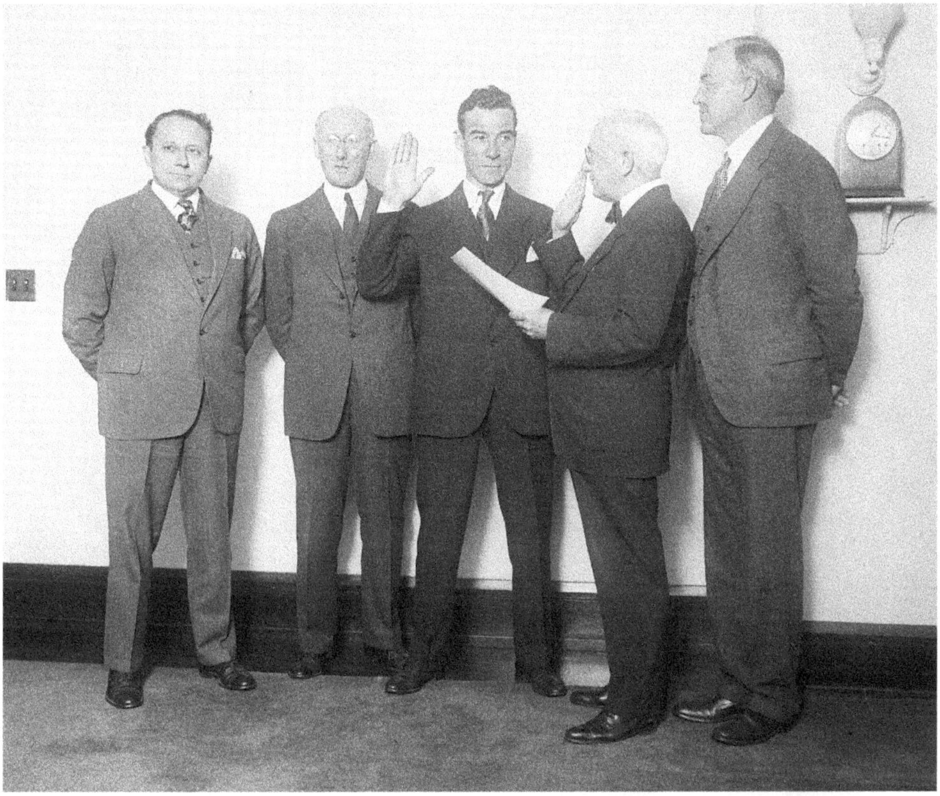

Clarence M. Young (*third from left*) is sworn in as assistant secretary of commerce for aeronautics, succeeding William P. MacCracken Jr. (*far right*), 1929. (Courtesy Library of Congress Prints and Photographs Division, Washington, DC, http://www.loc.gov/pictures/item/hec2013005580/.)

Postmaster General Walter F. Brown. (Courtesy Library of Congress Prints and Photographs Division, Washington, DC, http://www.loc.gov/pictures/item/npc2007017419/.)

Hugo Black. (Courtesy Library of Congress Prints and Photographs Division, Washington, D.C., http://www.loc.gov/pictures/item/hec2009008203/.)

Benjamin Foulois poses in front of an early army aircraft. As a major general, Foulois would serve as chief of the US Army Air Service, heading the army's airmail operations following Franklin Roosevelt's cancelation of commercial contracts in 1934. (Courtesy Library of Congress Prints and Photographs Division, Washington, DC, http://www.loc.gov/pictures/item/ggb2004005926/.)

Captain Edward "Eddie" Rickenbacker (*left*), president of Eastern Air Lines, helps a passenger disembark from an airliner, 1935. (Courtesy Library of Congress Prints and Photographs Division, Washington, DC, http://www.loc.gov/pictures/item/hec2013008259/.)

Harry Hopkins, one of Franklin Roosevelt's closest advisors, headed the Works Progress Administration and later served as secretary of commerce. (Courtesy Library of Congress Prints and Photographs Division, Washington, DC, http://www.loc.gov/pictures/item/hec2009014761/.)

The first municipal airport of Knoxville, Tennessee—Bearden Field—lacked adequate runways and facilities for commercial air traffic, prompting the city to construct a larger airport on rural land with the support of the WPA. (Courtesy Calvin M. McClung Historical Collection, Hodges Briscoe Collection, East Tennessee History Center, Knoxville.)

An aerial view of McGhee Tyson Airport, Knoxville's new WPA-funded field, which included multiple paved runways, a three-story terminal building, and a large hanger, 1937. (Courtesy Calvin M. McClung Historical Collection, Hodges Briscoe Collection, East Tennessee History Center, Knoxville.)

4

"Chicanery, Manipulation, and Fraud"

Senator Hugo Black's Air Mail Investigation, 1933–1934

In February of 1934 the US Army Air Corps (AAC) found itself at the center of the most contentious events in American aviation history. Senator Hugo Black's Senate Special Committee to Investigate Ocean Mail and Air Mail Contracts had been increasing its calls that something be done about the allegedly corrupt and collusive airmail contracts granted during the Hoover administration. As a result, on February 9 President Franklin Roosevelt signed Executive Order 6591, which annulled all existing airmail contracts and ordered the AAC to assume responsibility for the nation's airmail. Underfunded, ill-trained, and equipped with inferior aircraft, the AAC had but ten days to inaugurate service.

Not surprisingly, disaster ensued. On February 19, the first day of AAC operations, a blizzard swept across the eastern half of the United States, delaying and canceling many flights. Six army pilots perished in crashes during the first week of operations alone. Even pilots who were able to complete their routes faced unexpected and dangerous challenges. On the first day of AAC operations, C. R. Springer took off from Cleveland on a nighttime flight in his P-12 pursuit plane only to return to the field fifteen minutes later. Taxiing to a hanger, Springer hailed a mechanic with a request that he "get me a flashlight so I can find my way out of this damned town." Upon taking off into the dark sky the pilot had realized that his directional gyroscope was not working, and the plane's cockpit lights were so poor that he could not see his compass to navigate. Springer's trouble suggested that army pilots would continue to battle poor equipment and a lack of preparation in addition to the weather.[1]

Air Corps pilots also continued to crash. On February 22, three more planes went down, resulting in two more fatalities. The following day witnessed another crash and another death. While only two of the four crashes occurred during mail flights—the other two took place during an airmail supervisor's flight to observe pilots at a new field and during a training flight, respectively—the rapidly rising death toll quickly prompted a backlash in the media, in Congress, and among many leading aviation figures.

That criticism fanned the flames of a media firestorm that began immediately in the wake of Roosevelt's executive order. Two days after FDR issued EO 6591, Charles Lindbergh sent the president an angry telegram charging that the cancellations condemned airmail carriers "without just trial." Lindbergh claimed that the president's actions placed "no premium on honest business" and would "unnecessarily and greatly damage all of American aviation." While Roosevelt may have been inclined to listen to Lindbergh's private concerns, the president could not abide the fact that Lindbergh had simultaneously released the telegram to the press. The Roosevelt administration responded with its own press release, questioning Lindbergh's motives by stating that the pilot had "obviously" sent the telegram "for publicity purposes" rather than from a genuine desire to aid commercial aviation. The spat quickly escalated, much to the media's glee, and initiated a very public feud between the two most famous men in the country.[2]

As the army death toll mounted, other figures expanded upon Lindbergh's criticism. Eddie Rickenbacker called the Air Corps operation "legalized murder"; Representative Hamilton Fish (R-NY) charged the Roosevelt administration with assuming "dictatorial power"; *Time* magazine questioned Roosevelt's decision and the army's capabilities; and *Newsweek* decried the army operation as "the worst political blunder of the [Roosevelt] administration." In response, on March 10 Roosevelt suspended Air Corps airmail flights for a period of nine days. On March 19 the army resumed carrying the mail, but on radically truncated routes with far less poundage, and Air Corps chief Major General Benjamin Foulois forbade pilots with less than two years of experience from flying nighttime routes and mandated that those flights go forward only during good weather following a satisfactory check of all of the planes' instruments. At the same time, Roosevelt began working to return airmail routes to private contractors, a desire that would be realized at the beginning of June.[3]

Until then, Air Corps pilots continued to crash, in spite of the best efforts of Foulois and his commanders. The second week of March witnessed four more fatalities, and while moderating weather eased AAC pilots' burdens by the end of the month, their overall record demonstrated just how unprepared the service had been to assume responsibility for airmail. Between February and June, AAC pilots experienced sixty-six crashes; twelve pilots lost their lives. AAC airmail operators completed only two-thirds of their scheduled flights, a number that would have been even lower had not the service scaled back operations at the beginning of March. These realities demonstrated in the starkest terms the separation existing between military and civilian aviation by the mid-1930s. Fortunately for the Air Corps, the trials of its airmail operations bolstered support for increased training, larger appropriations, and new aircraft, suggesting that an easier road lay ahead.[4]

The Air Corps airmail fiasco formed the most visible—and controversial—aspect of the 1934 airmail scandal, a series of events encompassing the most contentious period in American commercial aviation history. During the depths of the Great Depression, in the wake of the sweeping Democratic victories in 1932, Democratic senator Hugo Black's Senate Special Committee to Investigate Ocean Mail and Air Mail Contracts served as a litmus test for US commercial aviation policy. Black and his allies charged that during the Hoover administration Walter Brown and his allies oversaw a corrupt, collusive, and illegal airmail policy that threatened the Post Office, the airlines, and, in more than a bit of hyperbole, the very foundations of the American way of life. Black's committee engaged in a comprehensive investigation, sponsored public hearings, and made recommendations that eventually led to the passage of new airmail legislation. Superficially, these events suggested a direct challenge to the prevailing Republican vision for federal aviation policy. In reality, however, under the leadership of Franklin Roosevelt, James Farley, and Hugo Black, this tumultuous period to a great extent served to validate that vision. In spite of the angry rhetoric and media firestorm, by mid-1934 US airlines returned to flying the mail under contracts broadly similar to those let by Walter Brown five years earlier while continuing to benefit from Commerce Department efforts to regulate and promote the industry. If anything, the uproar suggested the need for a more focused and coherent federal policy encompassing expanded governmental engagement with aeronautics—circumstances redressed four years later by the passage of the Civil Aeronautics Act of 1938.

Black's investigation provides the clearest lens through which to examine the content and context of contemporary federal policy debates concerning aviation. The Senate investigation focused attention on federal aviation policy for both legislators and the American public, prompting Democrats and Republicans, supporters and opponents, to marshal their most powerful arguments concerning American commercial flying. During the proceedings Black, Farley, and Roosevelt publicly stated their views on aviation policy and sought to gain support from both legislators and the public. The media offered exhaustive coverage of the committee's investigation and the events associated with the president's cancellation of commercial contracts. The committee itself subpoenaed financial records, correspondence, and memoranda from the Post Office and airlines. The investigation also called for major players—including Walter Brown, William MacCracken, and leading airline executives—to testify before the committee. These events thus exposed and clarified the most significant policy debates concerning aviation, offering an opportunity to examine the specific arguments marshaled by Brown, Black, and their respective supporters.

Ultimately, the history surrounding Black's investigation highlights the surprising continuity in federal aviation policy during the upheaval of the early 1930s. While on the surface Black's strident denunciation of Walter Brown's policies and his supposed antipathy toward Republican promotion of close connections between government and business suggest a desire to break from Hoover's vision for US aeronautics, a closer examination of Black's and his allies' actions reveals a different story.[5] Although Black's rhetoric was undoubtedly antimonopoly and anti–big business, he favored governmental action to support aviation. In fact, Black appears to have shared much of Hoover's vision regarding aviation's central role in America's future and government's responsibility to promote aeronautical growth. These facts necessitate a reevaluation of the lessons to be drawn from the Senate special committee's actions. Ultimately, the Black committee served to confirm the value of Hoover's vision and the effectiveness of federal policies in the years before 1932.

The roots of Black's Senate investigation traced to the Democratic landslide in the 1932 elections but also reflected ongoing upheavals in the industry itself. As the Great Depression deepened, the economic downturn affected the aeronautics industry unevenly. Airframe and engine manufacturers felt the pinch almost immediately; the number of nonmilitary aircraft produced in the United Stated dropped from a total of 5,414 planes in 1929 to less than 900 three years later, while the total value of all aeronautical goods produced declined by almost two-thirds. As most Americans' disposable income evaporated, general aviation also witnessed a precipitous decline. Total flying hours dropped by almost a third, and the Commerce Department issued just over half the number of student pilot certificates in 1932 that it had in 1929. As a result of these conditions, flying schools, mechanics, and countless other aviation-related industries struggled mightily.[6]

The airlines, in contrast—at least those fortunate enough to possess airmail contracts—bucked the trend. Between 1929 and 1932 airmail revenues doubled, passenger numbers tripled, and airlines increased their workforce by more than 250 percent. These figures, while astonishing in light of the larger economic climate, formed a rational outgrowth of Hoover's and Brown's focus on promoting commercial aviation. Airlines flying the mail for the US government could count on guaranteed revenue and ongoing promotion efforts from the Commerce Department. The Watres Act disbursed airmail payments on the basis of an airline's space available, so a reduction in airmail volume had little effect on carriers' profits. Further, Brown's reward system continued to provide increased revenue for those carriers embracing larger, faster, more technologically advanced planes. By the end of Hoover's presidential term these policies had borne fruit, as airlines benefited from rapidly increasing numbers of passengers even as they were able to reduce ticket prices and, for the first time, compete with railroad Pullman service.[7]

Not all airlines benefited from federal largesse, however. In his effort to encourage passenger service and technological development, Brown worked to restrict airmail contracts to those carriers he felt had the greatest potential to push the industry forward. Those operators received invitations to the 1930 operators' conferences that split up the national airway map and benefited from Brown's ongoing efforts to extend and consolidate routes. While the postmaster general also continued to reduce airmail payments with the ultimate goal of creating a self-sustaining airline industry—often to the frustration of the airlines affected—by 1932 a yawning divide existed between Brown's chosen airlines and those struggling to survive without airmail contracts. The latter, independent airlines, had for years struggled to gain access to airmail revenue with little success, their executives growing more and more frustrated by Brown's apparent favoritism. In point of fact the majority of those carriers simply didn't have the experience, equipment, or personnel to fly the mail safely, but their leaders nonetheless railed against Brown's "favoritism" for larger, more established lines. By the early 1930s the independents engaged in increasingly public attacks against the supposed corruption and collusion in the Post Office. They also worked to enlist the media in their crusade, most significantly finding a sympathetic ear in Fulton Lewis Jr., a reporter for the conservative Hearst-owned Universal News Service.[8]

Through 1932 the independents made little headway, but the sweeping Democratic victories in that year's elections created a host of new opportunities for those disenchanted with Republican policies. In fact, the independents had been lobbying Democratic senators and congressmen for years to little effect; in a 1931 letter to Frederick Rentschler, president of United Aircraft and Transport, P. G. Johnson alerted his superior that the independent air carriers had recently ramped up their lobbying efforts. Johnson reported that a group of these airlines had initiated a series of meetings designed to craft a strategy to "force the government to give them mail contracts." While those efforts came to naught in the short term, with the turn in political fortunes the independent carriers found a more receptive audience for their grievances. Brown also added fuel to the fire as his term as postmaster general wound down. Before vacating his office, Brown granted a number of route extensions to airlines already possessing federal contracts, refusing—legally, it must be said—to submit the new airway miles to competitive bidding. Coming as they did after the fall elections, Brown's actions drew sharp criticism from airlines hoping for a sea change in federal policy and from congressional Democrats who had chafed under Republican rule for twelve long years.[9]

These issues came to a head beginning in early 1933, when opponents of Brown's policies found an ally in the figure of Alabama senator Hugo Black. In January, Fulton Lewis Jr. submitted to Black a report outlining a long history of supposed corruption, collusion, and fraud connected to airline contracts. Lewis had compiled the report with the goal of publishing an exposé in the vein of Progressive muckrakers; unfortunately, Hearst refused to run the piece, forcing Lewis to seek an alternate audience for his work. Lewis was motivated to find one. He held a personal grudge against Brown, who had removed his father-in-law, Colonel Claudius Huston, from the chairmanship of the Republican National Committee, and Lewis hoped that his investigation would provide recompense for that perceived slight. Lewis's report had the full backing of the independent airlines and contained lurid charges against Brown and the pioneer operators; it also largely represented a work of fiction. Nonetheless Lewis, supported by lobbyists for the independents, piqued Black's interest.[10]

In Black, Brown's opponents found an individual passionately opposed to concentrations of wealth and power in any form, making the senator well disposed to listen to the charges against the postmaster general. Black hailed from rural Alabama and came of age during the Southern Populist uprising. While never a Populist himself, Black was sympathetic to their attacks on railroad, merchant, and financial monopolies that dominated the contemporary South. After graduating from the University of Alabama, he made a name for himself as a lawyer, judge, and prosecutor in Birmingham before running for the US Senate in 1926. In that campaign Black embraced a strongly Jeffersonian vision and firmly established his support for the common man, speaking forcefully against monopoly, concentrations of power and wealth, and Washington cliques. Interestingly, Black also expressed support for government-funded infrastructure improvement, one of the few areas in which he backed expanded federal power. Black won the election handily and traveled to Washington prepared to make good on his campaign promises. Casting himself—somewhat disingenuously—as a poor country bumpkin, Black proceeded to make a name for himself by acting aggressively against utility monopolies. In that effort Black consistently decried the nation's economic organization, arguing in a representative 1930 speech, "We are rapidly becoming a Nation of a few business masters and many clerks and servants." By the early 1930s his colleagues and the press knew Black as the Senate's "grand inquisitor"; the *Washington Post* referred to him as the chamber's "Chief Ferret." Black's background, then, made him the perfect candidate to take up the independent airlines' crusade against Brown, a mantle the senator assumed with a vengeance.[11]

With the approval of Senate Majority Leader Joseph T. Robinson (D-AR), Black began his investigation in February of 1933. Black picked his fellow committee members—Warren R. Austin (R-VT), William H. King (D-UT), Pat McCarran (D-NV), and Wallace H. White (R-ME)—and by the end of the month secured a Senate resolution empowering his special committee to "investigate and make a full, complete, and detailed inquiry into all existing contracts entered into by the Postmaster General for the carriage of air mail." Under that broad mandate the resolution identified four more specific goals: first, to determine why the Post Office granted airmail contracts to the carriers it did; second, to investigate under what auspices those contracts were granted; third, to examine the financial status of the companies receiving contracts; and fourth, to ascertain the status of federal cash subsidies paid out to airmail carriers. That information, Black believed, would concretely demonstrate the corrupt, collusive, monopolistic, and illegal activities undertaken by Brown, the Post Office, and the leading airlines.[12]

Black's desire to expose Post Office malfeasance represented a natural outgrowth of his larger political philosophy, but the senator also saw historical precedent for his actions. In an effort to forestall critics alleging that Black's actions merely represented partisan reprisals against the preceding administration, Black argued that his actions represented only the most recent in a long history of inquiries into Post Office impropriety. The senator suggested that in at least four previous instances—during the Lincoln, Garfield, Theodore Roosevelt, and Coolidge administrations—the Post Office had granted private mail contracts either without competitive bidding or under strictures that undermined the spirit of competition. In each case, Black argued, "the machinations, the methods, the means used have been identical." Tellingly, for him, in each case opponents charged investigators with acting out of a partisan desire to undermine the political opposition rather than any genuine effort to oppose corruption. Those charges, Black contended, had been groundless, as they were in the current case. In all four historical examples, Black highlighted the prompt cancellation of the fraudulent contracts and suggested that a failure to do so in the current case would be "un-American." This fiery rhetoric would pervade Black's investigation as the senator consistently emphasized his democratizing efforts to rid the nation of concentrated wealth and power.[13]

Black's special committee began its activities in the spring of 1933, though it did not formally convene until September 28. Black chose fellow Alabamian A. G. Patterson to be his chief investigator. Patterson, a member of the Interstate Commerce Commission, immediately created an investigations staff and proceeded into the field to interview airline executives and collect financial statements from airlines and their holding companies. Under Black's guidance, Patterson also created a questionnaire that the investigative team sent to all significant airlines operating in the United States. That questionnaire encompassed a detailed list of inquiries, requesting information on airmail routes served, any extensions or consolidations thereto, financial statements, the capital structure of the company, lists of officers and directors, names and addresses of all stockholders, information regarding whether directors and/or stockholders owned stock in other aviation companies, specifics regarding the amount of mail carried, rates and any changes thereto, and any connections between employees, directors, or stockholders and the government.[14]

With Fulton Lewis Jr's report grounding his understanding of the current airmail contract system, Black believed that Patterson's inquiries would expose several fraudulent practices in Hoover administration policies. First, the senator believed that Brown's actions at the "spoils conferences" had awarded airmail contracts without competitive bidding, violating the terms of the Watres Act. In doing so, moreover, Black hoped to demonstrate that Brown and the major airlines had illegally shut small, independent operators out of the proceedings and prohibited them from bidding on routes. Second, Black held that the three large aviation holding corporations possessed interconnecting directorates with connections to government officials. Black believed that these holding corporations represented illegal monopolies that encouraged collusion to the detriment of fair competition. Finally, the senator hoped to demonstrate that the postmaster himself owned stock in one or more aviation companies and thus benefited illegally from his ability to grant airmail contracts.[15]

As Black, Patterson, and the investigations staff began their inquiries, it became increasingly clear that a number of their assumptions regarding Brown's polices didn't bear scrutiny. Guided by Lewis's allegations, investigators looked to confirm what they already knew, at times displaying surprising myopia regarding the actual details of the airline industry and the airmail contract-letting process. Patterson himself clearly exhibited this shortsightedness during an interview with Hainer Hinshaw in June. Hinshaw—at the time employed by United—had been a leading airline executive since the mid-1920s and had attended Brown's conferences. According to the aviation executive, Patterson appeared uninformed about myriad legal issues relating to airmail contracts. Shockingly, Hinshaw related that he had to educate Patterson about basic facts relating to the investigation, including "the wording . . . of the Watres Act" and "the numerous mass meetings held by the then Postmaster General." Patterson also appeared to lack knowledge regarding the qualifications airlines had to meet in order to bid on airmail contracts. During the same interview, Hinshaw wrote that he had to remind Patterson that the Watres Act required prospective bidders to meet minimum qualifications, including "requirements in the matter of speed, equipment, and seats to be furnished." Emphasizing that in 1930 there were only five companies that did so, the United executive stressed that the airlines protesting the contemporary airmail structure almost universally failed to meet that bar. Further undercutting the independent airlines' objections, Hinshaw reminded Patterson that a majority of those corporations "were not in existence at the time of the advertisements; . . . their protests came long after the awards were made."[16]

Hinshaw also engaged in a vigorous defense of Post Office policies, in the process challenging Patterson's interpretation of events. He told Patterson that Brown's efforts to extend airmail routes—rather than subject the new mileage to competitive bidding—reflected a desire to stabilize the air commerce industry while simultaneously benefiting the bottom line. Echoing Brown's rhetoric almost verbatim, Hinshaw related that the postmaster general approved route extensions "on the theory that a few able companies would perform more satisfactorily than many smaller ones." Such a system would promote the growth of stable and profitable airlines while allowing the government to reduce airmail payments. Additionally, Hinshaw countered claims that the postmaster general had approved unnecessary airmail route extensions in order to generate additional revenue for select airlines. The United executive stated that the pressure to extend many of these routes in fact "came from the affected localities," which desired airmail service, and not from the postmaster general himself. Hinshaw clearly had reason to defend Brown's policies—after all, United profited handsomely from the airmail contracts it received at the 1930 conferences—but his meeting with Patterson nonetheless demonstrated the gulf between his and the investigator's interpretations of recent history.[17]

Although Black, Patterson, and the investigations staff became more familiar with the intricacies of the Watres Act and the mechanics of the Post Office bidding process as they continued gathering information through the summer and fall of 1933, they remained convinced that Brown and the large airlines had engaged in illegal behavior. In order to uncover evidence of collusion and corruption, Black and his staff undertook hundreds of interviews, subpoenaed mountains of corporate financial records, and engaged in exhaustive investigations of airline executives' and federal officials' personal finances. By the end of the year Black believed that he had sufficient evidence to initiate public hearings, during which he hoped to focus national attention on the scandalous practices of the Hoover administration.

In fact, the growing storm surrounding airmail contracts had already drawn significant attention from major media outlets. As early as February 1933, in reference to Brown's last-minute route extensions, *Time* reported that the postmaster general "drew the wrath of the House Post Office Committee and some operators by juggling airmail routes." Brown had done so "in precisely the manner which the law provides," the article admitted, but had nonetheless engaged in actions "his critics will call 'arbitrary.'" Looking forward, *Time* informed readers that Democrats had promised to enact a "new deal" for airline subsidies and were planning to break up the system forged under Brown's leadership. The *New York Times* also provided consistent coverage of the emerging scandal, reporting on February 16 that the Senate Post Office Committee had approved Black's special committee and throughout the month offering numerous articles on Brown's route extensions, Senate and House efforts to block Brown's actions and amend the Watres Act, and prognostications regarding the incoming administration's treatment of airmail subsidies. This coverage died down during the summer and fall as the committee proceeded with its investigation but returned in much greater volume in the winter as Black prepared to initiate public hearings.[18]

As those hearings began, Black embraced increasingly strident rhetoric as he took his message directly to the American people. Speaking to a national audience over the Columbia Broadcasting Service Network in February, Black castigated Brown and pilloried the aeronautics industry. Black told his audience that Brown's actions resulted in aviation being "greedily grabbed away from the control of those interested in aviation progress" and placed in the hands of a corporate and political elite primarily interested in lining their own pockets. As a result of aviation firms' consolidation into holding corporations and the mergers Brown helped push through, airlines were now "utilized by profiteers as a means of private gain through stock jobbing, speculation, and monopoly."[19]

Black's comments suggested that his committee was poised to expose what he later called "a network of intrigue, chicanery, manipulation, and fraud" pervading the airline industry. Beginning in January 1934 he attempted to do just that as the committee called forth a parade of witnesses. Described by one historian as a "comic opera," the hearings centered on testimony from investigators, airline representatives, and Post Office employees as Black attempted to draw out evidence of Brown's malfeasance.[20]

Black relied heavily on testimony from representatives of small airlines excluded from Brown's airmail map. These operators, still smarting from their inability to gain Post Office airmail contracts, were only too willing to detail the former postmaster general's supposedly illegal actions. Representative were statements from Thomas H. McKee, who until 1932 worked for the Wedell-Williams Air Service Corporation. Prompted by Black, McKee related details of his efforts in early 1930 to secure an airmail contract over a route from New Orleans to Fort Worth. The airline executive stated that he traveled to Washington and stayed for more than two months in a fruitless attempt to meet with Brown and secure Post Office subsidies. During that time, McKee testified, as his frustration grew, he did "a little scouting around" and discovered that a number of representative from large airlines were engaged in a "very mysterious meeting" at the Post Office Department—in fact, Brown's operators' conferences. Unable to gain access to the meetings through normal channels, McKee "crashed the gate" by claiming that he was an important representative from a large airmail contractor. Once inside, McKee described fourteen or fifteen airline representatives meeting in a proverbial "atmosphere of blue smoke." Discovering that William MacCracken was apparently in charge of the proceedings, McKee tried to get him to entertain Wedell-Williams's desire for an airmail route. MacCracken was, however, "very anxious to get rid of me," McKee related. After some further investigation, McKee concluded that Brown had tapped MacCracken to chair a meeting designed to split up the airmail map through collusion. Even more damning, the executive testified that at Brown's behest, "obviously, the independent passenger transport operators had been purposely excluded from this mysterious session."[21]

Other independent airline executives echoed and expanded upon the latter point. Erle P. Halliburton offered testimony that Post Office officials repeatedly rebuffed his efforts to secure an airmail contract and that Brown attempted to force his airline, Safeway, to merge with Transcontinental Air Transport (TAT). Theodore Taney, representing Pittsburgh Airways, Major William B. Robertson of Robertson Aircraft Corporation, and others informed the committee that Brown had conducted a series of secret meetings, colluded with a select group of airlines to grant airmail contracts without bidding, forced mergers upon unwilling operators, and bankrupted carriers unwilling to abide by his decisions.[22]

The special committee also subpoenaed representatives from the large airlines that took part in the operators' conferences, as Black hoped to expose concrete evidence of illegal dealings. Executives including Hainer Hinshaw and Paul Henderson—representatives of United Airlines and TAT, respectively—readily admitted that the postmaster worked with the airlines present at the conferences to create an airway map that conformed to his vision for the industry. They also confirmed that Brown excluded small, independent airlines from the proceedings and granted long route extensions without any bidding whatsoever. These actions, however, were perfectly legal under the dictates of the Watres Act. Nonetheless, Black's questioning stressed the unsavory aspects of Brown's actions, highlighting the postmaster general's apparent effort to subvert the free market and grant contracts to a chosen circle of associates.[23]

Perhaps unsurprisingly, Fulton Lewis Jr. emerged as a key figure during the hearings. Lewis submitted a statement to the committee that summarized his earlier findings and subsequently offered lengthy testimony expanding on his evidence against Brown and the airlines. Lewis told the committee that as a result of his investigation, "three salient factors appear evident without question." First, he argued, from the outset Brown had worked to grant airmail contracts through (collusive) negotiation with airline executives in an intentional effort to avoid competitive bidding. Second, the reporter emphasized, "Congress definitely and overtly refused to give [Brown] this authority, on the grounds that it was contrary to American traditions and principles of government," instead mandating that contracts be let through competitive bidding. Finally, Lewis argued that Brown had improperly applied the Watres bill's provisions for route extension in an effort to circumvent the bidding process.[24] These factors led Lewis to conclude that Brown had deliberately set out to subvert the law. After failing to get the bill passed with a provision to allow the postmaster general to award routes without bidding, he had unlawfully used the Watres bill's provisions to sidestep the issue, in express opposition to congressional wishes.

Lewis also presented evidence he believed demonstrated collusion between airline executives and federal officials. Drawing on his knowledge of the personal relationships between those groups, he testified that "Hainer Hinshaw refers to Postmaster General Brown as 'cousin Walter' and to President Hoover as 'cousin Herbert.'" While that information was far from damning in and of itself, Lewis then informed the committee that Hinshaw's brother Davis "played an active and prominent role in Mr. Hoover's 1928 campaign" and "Hainer also assisted." Lewis was forced to admit, however, that he could not find direct evidence that these relationships materially influenced Brown's granting of airmail routes. Flimsy though these charges may have been, Lewis's implications bolstered committee members' concerns about collusive practices in the industry. Lewis's prominent place in the media, moreover, assured him a ready platform from which to publicize his views, which served to further the case against the Hoover administration.[25]

Building on Lewis's charges, Black also used the hearings to focus attention on the large aviation holding corporations in an effort to expose monopolistic and collusive activities. Although he found little evidence of fraud or other illegal behavior, Black did uncover legal—but perhaps ill-advised—stock machinations that netted prominent airline executives large profits. Drawing the most attention were revelations surrounding the most famous man in the country: Charles Lindbergh. Black's investigation revealed that when Lindbergh agreed to become a "technical advisor" to TAT, he received generous stock options—eventually valued at more than $250,000. Not surprisingly, Lindbergh's association with TAT dramatically increased the stock's value, and the airline's president, Clement Keys, facilitated the quick sale of the stock, resulting in a substantial profit for the pilot. Black highlighted this profit taking while alleging that Keys instructed Lindbergh to keep the stock deal quiet—damning evidence in the senator's view.[26]

While the details of Lindbergh's stock dealings created a stir, they paled in comparison to those of Frederick Rentschler, founder of the Pratt & Whitney aircraft engine manufacturer and an executive in the United Aircraft and Transport Corporation (UA&T), at that time the nation's largest aviation holding corporation. Under Black's questioning, Rentschler revealed that when he formed Pratt &Whitney in 1925, he purchased 1,375 shares of the new company at $0.20 a share. After selling 110 of those shares at cost in 1927, Rentschler was left with 1,265 shares and a net investment of $253. The following year, Pratt & Whitney split the stock 79–1, raising Rentschler's total to 101,200 shares. Shortly thereafter, UA&T brought Pratt & Whitney under its corporate umbrella; Rentschler transferred his Pratt & Whitney stock to UA&T in exchange for 219,604 shares of the holding corporation. By May 1, 1929, UA&T stock was valued at $262 a share on the New York Stock exchange, making Rentschler's initial $253 investment worth more than $35.5 million. Even in early 1934, well after the stock market crash, Rentschler's shares were worth more than $7 million. Rentschler, however, no longer owned all of them, having sold 153,604 for a profit of more than $9.5 million, leaving the executive, as of December 1933, with 60,000 shares valued at $2.1 million, in addition to his profits. While Rentschler's and Lindbergh's profit taking was technically legal, it certainly appeared unseemly, particularly in light of the prevailing economic downturn.[27]

Although Black's efforts to implicate airline executives in illegal stock dealings largely came to naught, he hoped to strike paydirt in the financial records of his nemesis, Walter Brown. Patterson and his staff had spent significant time and effort attempting to link Brown to the airlines to which he granted Post Office contracts. Though the investigators failed to secure concrete evidence that Brown profited personally from his actions as postmaster general, Black was able to bring forward several witnesses who claimed to implicate Walter Brown in illegal stock dealings. Brown was able to counter the allegations with relative ease, but not before he found his reputation further discredited. Casting his net ever more widely, Black also attempted to prove that Brown and other Post Office officials offered select airlines preferential treatment in light of their political connections. These allegations, too, failed to hold up to scrutiny, but by this time the facts were largely immaterial, as Black had successfully painted Brown's Post Office as a corrupt department in bed with corporate interests.[28]

As the hearings progressed, they enjoyed a dramatic increase in media coverage from a press eager to expose governmental malfeasance. *Time* reported Black's investigation had "swept away the last remaining glory of the 1920s [the rise of American aviation] and consigned it to the nation's junk heap of lost illusions." *The Nation* focused on the Senate committee's exposure of supposed Republican wrongdoing, writing that the investigation confirmed the nation's worst fears about collusion in the Hoover administration, while decrying "all the waste, favoritism, and graft" exposed during the hearings. Two weeks later the magazine embraced even more strident rhetoric. Under a headline reading "So They Found the Body," Paul Anderson highlighted increasing public condemnation of "the favoritism, graft, and corruption of the Hoover Administration." Anderson continued by confidently stating, "Before the Congressional investigations are concluded the name of the Harding Administration will be a symbol of purity to the American people," quite the claim in the wake of the Teapot Dome scandal.[29]

The *New York Times* exhibited more sympathy for Hoover and Brown but remained focused on the ongoing drama in a steady stream of articles during the winter and early spring of 1934. In early January the paper referenced "sensational" revelations supposedly to come from Black's focus on mail contracts. In the following weeks the paper reported on numerous individuals' testimony, published transcripts of letters and other documents unearthed by Black's investigation, and highlighted the drama of Brown's testimony before the committee. The *Times* did, at times, appear less inclined to pillory Brown than did many other publications; a January 21 article reported that the Watres Act accomplished "a great deal for aviation." Nonetheless, the *Times*' coverage continued to follow the unfolding events in Washington, particularly during and after Roosevelt's decision to cancel airmail contracts in early February.[30]

While the growing public clamor undoubtedly forced Roosevelt's hand with regard to the ongoing airmail operations, the president was also reacting to more direct influences. In late January, Black met with the president and urged him to cancel all domestic airmail contracts. Early the following month Post Office Department solicitor Karl Crowley released a report—based on documents uncovered during the Senate investigation—strongly recommending that the Post Office do the same. Following a meeting between Crowley and Postmaster General James Farley on February 7, Farley, Crowley, First Assistant Postmaster General William Howes, and Second Assistant Postmaster General Harllee Branch met with the president to determine a plan of action. Eager to avoid a disruption in service and worried that any delay in canceling the existing contracts would reflect poorly on the administration in light of the recent revelations, the men turned to the Army Air Corps as a possible solution. Hoping that the AAC could step into the breach and carry the mail until the Post Office could bid out new contracts, Harllee Branch contacted Major General Benjamin Foulois, chief of the Air Corps, to ascertain whether the AAC could do so. Branch met with Foulois on February 9, 1934; faced with the question of the Air Corps' ability to fly the mail, Foulois responded, "If you want us to carry the mail, we'll do it." The general indicated that the AAC would need "a week or ten days" to prepare for the new assignment and returned to his office to draw up plans to that effect should the president and postmaster general decide to task the Air Corps with flying the mail.[31]

Unbeknownst to Foulois, his discussion with Branch was not theoretical in the least. Acting on Foulois's assurances, that very afternoon Roosevelt signed Executive Order 6591, canceling all domestic airmail contracts effective at midnight on February 19. Farley promptly announced Roosevelt's decision at an afternoon press conference, and word of the administration's dramatic action spread quickly—so quickly, in fact, that news of the Air Corps' new mission actually preceded Foulois back to his office in the War Department. Upon arriving, Foulois found himself confronted by army chief of staff General Douglas MacArthur, who angrily related that he had just heard from a journalist that the Air Corps was now in the airmail business. Surprised by the turn of events, Foulois assured MacArthur that he had not known that he was committing the AAC to the new task, but nonetheless promised his superior that the AAC was up to the challenge. MacArthur, though mollified by the Air Corps chief's explanation, left Foulois with a warning. "You're on your own now," the chief of staff stated, "It's your ball game."[32]

Foulois then turned to the task of preparing the Air Corps for its unexpected new challenge. In telling Branch that the AAC was capable of assuming responsibility for US airmail, Foulois had at least in part acted in the hope that flying the mail would create new opportunities for the Air Corps. Although Foulois was aware that the AAC's planes and pilots were "in sad shape" in early 1934, he hoped that flying airmail routes would allow army pilots to get badly needed flight time and increase funding for gasoline, equipment, and spare parts. Moreover, Foulois hoped that flying the mail would garner national attention and lead to increased appropriations moving forward. Prophetically, he believed that even should the AAC struggle, any trials the Air Corps experienced would only highlight the service's contemporary plight and confirm the need for new funds and equipment.[33]

Foulois was correct to question the AAC's capabilities; in point of fact the service was woefully unprepared to assume control of the nation's airmail routes. Since 1926 commercial operators had been working diligently to master the many challenges associated with flying the mail night and day, in all seasons, in all weather, in diverse terrain all around the country. Building on the progress made by the Post Office between 1918 and 1926, airlines improved their weather forecasting abilities with the help of the Commerce Department, mapped out their routes in intimate detail, and continuously improved maintenance and pilot training. Perhaps even more importantly, the airlines embraced new technologies. Flying at night and in all types of weather, airlines moved to install instruments such as altimeters, turn and bank indicators, and, eventually, radios in their planes to ease the task their pilots faced. In the early 1930s airlines also took advantage of new radio guidance systems pioneered by the Commerce Department that aided navigation at night and in bad weather. Moreover, following Walter Brown's takeover of the Post Office Department and the passage of the 1930 amendment to the Contract Airmail Act, federal policy facilitated airlines' embrace of larger, faster, more technologically advanced aircraft. By 1934 the first Boeing 247s were entering service, and the Douglas DC-2 was about to make its debut. By the late winter of 1934 the airlines carrying the US mail had, through hard work and continuous development, created a relatively safe, reliable, and effective air transport network.

The Air Corps, in contrast, had little experience with the types of flying required to carry the mail. AAC pilots rarely flew in adverse conditions. Funding shortages restricted training time, and because of worries about accidents, military aviators generally restricted their time aloft to periods of good weather during daylight hours. Virtually all contemporary AAC aircraft were open-cockpit types—unlike their civilian counterparts—and they rarely carried radios, navigation or landing lights, or instruments for blind flying. Air Corps pilots lived lives of relative leisure; the workday began around 7:30 and ended before 4:00, and pilots had weekends off. Though the schedule was much more rigorous during maneuvers, as a result of funding shortages those activities occurred rarely; the last major exercise had taken place in 1931. These conditions augured badly for an Air Corps now committed to flying regularly scheduled airmail routes with inferior equipment during the depths of winter in conditions with which most of its pilots were unfamiliar.[34]

Foulois and his subordinates worked to redress these shortcomings in the ten days between Farley's announcement and the start of the AAC's airmail flights. Following conferences with Harllee Branch and Eugene Vidal, the director of the Bureau of Air Commerce, a consensus emerged that the Air Corps would give priority to airmail routes linking the twelve cities containing Federal Reserve banks. The AAC did not have the men or equipment to fly all of the remaining routes; many would have to be discontinued. Foulois also ordered that instruments for blind flying and radios be installed in all aircraft assigned to mail-related duties. Unfortunately, the Air Corps did not possess sufficient radios and flight instruments to equip all of the relevant planes, and even when the instruments were available, maintenance workers unfamiliar with the gauges sometimes installed them incorrectly. Air Corps pilots, moreover, often lacked the training to use these aids and were woefully unprepared for flying at night and in bad weather. Foulois also faced the challenge of moving men and equipment from their bases to airports along the airmail routes, acquiring hanger space and living quarters and arranging for refueling and maintenance operations. With funds in short supply, many solutions were haphazard, at best. Foulois recalled that officers had "to sleep in the hangers because they couldn't get quarters"; money was so tight that AAC personnel could not get funds for basic necessities. Those challenges notwithstanding, by February 19, 1934, the Air Corps deployed 200 officers, 324 enlisted men, and 122 planes to fly twelve airmail routes encompassing seventy individual stops over a total of 13,284 airway miles.[35]

Unfortunately, the Air Corps operation experienced disaster even before its airmail flights began. On February 16, even as General Foulois issued strict orders that his pilots take no unnecessary risks when flying the mail, three army pilots perished in training flights. Two, Lieutenants J. D. Grenier and E. D. White, crashed in a snowstorm. The third, Lieutenant J. Y. Eastham, crashed while flying at night in foggy conditions. These deaths established a trend that, sadly, was to continue for the duration of the Air Corps' airmail responsibilities.[36]

AAC pilots' lack of adequate training and use of inferior equipment made a bad situation even worse. Joseph Atkinson, one of the pilots responsible for the Salt Lake City to Portland, Oregon, route, highlighted what a hectic time it was for the Air Corps. Calling the AAC's lack of funds for flight training and new aircraft "quite evident" in the period leading up to the airmail fiasco, Atkinson lamented the poor quality of the aircraft pressed into service to fly the mail. His superiors shared his concern. Colonel Henry "Hap" Arnold, the officer in charge of airmail operations in the western third of the country, believed the army aircraft "were entirely unsuited" to airmail responsibilities, an opinion echoed by Lieutenant Elwood "Pete" Quesada, one of the most experienced pilots in the Air Corps.[37] Tragically, Arnold's and Quesada's predictions were more than borne out in the disastrous events to come.

As Foulois and the army prepared to begin their airmail flights, Postmaster General James Farley, former head of the Democratic National Committee and a man with close personal ties to Roosevelt, explained his and the president's rationale for canceling the contracts in an open letter to Senator Black, in the process allying the administration with Black's investigation. Farley's letter found ready reception with the media and, combined with the unfolding disaster that was the army's airmail operation, brought yet a new level of interest in Black's investigation. Unsurprisingly, Farley's analysis echoed the senator's almost exactly. He began by stating that he opposed using Post Office airmail payments "for the benefit of a few favored corporations," particularly when those corporations used the funds as a basis for "wild stock promotions resulting in profits of tens of millions of dollars to promoters who invested little or no capital." Like Black, Farley argued against letting airmail contracts "by convenience and agreement" and emphasized the need for open and honest competitive bidding. The postmaster general also found fault with his predecessors' efforts to rationalize the airmail map during the 1930 operators' conferences. Farley contended that Brown illegally used route extensions to bolster the airmail revenues of major carriers; he was "convinced," moreover, Brown and his chosen airlines "held meetings for the purpose of dividing territory and contracts among themselves." Farley pointed to the conferences in May and June of 1930 as proof of this collusive behavior, arguing that "these meetings resulted in . . . the practical elimination of competitive bidding."[38]

With clear support from the Post Office and the Roosevelt administration, Black continued his investigation through the end of the month and into March and April. The parade of witnesses largely confirmed what Black had already concluded, with the notable exception of Walter Brown himself. Brown testified over the course of four days in late February, just as army pilots began flying the mail. During the first three days of his appearance, Brown found himself parrying questions from Black, the senator intent on forcing Brown to incriminate himself, to little effect. On the fourth day, however, Brown went on the offensive, beginning with an "emphatic denial" that he had acted improperly during the 1930s operators' conferences. In spite of Black's wishes, Brown defended himself ably, and, according to the *New York Times*, "turned the course of his testimony." Brown specifically addressed James Farley's letter, countering the new postmaster's charges by referring back to the wording of the Watres Act, under which, he argued, his actions were perfectly legal. Brown also offered a comprehensive articulation of his rationale in crafting the Watres bill and his efforts to promote commercial flying under the dictates of that legislation. While Black and his allies remained unconvinced, Brown's testimony drew praise from airline executives and sympathy from media outlets, including the *Times*.[39]

Although Brown's testimony heartened supporters of the Hoover administration and the former postmaster general, it did little to change the course of Black's investigation. By the middle of April, as the public hearings wound down, Black prepared to make public his findings. As the committee prepared its report, Black summarized those findings in a speech delivered to Congress on April 25 and 26, 1934, in the process offering the clearest articulation of his conclusions. Beginning with the assertion that Brown and the large airlines had engaged in a "deliberate effort" to mislead the public about the nature of federal airmail policy, Black proceeded to explain his interpretation of the former postmaster general's actions. According to the senator, from the outset Walter Brown had engaged in a "scheme" to let Post Office airmail contracts without competitive bidding. Black outlined how in 1929 the postmaster had authored a bill that would have allowed him to award contracts without bidding and taken it to Clyde Kelly in the hopes that Kelly would introduce the bill to Congress. According to Black, Kelly rejected the bill because "it made the Postmaster General practically a czar." After Kelly's rejection, Brown took his bill to Lawrence Watres, who eventually introduced it to a Congress that, much to Brown's frustration, eventually agreed on a compromise version of the Watres bill that provided for competitive bidding.[40]

Black also focused on airlines' culpability in the legislative and contract granting processes. The senator related that after Watres introduced the airmail bill, "the air-mail operators got busy," and he proceeded to outline what he felt was a concerted effort by big businesses to push the bill though Congress in the hopes of securing financial benefit. Black referenced a record "filled with telegrams and letters" from and to airline executives urging the employment of lobbyists and a redoubling of activities in connection with the proposed legislation. Airline executives were not satisfied that their "regular" lobbyists in Washington could win passage of a bill reflecting airline interests, the senator told his audience. They went to the lengths of hiring new, more powerful lobbyists; Black cited lobbying efforts that were "not the work of no $50 a month lobbyist" but instead emerged from powerful—though nameless—figures bent on corrupting the legislative process and winning concessions for their clients that would result in tremendous profits.[41]

Black then turned his attention to Brown's conferences in May and June 1930, which for him exemplified the core of the postmaster general's collusive agenda. Black argued that while the postmaster purportedly called the airlines to the capital for a series of informational meetings to educate them about the specifics of the new airmail legislation, in fact Brown's goal was to subvert the bidding process. Black claimed that, publicly, Brown strove to convince the airlines that "he had played fair in the passage of the Watres Act"; his real aim, however, was to create an environment in which the airlines would disagree about how to split up the airway map, allowing Brown to do away with competitive bidding entirely and remake the airway map according to his own wishes. For Black, this was the preeminent example of Brown's deceitfulness. The postmaster "called [the airlines] by deception," Black related in fiery tones, with the end goal of illegally granting the most lucrative contracts to his chosen airlines, to "give more to him who had something and take away from him who had not."[42]

In the remainder of his address the senator continued to emphasize that the whole process, from Brown's push for a new airmail bill to the granting of contracts in the summer of 1930, represented a fraudulent, collusive effort to undermine open and fair competition and benefit large businesses with ties to the government. Black presented evidence from airlines' records and from the Post Office documenting Brown's actions at the conferences. He argued that the airlines colluded with one another to split up routes without resort to bidding and that large airlines received preferential treatment from the Post Office in light of their political connections. The senator claimed that the postmaster general had overstepped his authority by granting long route extensions, used his control over airmail contracts to force consolidations in the airline industry, and schemed to confer routes without competitive bidding. Black also highlighted rulings from Comptroller General McCarl prohibiting Brown from granting route extensions and forcing Brown to put several routes up for bid. The postmaster did so, according to Black, but under restrictions that assured that Brown's chosen companies would receive contracts, again highlighting Brown's concerted effort to undermine fair competition.[43]

Black's two-day address displayed all of the passion and zeal he brought to the investigation as he highlighted the supposed laundry list of Walter

Brown's crimes; his revelations, however, were not revelations at all for anyone familiar with the relevant events. Brown never disputed that he had authored new airmail legislation with the initial goal of avoiding competitive bidding, bidding that in his mind would introduce harmful competition to the airline industry and undermine pioneer carriers' efforts to invest in new technology with the goal of inaugurating faster, safer, more reliable passenger service. Brown also readily admitted that he called the operators' conferences with the express desire of splitting up the airmail map through voluntary cooperation between the airlines and the Post Office, without recourse to destructive competitive bidding. He did so, moreover, with the consent, and indeed the support, of the major airlines. Both sides acknowledged the need for focused federal support to promote the growth of passenger service, and both sides worked toward that end. These actions, while anathema to Black's populist antimonopoly stance, represented a perfectly rational modus operandi for Brown—collusion, yes, but collusion for the greater good of the industry. As such, the senator and the postmaster did not disagree materially about the events themselves, only their implications.

Black's testimony also demonstrated a lack of appreciation for the intricacies of the airline industry even as the senator appeared to engage in faulty reasoning. As he condemned the parties involved in pushing to pass the Watres bill, Black implied that the airlines were simultaneously perpetrators and victims in the legislative process. The senator pilloried airlines for their efforts to lobby for the Watres bill, only to then suggest that Brown used that very bill to avoid competitive bidding at the airlines' expense. Much of this apparent inconsistency resulted from Black's failure to distinguish between the larger, more established airlines lobbying for the Watres bill and attending the conferences and small independent operators cut out of Brown's vision. Brown's actions did benefit some airlines at the expense of others, but those cut out of the airmail map—and those arguing most stridently for the investigation—were for the most part unprepared to undertake regularly scheduled mail service, and certainly not able to carry passengers. Perhaps Black simplified his message for rhetorical effect in this instance, as he was no doubt aware of the distinction between the large airlines and the independent operators who had lobbied for his investigation. Nonetheless, his focus on attacking monopoly and collusion, in this case at least, appeared to ignore important contextual factors familiar to anyone with knowledge of the commercial aviation industry.[44]

Inconsistencies in Black's rhetoric notwithstanding, his investigation did lead to noteworthy—though by and large temporary—changes for commercial aviation. The Senate special committee largely discredited Walter Brown's actions as postmaster general and for a time cast a shadow over the entire Hoover administration. The investigation led Roosevelt to cancel existing airmail contracts and forced a reorganization of the industry. That process began shortly after the army began flying the mail. On March 7 Roosevelt contacted Black, along with Senator Kenneth McKellar (D-TN) and Representative James Mead (D-NY)—the chairs of the Senate and House Post Office Committees, respectively—in the hope that airmail contracts could be returned to commercial carriers "as soon as possible." In support of that end, the president embraced a two-headed approach. First, he pushed Congress to pass temporary legislation authorizing the Post Office to accept private bids on short-term, three-month airmail contracts as soon as possible. This temporary legislation would return the mail to airlines and end the army debacle while Black, McKellar, and Mead could embrace the second part of FDR's plan: the creation of new, permanent airmail legislation.[45]

Roosevelt saw the first aspect of his plan enacted in less than three weeks. On March 28 James Farley announced that the Post Office would accept bids on temporary airmail contracts by the middle April. Prohibited from bidding were any individuals present at the 1930 operators' conferences or the airlines that employed them. Those dictates were, however, largely semantic, as the large airlines that dominated Post Office routes under Brown's leadership submitted bids under—slightly—different names. American and Northwest swapped the "Airways" in their titles for "Airlines," and Eastern Air Transport became Eastern Air Lines; other major carriers followed a similar script. On April 20 Farley announced the winners of the new temporary bids. Perhaps not surprisingly, the Post Office overwhelmingly awarded contracts to the same carriers that had possessed them in February, in most cases for the same routes. The "pioneer" operators remained the airlines with the skill, experience, and infrastructure to fly the mail; independent lines were simply unable to compete, largely discrediting their protests against the former regime's supposed favoritism. Private airlines returned to carrying the mail on May 8.

As the Black committee wrapped up its hearings and Roosevelt and Farley frantically worked to return the mail to private carriers, Senators

Black and McKellar began to craft new, permanent airmail legislation. Acting in large part on instructions from the president, they quickly drafted the new law and introduced it to Congress in the second week of March. What was to become the Airmail Act of 1934, S. 3070, or the Black-McKellar Act, broke little new ground, considering the uproar embroiling commercial aviation at the time. The bill made permanent the Post Office's temporary three-month contracts, established a three-year limit on all airmail contracts moving forward, mandated that those contracts be let only through competitive bidding, established minimum speed, load capacity, and safety requirements for bidders, and limited route extensions to no more than one hundred miles. Like the temporary legislation, the Black-McKellar bill prohibited awarding contracts to executives or corporations present at the 1930 conferences as well as any company connected to subsidiaries, affiliates, or holding companies in the industry—in effect, forcing the breakup of the large aviation holding corporations. Finally, the new law granted to the Interstate Commerce Commission (ICC) control over airmail rates, removing that responsibility from the postmaster general. On June 12, 1934, Roosevelt signed the new bill into law, bringing the most tumultuous period in American commercial aviation history to a close.[46]

On the surface, the dramatic events of 1933 and 1934 suggested a sharp break in federal aviation policy. Democratic activism, Hugo's Black's strident rhetoric, the Senate investigation and hearings, and new legislation did much to discredit Herbert Hoover and Walter Brown's corporatist vision for US airline development, at least in the eyes of the American public. Behind the scenes, however, these events did little to change the foundations of federal policy; in many ways the uproar served to confirm the fundamental agreement policy makers shared regarding the proper governmental responsibilities toward commercial flying. Although that consensus would emerge most clearly four years later with the passage of the Civil Aeronautics Act of 1938, even in 1934 it was clear that Hugo Black and his supporters opposed the basic assumptions of Republican policy far less than their public words and actions might initially suggest.[47]

While Hugo Black was clearly no fan of Walter Brown and his actions as postmaster general, any suggestion that the senator therefore desired a wholesale reorganization of federal aviation policy ignores the substance of Black's words and deeds. Far from engaging in a narrowly destructive endeavor to uncover and stamp out concentrations of wealth and power, in the process dismantling the framework of Republican policy, Black acted in large part out of a desire to aid the development of US commercial flying. The senator maintained close connections to aviation independent of his relationship to the special committee. In his correspondence and public pronouncements, moreover, Black reaffirmed Hoover's and Brown's vision regarding aviation's place in America's future, while his actions preserved the core of the Republicans' policies. As a party interested in aeronautical development, Black's actions emerged from a desire to cleanse the aviation industry of corrupt elements that in his mind presented a barrier to future success. Viewed through this lens, the airmail scandal served as a key chapter in the ongoing debate regarding aviation's proper place in America's future, and Black, commonly depicted as aviation's biggest opponent, emerges as an important party interested in promoting aeronautical development.

Black's focus on promoting commercial aviation comes through clearly in his public statements. Speaking to a national radio audience in February 1934, he offered a powerful articulation of aviation's value to the nation. Echoing many of the points embraced by Hoover, Brown, MacCracken, New, and other aviation proponents, Black highlighted his "belief that aviation is destined to have a most important place in our National progress." Black believed that commercial flying would play an increasingly key role in commerce; he also emphasized aviation's military value. "Our people," he argued "realize that if war should ever be forced upon us, we could not today defend ourselves, without a modern, well equipped, efficiently manned, aviation system."[48]

As he embraced rhetoric similar to that of Hoover and his allies, Black also drew similar conclusions regarding the government's responsibility to support aeronautical progress. Citing aviation's value to both commerce and national defense, the senator told his audience that commercial flying's growing importance "imperatively demands that this Nation take whatever steps are necessary to foster, encourage, and maintain this great peacetime servant of progress; this indispensable war necessity." Black, like his Republican forbears, believed that those steps included airmail payments to protect airlines' solvency and encourage the expansion of commercial service. He also supported the Commerce Department's regulatory and promotional activities. With appropriate federal involvement, he suggested, aviation was "destined to become a great and integral part of the commerce of this nation."[49]

Black's antipathy to Walter Brown's actions, then, concerned the means of achieving that goal, not the goal itself. In order to secure aviation's ultimate success, Black argued that the industry needed to be cleansed of its corrupt, collusive, and monopolistic elements. His investigation, in this context, emerged from a desire to do just that, embodying a necessary step to assure aviation's commercial future. In a similar vein, Black told the nation that Roosevelt's order canceling existing airmail contracts would accelerate aviation's "orderly progress. . . . A reorganized industry, with honest stock capitalization; fair profits, contracts that are just; and controlled by operators instead of speculators is the way to succeed in aviation."[50]

Black's sponsorship of the Airmail Act of 1934 displayed a similar focus and offers perhaps the strongest evidence of his fundamental agreement with Republican policy. With FDR's guidance, Black—with Senator McKellar—crafted and oversaw the passage of legislation ensuring foundational continuity in the federal government's engagement with commercial flying. The Airmail Act of 1934 maintained federal responsibility for subsidizing airlines through airmail contracts, a core aspect of Hoover and Brown's program. The new legislation also maintained Brown's basic route structure; mandated minimum requirements for bidders, virtually guaranteeing that the same airlines that had dominated the airmail map before 1934 would continue to do so; and encouraged the continued expansion of commercial flying by providing for ongoing route extensions. While the new law did embrace change—including unfairly banishing executives present at the 1930 conferences from the industry, forcing the breakup of aviation holding companies, reducing airmail contracts from ten to three years, reducing the postmaster general's power to approve route extensions and consolidations, and transferring rate-fixing abilities to the Interstate Commerce Commission—for the most part those modifications represented changes of degree, not kind. Black's long-standing focus on opposing concentrations of power and wealth comes through in the details, but the most striking thing about the new legislation was how little it actually altered. Considering the uproar surrounding the Black committee hearings and the vitriolic rhetoric defining the national debate over airmail policy, the 1934 law's foundational coherence with preexisting policy highlights the basic agreement between policy makers in regard to aviation policy.

Tellingly, Black maintained an interest in aviation long after the end of his special investigation. The following year, Roosevelt again called on Black's support in crafting aviation legislation. Writing to the senator in June, the president requested that Black "run down and talk with me about" the next step in federal engagement with aeronautics and expressed his hope that Black would support an effort to craft an all-encompassing new law. The following year, James Farley contacted Black regarding the same issue. Noting the senator's ongoing interest in airmail legislation and Post Office policy, Farley hoped that Black would review correspondence between Farley and James Mead regarding a new law. The effort to secure the passage of that legislation did not reach fruition until 1938, but FDR's and Farley's desire to include Black in the legislative process is instructive.[51]

Black also maintained an active correspondence with numerous airline executives and industry figures. Paul Brattain, assistant general manager of Eastern Air Lines, was particularly close to Black; the two became acquainted during Black's investigation and stayed in touch thereafter. In 1935 Brattain wrote to Black to ask a favor. Noting Black's "active interest in aviation," Brattain hoped that the senator could use his influence to secure federal support for aviation-related infrastructure development in Black's home state. Specifically, Brattain asked Black to look into installing lighting and a new radio beacon in Montgomery. It remains unclear whether Black was able to secure funding for the new infrastructure, but Brattain was nonetheless thankful for Black's interest in the matter. The same year, Black's name surfaced as the leading candidate for the chairmanship of a stillborn Senate committee on commercial aviation; he also responded to numerous requests to address airmail-related issues and maintained an expanding library of aeronautical literature.[52]

Black was most active, however, in aviation-related labor issues. The senator played a crucial role in facilitating the passage of S. 2486, an amendment to the Railway Labor Act in 1935 that secured additional rights regarding hours and pay for commercial pilots. Black also maintained a close relationship with David L. Behncke, president of the Air Line Pilots Association (ALPA). Behncke wrote Black on a variety of topics, including pilots' pay and hours, legislation, hiring and firing practices, and the organization of the commercial industry. Illustrative of their close relationship is an ongoing correspondence between February and May 1935 concerning the allegedly improper firing of seven Northwest Airlines pilots. According to Behncke, Northwest had acquired a smaller carrier, Hanford Airlines, and promptly fired seven of the former carrier's pilots. The ALPA president wrote, "We strongly suspect that it was a tacit understanding between

Northwest and Hanford . . . that Northwest Airlines was not to reemploy any of the Hanford pilots because they were strong union men." Two days later Black wrote to F. W. Wittemore, Northwest's vice president in charge of operations, to request an explanation for the terminations. This began more than two months of ongoing correspondence, during which Black worked diligently to secure the reemployment of the seven pilots in question. Eventually his efforts were rewarded, and Northwest agreed to rehire the pilots.[53]

Black's ongoing interest in labor issues made the senator a consistent advocate for pilots and aircrews. He worked with Behncke and Senator McKellar to expose endemic airline underpayment of pilots and aircrews, sought greater pay equality between pilots flying foreign and domestic airmail routes, and took an active role in investigating the TWA crash that killed Senator Bronson Cutting (R-NM) in May 1935—a crash attributed to pilot fatigue brought on by overly generous limits on flight time. Black also wrote the National Labor Relations Board on behalf of the ALPA and contacted Eastern Air Lines directly in an effort to protect unionized pilots. The last effort included a focused effort to win over Francis Biddle, the board chairman, prompting a generous letter of thanks from Behncke and the ALPA leadership. A year earlier, Behncke sent Black an even more effusive note; in a June 1934 telegram Behncke thanked the senator for his "splendid and invaluable support" in efforts to improve pilots' wages and working conditions, assuring Black that his "persistent and untiring efforts [o]n behalf of workers will not soon be forgotten."[54]

Black also maintained an interest in aviation's military significance. In March 1936 Paul Thomas, general director of the Air Defense League—a nonpartisan organization devoted to raising awareness of America's pressing need to accelerate aeronautical development to bolster national defense—wrote Black regarding the need for an "adequate air defense program." Black responded positively, writing that he was "thoroughly in accord with the idea[s]" Thomas put forward. The same month, Black received a note from Judge Lee Smith—like Black a native of Alabama—expressing concern that US air defenses were inadequate when compared with those of other nations. Black responded to the query encouragingly, writing that he strongly favored "sufficient Congressional appropriation to see to it that we have an air force adequate for our protection."[55]

Combined with his legislative efforts, Black's ongoing engagement with US aeronautics provides powerful evidence of policy makers' fundamental agreement regarding the federal government's responsibilities toward commercial aviation. Black, often depicted as commercial aviation's most vitriolic opponent, on closer examination worked hard to maintain airmail subsidies, promote stable commercial growth, secure pilots' rights, and assure aeronautical development as an aid to national defense. In doing so he and his Democratic allies validated Hoover's vision for American aviation. While Black's opposition to monopoly and concentrated wealth and power grounded his efforts to discredit Brown and expose fraudulent practices within the industry, those efforts did not reflect a fundamental disagreement about the ends federal policy should serve. Black, in fact, echoed many of Hoover's ideas concerning the role aviation should play in America's future. These facts suggest a remarkable unanimity among American policy makers regarding aviation.

Similarly the airmail scandal, for all of its drama, largely served to confirm the status quo. Though the press focused on an emerging spectacle that some believed would eventually surpass the Teapot Dome debacle and the army's disastrous attempt to assume airmail duties, the Senate investigation and resulting legislation changed relatively little. True, by the summer of 1934 the aviation holding corporations were no more, and the postmaster general lost the power to fix airmail rates. These changes, however, paled in comparison to the basic continuity federal policy enjoyed. After the uproar for the most part the same airlines flew the same routes and benefited from a similar level of federal support. Democratic rhetoric notwithstanding, policy makers maintained their focus on using airmail subsides to encourage commercial development and continued to look to the Commerce Department to regulate the skies and promote American aeronautics. Ultimately the scandal, though it encompassed the most contentious period in US aviation history, served primarily to clarify the fundamental soundness of Hoover's vision for federal aviation policy.

Moving forward, Franklin Roosevelt increasingly came to dominate federal engagement with aeronautics as his New Deal programs took an ever more active role in promoting commercial progress. Roosevelt's actions, however, largely stayed true to the foundations set down by Hoover and confirmed by Black. Although Roosevelt's relationship with aviation was defined by the exigencies of the Depression, the president's policies provided powerful evidence of aviation's centrality to America's future.

5

Enacting a New Deal for Aviation

Franklin D. Roosevelt and US Aviation Policy

Franklin Roosevelt found himself in an unenviable position in the late winter of 1934. As Hugo Black's Senate Special Committee to Investigate Ocean Mail and Air Mail Contracts focused attention on the supposed fraud, graft, and corruption associated with Post Office airmail contracts, the president's decision to annul those contracts and order the army to fly the mail resulted in a media firestorm and increasing criticism over the deaths of army pilots. Pressed to take action, the president initially reduced the scope of army airmail operations. Quickly, however, he moved to return those operations to private contractors. Ultimately, Roosevelt's measures, largely made permanent in the 1934 Airmail Act, confirmed the foundational assumptions underlying US aviation policy. Those assumptions, however, were very much in the global minority by the mid-1930s. In fact, the majority of nations working to foster the growth of commercial air transportation were blazing a very different path, a path predicated on explicit governmental subsidization.

Outside the United States, the center of commercial aeronautical development resided in Europe. There, a very different set of political, economic, and geographic conditions held sway, resulting in airlines developing along very different lines than their American counterparts. Across the Atlantic, national borders lay much closer together—the distance from London to Paris is roughly comparable to the distance from Washington, DC, to New

York City. That fact, combined with significantly greater population density, provided a larger market and fewer technological hurdles for early airlines. Additionally, European governments expressed more willingness to provide explicit and ongoing technological and fiscal support, national rivalries provided an impetus for focused governmental engagement with commercial flying, and at least initially, the aftermath of the Great War provided a large surplus of aircraft to jump-start passenger service. As a result of these conditions, European airlines emerged much earlier and more successfully than did those in the Western Hemisphere. Although problems of weather, load carrying, speed, and reliability were universal, European carriers made the most of their advantages and, for at least a decade after the end of World War I, enjoyed marked superiority over American operations.

European airlines began to proliferate immediately after the Armistice. As R. E. G. Davies has demonstrated, at the end of the war most European nations possessed a surfeit of aircraft. "Either in a conscious attempt to put idle machines to useful work, or by turning to advantage the convenient supply of cheap vehicles," he writes, "the first airlines were born." Only two months after the cessation of hostilities, in January 1919, the German government authorized civil airline operations, and the first German commercial flight took to the sky the next month. The first French carrier followed in March, and the British, in August. By 1920, when the US Post Office had yet to attempt a transcontinental airmail flight, the majority of European countries had regularly scheduled national and international routes, including a popular and profitable cross-channel run. This growth continued and, in fact, accelerated into the early 1920s as European nations created a comprehensive network of air transport in Britain and on the Continent.[1]

This growth was, to a large extent, underwritten by direct government subsidies. In the cases of Germany and France, local, state, and national subsidization assisted the growth of airlines virtually from their inception. As Davies argues, both German and French leaders realized "that to promote a new transport medium money had to be spent on research, manufacture, development, and operation." Almost unilaterally, that money came from national coffers. Britain initially eschewed subsidization but ultimately became the exception that proved the rule in the European context. British airlines did not receive subsidies in the years immediately following the Armistice, and as a result they stagnated during a period of rapid growth for their French and German counterparts. The British government found itself forced to reexamine its policies when British carriers found themselves unable to compete on the lucrative London-to-Paris run. French leaders, recognizing the prestige of that important route, heavily subsidized cross-channel operations, and British carriers quickly found themselves marginalized. Eventually the two largest British competitors—Handley Page Transport and Instone Air Line—raised the white flag and suspended operations. In the wake of that embarrassment, in March 1921 the British government authorized appropriations to support air commerce. This reversal of policy signaled, in Davies's words, "the recognition by a government of the United Kingdom that in an environment of cut-throat competition a new industry must be helped if it is to have a reasonable chance of reaching maturity."[2] Moving forward, even Britain, which had traditionally embraced a more liberal economic philosophy than had her Continental counterparts, saw subsidy as the path to success for air transport.

Subsidies helped European carriers grow much more quickly than did American operators; those same policies, moreover, pushed European governments down a path that eventually led to nationalized airlines. Britain began this trend with the consolidation of a number of smaller carriers into the overseas line Imperial Airways in 1924. Germany established Deutsche Luft Hansa for national and international routes in 1926, the French created Air France in 1933, and the British moved to create British Airways in 1935.[3] Nationalized carriers received substantial governmental support for research, manufacturing, and infrastructure development. At the same time, European governments moved aggressively to subsidize operating costs. Whether this resulted from a desire to use air commerce as an aid to national defense or to bolster national pride, or because of European governments' desire to support an emerging industry and promote faster, more efficient commerce, the net result was, by the mid-1920s, the creation of a comprehensive air transport network across the Continent with links to many imperial destinations. Before Americans could fly from coast to coast on a single airline, European passengers could fly from Europe to India, Africa, and the Middle East in well-appointed planes owned and operated by national carriers.

Those circumstances highlight the sharp contrast between US and European air transport policies. It seems likely that large European carriers would not have survived without subsidies; certainly, without governmental backing they would not have prospered as they did. Their American counterparts, without access to government monies before 1925, were almost unilaterally unsuccessful in the postwar era. Not until the Kelly Act authorized the privatization of government airmail contracts did US operators begin to realize steady income. Before that time the only successful large-scale American air carrier was the US Post Office—ironically operating an airmail network owned and operated by the federal government. With the Kelly Act and subsequent legislation, US policy makers embraced the somewhat contrived policy of informal subsidization. Doing so allowed them to highlight the value of the free market while continuing to support de facto federally funded aeronautical growth. Particularly under the direction of Walter Brown, Post Office airmail payments functioned as an explicit inducement for airlines to embrace a federally approved path.

The debates engendered by the Black committee hearings and the challenges posed by the ongoing Great Depression threw those issues into sharp relief. On the one hand, Black and his allies embraced a passionate defense of competition and the free market, pillorying the Hoover administration for providing collusive support for a chosen set of air carriers. On the other, Franklin Roosevelt's maturing New Deal oversaw a radical expansion of federal responsibilities, particularly with regard to intervention in the economic sphere, encompassing both new regulatory authority and increased federal spending. Those pressures notwithstanding, new legislation largely confirmed the status quo. Roosevelt embraced policies that eschewed a truly free market and the lure of formal subsidies alike to stay the course for American air transport. Moving forward, his administration would play an increasingly central role in defining the future for US airlines, in the process charting a markedly different course than that followed by European governments and demonstrating a significant point of continuity with his Republican predecessor. Roosevelt's consistent advocacy for commercial development culminated in the passage of the Civil Aeronautics Act of 1938, legislation that codified the basic soundness of Hoover's vision and laid the foundation for American airline development for the next forty years.

Franklin Roosevelt's engagement with aeronautics began long before he assumed the presidency. Only twelve years after the Wright brothers' first flight, Roosevelt penned an article for *Flying* magazine highlighting aviation's military value. Writing for the September issue, Roosevelt decried the state of US military aviation, arguing that is was "absolutely essential that the aeronautics arms of the Army and Navy be increased, not by doubling, but a hundred fold." In the same article he emphasized the leading role Americans had played in aviation's development, praising the "pioneer work" and the "time and thought" Americans had devoted to perfecting practical uses for aircraft. For Roosevelt, that history assured America's readiness to "build up this branch of essential national defense."[4]

In the same year, Roosevelt published an additional piece that spoke directly to how the navy could—and should—use aerial platforms. In "Scouts and Aircraft" he presciently argued that spotter planes would revolutionize naval warfare, allowing surface forces to extend their reconnaissance abilities dramatically and changing the strategic and tactical context in future engagements. In 1918, while serving as the assistant secretary of the navy, Roosevelt attended the inauguration of US airmail service, joining President Woodrow Wilson in seeing off the first mail flight from Washington, DC, to New York. Roosevelt famously flew to Chicago to accept the 1932 Democratic presidential nomination in person—this in spite of the discomfort that flying caused the polio-disabled governor. He was also the first president to fly while in office, traveling on a Pan Am Clipper across the Atlantic in 1943 to meet with fellow allied leaders.[5]

While anecdotal, these examples suggest that Roosevelt maintained ongoing connections to American aeronautics for the duration of his political career. More importantly, however, Roosevelt's interest in aviation resulted in consistent efforts to shape the development of federal policy for both military and commercial ends. Those efforts began in 1934 with his engagement with Hugo Black's Senate special committee but quickly expanded to encompass more wide-ranging efforts. In 1935 Roosevelt created the Federal Aviation Commission (FAC), which he tasked to examine all aspects of American aeronautics and to develop a focused, forward-looking national policy. In the wake of the commission's activities, Roosevelt worked closely with members of Congress to shape new legislation that would ultimately take the form of the Civil Aeronautics Act of 1938. This pivotal bill created the legislative foundation that would direct American aviation until deregulation more than forty years later. As part of that process, the president also promoted the creation of the Civilian Pilot Training Program, which introduced thousands of Americans to flying and helped create a pool of licensed pilots who would play a crucial role for both the military and commercial carriers. Finally, under the auspices of numerous New Deal agencies, including the Civil Works Administration, Public Works

Administration, and Works Progress Administration, Roosevelt used federal public works projects to promote the development of aviation-related infrastructure throughout the country. These actions resulted in tens of millions of federal dollars being spent to build airports around the country, literally creating the foundations of the postwar air transport boom.

Within this larger context, the basic continuity Roosevelt's aviation policy shared with his predecessor's is particularly noteworthy. In fact, Roosevelt's actions represented a natural outgrowth of the foundations set down during the preceding Republican administrations. FDR maintained a federal focus on Post Office subsidies to passenger carriers, continued to promote close cooperation between the government and the industry, organized numerous forums through which he attempted to determine the proper path for future growth, and worked to pass legislation that would place American aviation on a firm commercial footing. While Roosevelt ultimately expanded federal control over aviation, the basic continuity between his policies and Hoover's highlight a significant point of convergence in at least one aspect of their respective economic agendas.

In spite of Roosevelt's noteworthy contributions to aeronautical development, historians of both American aviation and Roosevelt himself have consistently overlooked his actions. Scholars cite the president's supposed error in canceling commercial airmail contracts in 1934 and point to the lack of consistent policy statements as evidence that Roosevelt lacked a consistent policy focus. Epitomizing this view, in his book *Airlines and Airmail* Robert van der Linden argues that "Roosevelt never had a coherent national aviation policy."[6] By that definition, however, FDR lacked almost any "coherent" policies at all.

Famously reticent to put his thoughts and opinions in print, Roosevelt rarely engaged in the type of focused policy making that dominated the Hoover administration. FDR was, ultimately, a pragmatist, often authorizing multiple, at times contradictory programs designed to achieve similar ends. Further complicating the issue, Roosevelt took office in the midst of the Great Depression and, as a result, spent his first months in office focused on the banking crisis, rising unemployment, and the implosion of the world's economy. In his flurry of activity during the famous hundred days, and indeed for the duration of the New Deal, the president demonstrated a consistent willingness to embrace creative policy making, throwing ideas at the proverbial wall to see what stuck. Bearing those tendencies in mind, any focus on the coherence—or lack thereof—of Roosevelt's aviation policy misses the point. FDR wanted results, and it is the result of his actions that most clearly demonstrate his contributions to American aeronautical development. Clearly, Roosevelt lacked the consistent, activist vision that defined Hoover's commitment to promoting aviation's progress, but that should in no way obscure the gains he worked to foster or the basic similarities between his actions and those of his predecessor.[7]

Those actions suggest a need to reevaluate Franklin Roosevelt's contributions to the development of American aeronautics. His constant engagement with aviation policy highlights his ongoing interest in the progress of the commercial industry. FDR also focused on aviation's military value, highlighting the need for more and better-trained pilots, continued research and development, and a mature manufacturing sector.[8] These foci belie the image of a president uninterested in aviation, whose most significant actions with regard to aeronautical policy resulted in a public relations disaster following the deaths of twelve army pilots. Ultimately, Roosevelt's relationship to aviation must be viewed in a different light than Hoover's; the coherence of his policy derives from the results of his actions rather than their philosophical bases. Those actions, moreover, resulted in the greatest gains American aviation had yet experienced and in large part created the foundations of our modern air transport network.

As president, Roosevelt first turned his attention to American aeronautics as a result of the Black committee hearings of 1934. Though he had taken the unprecedented step of flying to Chicago to accept the Democratic nomination for president in 1932, Roosevelt made no significant policy statements related to aviation during his candidacy or in the first months after taking office. In large part this reflected the prevailing conditions the country faced at the time: the banking crisis, worsening unemployment, and the collapse of the European credit structure. Although many Democrats viewed their victory in the 1932 election as an opportunity to challenge Republican airmail policies, particularly those introduced by Walter Brown, it appears that, at least initially, Roosevelt did not involve himself in these machinations.

Roosevelt's decision to cancel Post Office airmail contracts in February 1934, however, thrust the president squarely into the center of the debate over aviation policy. Immediately confronted with crashes, dead army pilots, and a scathing critique from Charles Lindbergh, FDR struggled to respond to mounting criticism. Lindbergh's criticism in particular placed the president in a difficult position. Writing to the president in a telegram that Lindbergh simultaneously released to the press, the aviator warned that "unless the facts leave no alternative the condemnation of commercial aviation by cancellation of all mail contracts and the use of the army on commercial air lines will unnecessarily and greatly damage all of American aviation." The *New York Times*, which published Lindbergh's telegram in its entirety, also reported that Lindbergh and "veteran mail pilots" alike agreed that Roosevelt's actions placed the lives of "inexperienced" army pilots at great risk—a warning borne out in the mounting death toll during the first weeks of army operations.[9]

Roosevelt responded by curtailing the scope of army airmail operations and turning his attention to the pressing need to craft legislation providing for private contractors' resumption of airmail operations. As he did so, however, the White House mailbox increasingly overflowed with letters from Americans weighing in on the emerging scandal. By early April, Harllee Branch reported that Americans had sent Roosevelt and the Post Office more than two thousand letters or telegrams specifically addressing the president's actions. Of those, more than one hundred spoke directly to the emerging feud between Roosevelt and Charles Lindbergh. Almost all of those unsolicited missives exhibited strong feelings about the airmail scandal, though there was little unanimity regarding Roosevelt's decision. Regardless, the president quickly found himself forced to address a rising tide of concern not just from the Post Office, army, and Congress, but from the American people as well.[10]

Many of the most passionate letters the White House received responded directly to the growing rift between Roosevelt and Lindbergh. Americans pilloried the president and his staff for "slurring" Lindbergh's name and publically airing a "very gratuitous and unwarranted insult" against the famous aviator. A letter from one Emma Dillon offered perhaps the sharpest rebuke: Dillon angrily criticized Roosevelt's "cowardly personal attack" on Lindbergh, according to her an action that "convinced many that you cannot meet the issue squarely." Opinion ran just as strongly in the president's favor, however, as Americans congratulated FDR on taking "the bravest stand I have ever known a man to make" and highlighting Lindbergh's duplicity in using a press with which he had engaged in a number of public battles to advance his arguments against the president. Other letters embraced a more personal tone. One Sallie Stockard asked FDR to let her "handle Lindy"; according to her the pilot had shown "the Ass's Ears" and needed a firm hand to counter his "overweening pride." Tensions between Roosevelt and Lindbergh continued to escalate through the spring of 1934; in March *Newsweek* reported that the growing feud represented a "dramatic shadow-boxing exhibition" between the nations' two foremost heroes.[11]

Americans' concerns, however, extended beyond the specific dictates of Roosevelt's ongoing feud with Lindbergh; in fact, far more Americans wrote FDR to weigh in on the larger issue of federal airmail policy, even before army flights began. While those letters and telegrams exhibited a rough parity between support for and opposition to Roosevelt's actions, their consistency and passion highlighted Americans' perceived ownership of aviation policy. Even more significantly, the growing correspondence included letters from both lawmakers and members of the aviation industry. Immediately following Roosevelt's decision to cancel existing airmail contracts, Representative Harry Musselwhite (D-MI) wrote the president to express approval for FDR's actions. A member of the House Committee on Post Office and Post Roads, Musselwhite was well inclined to stand behind the president. His message, nonetheless, was representative of the opinions expressed by a number of other lawmakers.[12]

Several airline executives also penned quick responses to the cancellations. Croll Hunter, the general manager of Northwest Airways, wrote the president on February 15 to express his worry that unless Roosevelt was willing to modify the existing cancellation order, "this great airways system faces certain destruction." Hunter's worries were well founded, as his airline, like every other that had formerly flown the mail, struggled to make ends meet flying passengers without the aid of airmail revenue. Nonetheless, Hunter's letter exhibited a remarkably balanced tone, closing by telling the president that "we, as good citizens, find no fault with your great effort to clean up the airways situation, and to provide for the people of this country an efficient, comprehensive, and honest system of airway development."[13]

Public scrutiny of White House airmail policy grew much more intense as the army began its first airmail flights. Although the American public initially supported Roosevelt's actions by a slim margin, this began to change as army pilots started to fall from the skies. By late March the president was receiving an increasing number of angry letters decrying his actions. On March 19, one E. F. Gillespie wrote that "ten dead and fourteen injured suggests an almost irretrievable error of judgment" and suggested that the president "send Jim Farley on a few night air mail flights" to see how the postmaster general would fare. Americans also worried what the army's lack of preparedness to fly the mail heralded for national security. "If the army can not carry the mail, how can it win a war?" wrote a veteran of the Spanish American War and World War I in a representative communication.[14]

The army's failure also attracted increasing attention from some of the most well known figures associated with American aeronautics. No less an authority than Billy Mitchell weighed in on the controversy in early March. Mitchell expressed support for Roosevelt's actions, writing, "The President and the government should be justly proud in the position they have taken with respect to our aeronautics. The people of the United States had the right to expect that the Army Air Corps could fly the mail with ease." With regard to the growing death toll, the general suggested that the debacle represented a blessing in disguise, for without such a wakeup call the nation would have been unprepared in the event of war.[15]

Mitchell, however, was in the minority. Their attention fed by increasing press coverage of crashes and fatalities, most Americans focused on the president's culpability for the rising death toll as the media drew attention to the fallout from FDR's actions. In early March a *Time* article reported that Americans had begun to wonder if "President Roosevelt was not wrong on his airmail policy." Highlighting the fact that commercial operators had "warned Washington and the country that the Army . . . was not equipped or trained to step into the breach [flying the mail]," the magazine suggested that Roosevelt and his advisors had willfully ignored that counsel, sweeping it as aside as "sour grapes." By late April, *Newsweek* referred to Roosevelt's decision as "the worst political blunder of the administration," hardly the legacy Roosevelt had hoped for regarding his first significant involvement with aviation.[16]

FDR, however, had never considered the army to be a permanent solution. Driven by the mounting wave of criticism from the media and the American public, Roosevelt began to work toward the creation of new legislation that would return airmail operations to private contractors. On March 7 the president wrote Senators Hugo Black and Kenneth McKellar (D-TN) and Representative James Mead (D-NY) to express his desire to see new legislation emerge from Congress. In that letter Roosevelt expressed hope that airmail contracts could be returned to commercial airlines "as soon as possible." The president argued that new legislation would allow the government to "avoid the evils of the past" while encouraging "the sound development of the aviation industry." He ended with the fervent hope that enacting new legislation would "establish a sound, stable, and permanent air-mail policy."[17]

With that goal in mind, Roosevelt put forward a number of concrete policy proposals he hoped the congressmen would incorporate into forthcoming legislation. First, the president argued that the Post Office should limit the term of airmail contracts to three years in order to encourage more active competition between air transport operators and that operators seeking contracts should do so through a process of "open competitive bidding." FDR also highlighted the necessity of establishing a maximum rate of compensation "above which no contract will be awarded." Within that framework, Roosevelt articulated his desire that a specific set of qualifications govern bids. Only "speed, useful load capacity and safety factors and devices should be considered" in equipment specifications, he argued; bidders should be granted six months to qualify for the specific performance requirement dictated by contracts. A further series of dictates spoke directly to the perceived collusion sanctioned by Walter F. Brown. The president hoped that new legislation would prohibit any air transport operator "affiliated with any other company having connections with subsidiaries, affiliates, associates, or holding companies" in the aviation industry from bidding and forbade the merger of mail contractors or the subletting of any contract. FDR also pushed the congressmen to eliminate from the bidding process any company whose officers were party to the "spoils conferences" of 1930. Finally, Roosevelt pushed aggressively for changes to labor policies and pay scales. He emphasized the need for safeguards to prevent profit taking from stock deals, excessively high salaries, and "unearned bonuses and illegitimate personal expense accounts" in order to protect "legitimate stockholders and the public." Addressing the well-being of pilots, mechanics, and line workers, Roosevelt hoped each airmail operator would establish "maximum flying hours, minimum pay and a pension system."[18]

Roosevelt quickly found his efforts rewarded. Two days after the president wrote Black, McKellar, and Mead, the two senators jointly introduced what *Time* called "the administration bill." That bill, which ultimately became the Air Mail Act of 1934, "made all of the president's points" and embraced the framework Roosevelt articulated to his congressional allies.

On June 12, 1934, Roosevelt signed the bill into law, bringing the airmail scandal to an end and providing the legislative foundation for commercial airmail contracts that would hold sway until the passage of the Civil Aeronautics Act of 1938.[19]

Roosevelt's actions were not without controversy, however. To many they appeared to represent a dangerous divergence from the broadly associationalist policies that had governed the federal government's engagement with commercial flying since the early 1920s. Many leading aviation executives in particular sharply disagreed with the president's legislative focus. Ernest R. Breech, president of North American Aviation, in a statement to the House Post Office and Post Roads Committee, argued that FDR's policies "would result in the greatest possible confusion within the industry." TWA president Richard Robbins expressed a similar sentiment, stating, "President Roosevelt has been cruelly misinformed as to the facts of the airmail situation."[20]

Industry opposition was motivated primarily by the president's emphasis on transparent, competitive bidding. Breech argued that "the strong, well-managed and adequately financed companies now face the prospect of having their investments wiped out by the opening of these routes" to new bidders. According to the NAA president, this "would throw the industry back to the conditions existing in the early stages of development, thereby sacrificing not only the results of pioneering efforts to date, but in effect confiscating the properties and investments of the air mail carriers prior to the cancellation order." Eddie Rickenbacker, North American's vice president, expressed similar concerns, arguing, "I feel it will be a serious mistake if the equalities of the present operators of the air transport lines of this country are not recognized and given preemptive rights on the routes which they have pioneered at great expense to their stockholders." Fundamentally, these executives' opposition reflected their belief that pioneer operators should be rewarded for their efforts to establish commercial air service.[21]

Breech's and Rickenbacker's criticisms spoke directly to several significant points of divergence between Roosevelt's policies and those of the preceding administration. First, and most obviously, FDR believed that competitive bidding would serve both public and commercial interests. He made it clear that proper equipment, speed, load capacity, and safety should be the only specifications considered when weighing airmail bids—a change from Brown's policy of emphasizing night flying requirements and other qualifications specifically designed to benefit pioneer operators. The president emphasized that limiting bidding requirements in this way would ensure "that the bidding shall be really competitive," not merely a method through which to exclude unwanted proposals. The president's focus on three-year contracts also ran counter to Brown's hope for longer, ten-year route certificates. Roosevelt's most contentious point of divergence with the Hoover administration emerged from his efforts to force changes in the structure of the aeronautics industry. He argued that holding corporations and other industrial conglomerations were "clearly contrary to good faith and public policy" and pushed to exclude any such organization from bidding on airmail contracts—a desire codified in the 1934 Air Mail Act and representative of the broader New Deal focus on combating the worst excesses of industrial conglomerations.[22]

While Hoover and Brown opposed airlines' purchasing of "substantial interests" in other operations, they were more sanguine regarding the vertical integration that dominated the industry by the early 1930s. Brown in particular saw this type of industrial organization as containing the potential to streamline research and development, promote technological progress, and maximize efficiency in production and airline operations. Finally, in line with his broader New Deal philosophy, FDR pushed for new labor provisions that would protect pilots, maintenance men, and line workers from unfair employment practices through standards for maximum hours, minimum pay, and pension systems for airline workers.[23]

Those differences, however, should not overshadow the remarkable continuity between Roosevelt's policy focus and that of his predecessors. Roosevelt's emphasis on competitive bidding and three-year contracts, and his efforts to eliminate interlocking directorates and enact new labor provisions, represented differences of degree rather than kind. Like Hugo Black's, FDR's actions emerged from a desire to promote the continued growth and expansion of American aviation. His efforts, in fact, played a crucial role in preserving and ultimately expanding the government's central role in supporting airline development. Debates over the proper qualifications for airlines bidding on airmail routes assumed the inherent value of government airmail subsidies, confirming the essential continuity of federal policy. Roosevelt must also get credit for successfully returning airmail contracts to private operators. While in retrospect doing so may appear to have been inevitable, contemporary conditions militated against an easy return to commercial airmail. Black's Senate investigation had thrown the industry into chaos and drawn negative attention to the airlines and federal contracts. The army debacle further exacerbated the problem and placed Roosevelt in a difficult situation. In spite of the prevailing turmoil, Roosevelt never considered nationalization or doing away with governmental subsidies.[24]

Faced with a difficult political situation, Roosevelt worked diligently to create a compromise that addressed the harshest criticisms of the Watres Act while preserving its central policies. In so doing, he validated the central aspects of Hoover's aviation policy and confirmed his commitment to fostering aeronautical growth along essentially similar lines. Concluding his letter to Hugo Black, Roosevelt summed up his goals for commercial flying, writing, "Competition . . . will stimulate inventive genius, and should give to our people safer and better equipment both for commercial and military purposes." Like Black's ongoing efforts to support aviation's continued development in the wake of the Senate investigation, the president's statement highlights the remarkable unanimity of opinion among policy makers regarding aviation's significance and the federal government's role in promoting aeronautical growth.[25]

Franklin Roosevelt's engagement with the tumultuous events of early 1934 represented the first in a series of ongoing efforts to nurture the development of US aeronautics. In the short term, the president's actions returned airmail contracts to private hands and helped establish a new bidding and airmail rate system that FDR believed would promote commercial growth. More broadly, however, the airmail scandal motivated Roosevelt to play an increasingly central role in defining the proper course for American aviation policy. Stung by criticism from the public and media over his handling of army airmail operations and, like Hoover, Brown, Black, and others, viewing aviation as a key player in commerce and national defense, FDR embarked on a series of initiatives designed to ensure that US aeronautics could and would achieve its full potential. The president's creation of the FAC and his focused efforts to shape the Civil Aeronautics Act represent the two most significant of those efforts. Together, they brought US aviation policy full circle and established a paradigm for commercial flying that lasted more than forty years.

Roosevelt began looking beyond the events of early 1934 even before the conclusion of the Black committee hearings. As Black's activities were winding down, the president grew increasingly worried that the United States did not currently have a "broad aviation policy." In an effort to redress that dearth, FDR penned a memo laying out his desire to gather information about all aspects of American aeronautics in order to lay the foundation for future policy. Congress should, he wrote, "authorize the appointment of a commission" to gather information and recommend "a broad policy covering all phases of aviation and the relationship of the government thereto." Leaving little to chance, the president pushed for and secured the inclusion of a provision in the 1934 Air Mail Act authorizing him to designate the members of an investigative board tasked to report on the state of US aviation and make recommendations regarding future policy—what became the FAC. Roosevelt encouraged the commission to cast its net broadly and request testimony from pilots, designers, manufacturers, airline executives, labor leaders, academics, and policy makers in an effort to provide a comprehensive portrait of US aviation and—it was hoped—concrete suggestions for federal policy moving forward.[26]

The FAC certainly achieved those goals. During the summer and fall of 1934, a parade of the most significant figures in American aviation testified before the commission. Charles Lindbergh, General William Mitchell, Juan Trippe, William MacCracken, Eddie Rickenbacker, W. A. Patterson, and others offered their perspectives on myriad aspects of American aeronautics and made suggestions regarding the proper course for federal policy. The depth and breadth of that testimony provides a singular opportunity to assess prevailing opinions about the state of American aviation at the time. Significantly, the commission's findings reveal a remarkable unanimity of opinion regarding the most significant aspects of federal policy, opinions that played an important role in shaping Roosevelt's evolving policy viewpoint and framed his efforts to craft new legislation.

From the outset Roosevelt immersed himself in FAC activities. He began by taking an active role in determining the makeup of the commission itself, first voicing his wishes in a June 1934 White House memo in which he outlined the structure he believed the commission should take. FDR pushed for a five-member board. Members would not require congressional confirmation, no more than three could represent the same political party, and they would be allowed to choose their own chairman. Perhaps to entice potentially reluctant commissioners, Roosevelt suggested that they receive compensation equivalent to "a Senator or Representative in Congress."[27] By July, Roosevelt's plans had come to fruition. The chosen chairman, Clark Howell, led the five-man commission, which included several noted aviation-related figures. Howell, a former editor of the *Atlanta Constitution*, had served the federal government before. In 1922 Warren Harding named him to a special mining commission, and Herbert Hoover had tapped Howell to be a part of a national transportation commission. This background, plus his Democratic affiliation and political connections, made Howell an excellent fit for the FAC's mission. Serving alongside Howell were Edward P. Warren, Albert J. Berres, Jerome C. Hunsaker, and Franklin K. Lane Jr. Both Warren and Hunsaker had long-standing connections to the aviation industry. Warren, a pioneer aviator in his own right, had served as chief physicist for the National Advisory Committee for Aeronautics in the years following World War I and from 1926 to 1929 had served as the assistant secretary of the navy for aeronautics. Hunsaker taught aeronautics at the Massachusetts Institute of Technology and had a history of designing key aircraft for the US Army Air Corps.

As they prepared to begin hearing testimony in September, the commissioners worked closely with Roosevelt to ensure that their agenda aligned with the president's wishes. On July 25 Howell wrote to FDR to request a face-to-face meeting before the FAC began its fact-finding efforts. Reminding Roosevelt that the commission's hearings began on September 17, Howell wrote that it was "advisable before we proceed with these hearings to have a conference with you." Howell suggested that the members of the commission meet with Roosevelt at Hyde Park on September 14—a request Roosevelt granted readily.[28] Roosevelt's willingness to invite Howell and his colleagues to his home highlights the significance with which he viewed the commission's mission. Hyde Park was the president's sanctuary; his desire to meet with the FAC members there was noteworthy and demonstrates how eager he was to ensure that the commission lived up to his expectations.

Both before and after that meeting, Howell and his colleagues worked diligently to ensure that the commission would be able to offer Roosevelt the most comprehensive overview of contemporary aeronautics possible. They formally requested testimony from virtually every significant player in American aviation and sent out hundreds of questionnaires and informational queries, individually contacting more than twenty airlines alone. Focusing their investigation on a broad range of topics—air transportation, civil aviation, airports, national defense, procurement of military material, coast guard, lighter-than-air craft, relations of government and industry, research and education, and aeronautical law—they brought scores of witnesses to Washington, DC, to provide insights into those individuals' respective areas of expertise.[29]

Witness testimony demonstrated a remarkable unanimity of opinion. Most strikingly—though perhaps not surprisingly—virtually every witness pushed for continued federal airmail subsidies. Representatives from the Post Office, the Commerce Department, private interest groups, and the airlines alike portrayed airmail revenue as a necessary precondition for continued commercial growth. Witnesses also pushed for increased coordination among the governmental authorities engaged with aviation. Some embraced the more radical step of creating an independent regulatory agency responsible for all aspects of aviation oversight. The push for increased federal engagement with flying was also manifested in a general desire for the government to more aggressively promote aeronautics to the American people, particularly with regard to research and education. Finally, testimony overwhelmingly emphasized that federal involvement with aeronautics was vital for both the commercial and military success of the United States.

Airmail subsidies naturally formed a focal point of the FAC's investigation in the aftermath of the airmail scandal and enactment of new legislation. As federal officials and industry insiders alike struggled to adjust to the new federal framework created by the Air Mail Act of 1934, individuals appearing before the commission unilaterally expressed firm support for continued subsidies. Federal officials represented some of the strongest voices highlighting the ongoing value of federal airmail payments. Appearing in the place of his boss, Eugene Vidal, and speaking for the Bureau of Air Commerce (the renamed Aeronautics Branch), Assistant Director Rex Martin argued that "adequate mail pay or subsidy for mail-passenger service is vital to the development of air transport and its safe operation." Like Herbert Hoover and Walter Brown, Martin emphasized that airmail payments provided "an incentive for the development of passenger and express business," therefore resulting in "a more rapid development" of commercial aviation in general. In particular, Martin highlighted airlines' ability to use profits accruing from federal support to fund "expansion and new equipment."[30]

Representatives from the Post Office seconded Martin's view almost verbatim. Second Assistant Postmaster General Harllee Branch told the commissioners that airmail subsidies represented the centerpiece of federal policy. "There can be no doubt," he argued, "that the support which the government has given air transport through air mail pay has been largely responsible for this remarkable development of the aviation industry itself." Emphasizing that the Post Office, more than any other government agency, was responsible for commercial development, Branch suggested that Post Office payments benefited airlines, aviation manufacturing firms, and the public. They allowed airlines to "buy modern equipment," manufacturers to outstrip their competitors in other countries, and the country to protect its preeminence in aeronautical development. Branch closed his testimony with a warning: he doubted whether any contemporary airline "could continue to operate . . . without this help which the government gives them."[31]

Not surprisingly, airline executives also argued for the continued necessity of airmail payments. Eddie Rickenbacker, vice president of North American Aviation, represented the loudest voice from the air transport industry. Arguing that Post Office subsidies offered the best and most fiscally responsible way to promote the continued development of commercial aviation, Rickenbacker suggested that in addition to normal airmail payments the government should grant an additional graduated subsidy "dependent entirely on the proved revenues from passengers and express to those lines that must have it to exist"—in other words a government-guaranteed profit. Airlines, he argued, were "rendering a genuine service to the traveling public, to the Post Office, and to the industrial life of this country" and had, in his view, actually "subsidized the government [and] people as a whole." Other executives, while less strident in their rhetoric, echoed Rickenbacker's call for continued federal support. Ernest Breech, president of North American Aviation; W. A. Patterson, president of United Airlines; and many of their peers viewed federal support as foundational to the continued growth of American air commerce. While a number of executives argued that the maturation of air transport would eventually remove the need for such payments, in 1934 the overwhelming majority of opinions strongly supported continued subsidization.[32]

Airline executives found a ready ally in Hiram Bingham, president of the nation's most influential aviation advocacy group, the National Aeronautic Association. Bingham, a former US Senator, early aviation pioneer, and explorer famous for publicizing the existence of Machu Picchu, maintained close connections to lawmakers and exerted significant influence over federal aviation policy, labor practices, and engineering through his work for the association. In his testimony he made clear that both airmail payments and "bonuses or direct subsidy for improved air transport in the carrying of mail, passengers, express, and so forth" were integral for the continued development of US flying. Bingham, in fact, went beyond even Rickenbacker, arguing that repealing the Watres Act had been a mistake and fervently supporting the reintroduction of policies broadly similar to those crafted by Walter Brown.[33] While he found little agreement regarding the latter point, Bingham's testimony nonetheless placed his organization firmly in line with the wishes of the Commerce Department, the Post Office, and the airlines.

While subsidies represented the single greatest point of consensus, witnesses also expressed broad agreement that the federal government should continue and, in fact, increase its regulation of American aviation. Members of both the government and industry argued for greater coordination among government agencies with ties to aviation and a stronger connection between military and civil aviation policy. Many witnesses went so far as to argue for the creation of an independent commission responsible for all aspects of aviation policy and regulation—an opinion that presaged the creation of the Civil Aeronautics Authority four years later.

Secretary of Commerce Daniel Roper took the lead in pushing for improved coordination among federal agencies. Arguing that aviation represented "an industry of the greatest importance to our future," Roper suggested that "an effort should be made more definitely to initiate a cooperative consultation among [government] agencies" in order to facilitate the creation of a "logical Federal aviation policy." To that end he argued that "the creation of an aviation commission entirely divorced from all departments of the government" would best serve both aviation and national interests.[34]

Representatives from the industry seconded Roper's proposal. Lester Seymour, president of American Airlines, told the commission that he favored the creation of a single "government body that gives its complete attention to the activities of the air transport companies." That body should, Seymour continued, have "complete control over our affairs," including, but not limited to, regulation, assistance, promotion, airmail rates, and navigation aids. W. A. Patterson expressed similar sentiments, testifying that commercial aviation would be best served by the government's granting "broad powers to a permanent, independent federal aviation commission" responsible for "the economic growth and supervision of civil aeronautics."[35]

On October 16 the FAC heard testimony from no less a figure than Charles Lindbergh, who powerfully expressed his support for the creation of an independent regulatory agency. Highlighting Lindbergh's stature and his intimate knowledge of the air transport arena, commissioners asked the pilot to lay out a concrete plan for aviation oversight. Lindbergh grounded his proposal in the need to establish safe and reliable airline service both nationally and internationally, arguing that close government regulation was a necessary precondition to achieving those goals. "I believe there should be a permanent aviation commission," he argued, "completely independent" of any other regulatory agency and with full authority over commercial flying. That commission, he suggested, should limit bidding on airmail contracts to "responsible operators" and engage in a comprehensive effort to regulate in the interests of passenger safety while aggressively promoting commercial flying to the American people.[36]

Support for promotional efforts appeared prominently in other witnesses' testimony as well. Daniel Roper went so far as to develop his own lexicon, arguing that the government needed to "aeorize" the nation in an effort to "stimulate proper school and educational endeavors among the youth of the land and cultivate air-mindedness among the people generally." Dr. Karl Compton, president of the Massachusetts Institute of Technology, offered a similar perspective. Compton had a long history of engagement with aviation, having served as an aeronautical engineer in the Army Signal Corps during World War I and having helped to establish MIT's groundbreaking aeronautical engineering department in 1913. Speaking in his capacity as an expert on engineering and as a member of President Roosevelt's Science Advisory Board, Compton contended that national interest "requires that the Government take whatever steps it can to encourage and stimulate any new developments" in aeronautics. Aviation, in his opinion, had "not come anywhere near realizing what its ultimate possibilities are for public service," a situation that mandated ongoing governmental promotion.[37]

A final thread flowing through the commission's hearings emphasized aviation's value to the nation. Virtually every witness argued that aviation was central to the continued development of the American way of life—a fact that necessitated comprehensive, sound federal policy. Speaking directly to this point, Eddie Rickenbacker encouraged the commissioners to remember aviation's "importance as a social, political, and commercial asset to this country." Daniel Roper seconded Rickenbacker's thoughts, arguing that aviation was "an industry of the greatest importance to our future national defense and for serving America[n]" society and economics.[38]

These men's explicit connection of aviation to the country's well-being suggests that by 1934 interested parties understood aviation policy to have implications far beyond airmail rates and routes. Rickenbacker, Roper, Lindbergh, and others understood the ongoing development of American aeronautics—in large part dictated by federal policy—to have implications for national security and social, political, and commercial progress; indeed, virtually every aspect of the country's future. Significantly, at least among the parties testifying before the FAC, there was virtually no countervailing opinion worthy of mention. Although the commission was certainly predisposed to request testimony from those with an interest in aviation's continued progress, the striking agreement regarding aviation's expanding influence remains noteworthy.

Contemporary periodical coverage echoed the FAC's focus on aviation's growing national significance. Although concerns over safety remained significant, by the mid-1930s a majority of Americans had embraced aviation's commercial possibilities. In 1936 *Newsweek* highlighted commercial aviation's maturation in an article entitled "Airlines: U.S. Report Shows All Types of Air Traffic Soaring." Commenting on the previous year's developments, the article happily reported, "All through 1935 airline officials, totting up payload manifests, beamed with satisfaction. Month after month their summaries showed passenger, mail and express traffic soaring to new records." Two years later, *Life* was confident enough in the industry's commercial stability to run the headline "Aviation Comes of Age." Highlighting airlines' growing national prominence, the article related that in less than two decades air transport had "advanced infinitely faster and more wisely than the railroads did in their early life." As these and myriad other publications suggested, by the midpoint of the decade Americans increasingly looked at flying as a mainstream transportation technology, a far cry from the associations with daring and danger that had dominated the country's relationship with aviation in the recent past.[39]

By the end of 1934 the commission concluded its hearings and began to formulate its official report. Given the broad consensus existing among the commission's witnesses, that report revealed few surprises—in fact, it primarily served to codify the widespread consensus expressed by the witnesses. Of note, however, was the commission's confirmation of the foundational concepts that underlay Herbert Hoover's engagement with commercial aeronautics; its findings also voiced support for key aspects of Walter Brown's program, exonerating the former postmaster general to at least some extent. While hardly groundbreaking, the FAC's advocacy for basic continuity in federal aviation policy remains noteworthy in light of the turmoil created by the events of the preceding year, and it formed an important motivator in framing policy discussions moving forward.

After highlighting the need for a federal policy that would allow the country "to maintain a position of world leadership in air transport," the commission laid out a series of focused policy recommendations. First among them was a call for continued airmail subsidies. The FAC recommended that the government provide payments sufficient to "maintain and develop adequate transport services," including direct subsidies above and beyond postal revenues, if necessary. Howell and his colleagues pushed for certificates of convenience and necessity to be issued to commercial carriers, for expanded federal support for lighting and navigation facilities, and for limited competition between airlines that would avoid "uneconomic paralleling of routes or duplication of facilities."[40]

Significant, though unsurprising in light of the consistent focus on the issue exhibited by witnesses, was the commission's call for an independent regulatory group. The FAC emphasized the pressing need for an "air commerce commission" appointed directly by the president, encompassing "broad supervisory and regulatory powers over civil aeronautics" with a particular emphasis on air transport. Beyond those broad outlines, however, the commission's report offered few clues as to the organization, function, and specific responsibilities such a commission would embrace. While the report did mention both "supervisory and regulatory" functions, Howell and his colleagues remained frustratingly mute regarding the extent to which the proposed body would supersede the activities of the Post Office or the Commerce Department. The commissioners did recommend that the Interstate Commerce Commission retain control over airmail rates, a point of clarification that in fact clarified little, as it appeared to fly in the face of the FAC's focus on granting the new agency broad, independent powers over air commerce.[41]

Finally, the commission's report included a host of recommendations for civil and military aviation, education, and promotion. These included a call for federal support for the development of more economical and easier-to-fly private aircraft—a "flivver" plane—that would allow more Americans to take to the air; a recommendation for ongoing coordination between civilian and military policy makers; an appeal for high-quality military aircraft; and a call for integrated manufacturing organizations. The commission also emphasized the value that the NACA brought to American aeronautics and recommended that the NACA work more closely with universities to foster aeronautical education and coordinate technological development.[42]

As the FAC wrapped up its work, Howell and his colleagues continued to work closely with the president. Before releasing the commission's findings to the public, the chairman contacted Roosevelt to ensure that the president was thoroughly briefed on commission activities. Writing to FDR on January 25, 1935, Howell summarized the FAC's findings, placing particular emphasis on the fact that "practically all" of the witnesses appearing before the commission urgently recommended the creation of a new aviation commission. The FAC chairman also sought Roosevelt's assistance in spreading word of the FAC's findings. Most notably, Howell emphasized the importance of Roosevelt's "sending a message to the two Houses of Congress" expressing support for the report and highlighting the need for new aviation legislation.[43]

Ironically, the release of the Federal Aviation Commission's final report did not spur the passage of new legislation—at least in the short term. Although the aviation community clearly supported the expansion of federal engagement with aeronautics, and the FAC report suggested the outlines of such a policy, barriers remained. In a surprising turn of events, Franklin Roosevelt erected one of the most significant. Though the president had been a key figure behind the FAC's creation and had maintained an ongoing and active interest in the commission's activities, upon the conclusion of its work he balked at implementing key recommendations. Most importantly, Roosevelt took issue with the committee's central recommendation: that the government create a new, independent aviation regulatory commission.

Roosevelt's opposition—or at least lack of support—appears to have emerged from a larger White House focus on executive reorganization. The president's interest in transportation policy extended beyond aviation alone; in 1935 Roosevelt was focused on the idea of creating a holistic transportation policy and placing responsibility for air, sea, and land transport under the auspices of a single federal agency. Obviously, a new, independent aviation commission flew in the face of that desire. Further, Roosevelt's wish for greater coordination also reflected a larger concern with the ballooning federal bureaucracy. The president was concerned with the proliferation of independence commissions, agencies, and organizations divorced from executive control. Eventually this would lead Roosevelt to launch an investigation designed to craft comprehensive recommendations for an overhaul of the executive branch. Headed by Louis Brownlow, the group completed its activities in 1936; Roosevelt forwarded its proposals to Congress in early 1937 and called for legislation authorizing a thorough reorganization of the executive branch granting the president increased authority over such organizations as the Federal Trade Commission and the Interstate Commerce Commission (ICC). That call met with widespread opposition; the ensuing battle cost Roosevelt significant political capital and, combined with his infamous "court packing" proposal, would go a long way toward spelling the end of the New Deal. Although those events lay in the future, FDR's unwillingness to act in support of a new aviation body reflected the same foundational emphases.[44]

Roosevelt had other reasons for failing to offer strong support for the FAC findings as well. For several years the president had exhibited indecision regarding the ICC's role (or lack thereof) in determining airmail rates. In 1934 he had supported expanding the ICC's jurisdiction, support that led to that agency's gaining control over airmail rates under the Black-McKellar bill and support that flew in the face of efforts to place those powers in a new agency. In 1935 he argued that economic regulation of air transport should fall under ICC control. By 1936, however, the president's stance was less certain, leading members of Congress to examine the proverbial tea leaves for clues as to the president's wishes—and Roosevelt provided few clues as to his position. In a similar vein, while FDR stood behind the FAC before and during its investigation, his attention waned in subsequent months. The reasons for this about-face are unclear; Roosevelt often ran hot and cold on initiatives—and with aides and colleagues—and was famously cagey regarding his actual desires. His sudden lack of interest could reflect his changing stance on the issue, a political play, or simple distraction.[45]

Regardless of the reason for Roosevelt's inattention, its effects were manifest. In the sudden absence of presidential advocacy and guidance, other interested parties stepped forward to oppose the FAC's recommendations. Most importantly, Post Office officials argued against changes to the status quo. Still smarting from the ICC's assumption of control over airmail rates and loath to surrender control over airmail payments and routes to any other agency, James Farley used the political vacuum to his advantage, calling on members of Congress to plead his case. Aviation, he argued, was not sufficiently developed to justify its own regulatory agency. Although he backed ongoing federal support for commercial flying, Farley opposed treating aviation as a mature transportation form. Airmail payments continued to play a foundational role in securing airlines' solvency; for Farley that fact mandated ongoing Post Office involvement in commercial flying.[46]

Further complicating matters were a host of legislative proposals percolating through Congress. The majority of these encompassed efforts to amend the basic structure of airmail rate payments and route organization without attempting to modify regulation or oversight; to a great extent they reflected the increasingly dire financial straits airlines faced in the wake of their resumption of airmail carriage in March 1934. Bidding for new contracts in the wake of the army debacle and during the turmoil of the ongoing Black committee activities, most carriers had entered low bids under the temporary system put in place by Roosevelt and Farley. In doing so they hoped to assuage some of the anger that had led to the airmail scandal; low bids also reflected the fact that the airlines were desperate to regain access to airmail subsidies in a newly competitive atmosphere, as they could not remain solvent without them. Most airline executives, however, assumed that rates could and would be revised upward at a later date, an assumption that proved to be erroneous. The Black-McKellar bill made the temporary bids binding for a period of three years and gave the ICC oversight over airmail rates from the end of that three-year period forward. As such, there was no short-term relief from the industry's financial peril, and the ICC gave airlines little indication that payments would increase in the long term. Fundamentally, the 1934 legislation embodied a makeshift effort that demonstrated little recognition of the complexities of the contemporary economic environment, conditions readily acknowledged by industry insiders, aviation interest groups, and political allies. As a result, the airlines struggled to make ends meet and increasingly looked to allies in Congress for aid.[47]

Although they found ready support from figures including Clarence Lea (D-CA), Pat McCarran (D-NV), Harry Truman (D-MO), and Sam Rayburn (D-TX), the absence of presidential guidance stymied legislative efforts as members of Congress hesitated to push new bills forward without knowing Roosevelt's wishes. Lea, for example, introduced a bill authorizing the creation of a new Civil Aviation Board in 1935 but later amended the legislation to vest regulatory functions in the ICC as FDR backed away from the FAC's findings. None of these bills found broad support, and even their sponsors expressed lukewarm advocacy as they waited to receive a clearer sense of the White House's wishes.[48]

Uncertainly reined until early 1937, when Roosevelt renewed his focus on aviation policy and began working aggressively to formulate new legislation. In February, Clarence Lea—chairman of the House Committee on Interstate and Foreign Commerce and the figure who would become the administration's primary ally in Congress—wrote to Roosevelt in the hopes of securing the president's support for new legislation. For more than two years Lea had worked consistently to craft a bill that would satisfy the industry and adhere to FDR's wishes; by 1937 his patience was running out. In an effort to discern the president's stance, Lea wrote that in his effort to "work out" a new model for aviation regulatory legislation, he "would be glad for any suggestion from you [Roosevelt] that would help us to express the Administration's viewpoint in this new legislation." Lea reminded Roosevelt that while the latter had expressed a desire for new legislation dating back to 1935, the administration's position at present remained murky at best, a situation that Roosevelt could easily redress. Lea's query elicited an emphatic response from Roosevelt: two days later the president wrote his secretary with a request "to get Clarence Lea down here right away."[49]

While Lea's missive did not immediately lead to Roosevelt's public clarification of his position, it did serve as a spur to action. The legislative situation in Congress also contributed to FDR's newfound engagement: by the spring Congress was beset by proposals for new aviation laws. More than half a dozen new statutes had been put forward during the session, the two most significant coming from Lea and Senator Pat McCarran. The situation called for executive leadership, and in May, Harry Truman wrote Roosevelt to brief the president on contemporary developments and request guidance. Roosevelt responded that while he had not had the opportunity to examine the "specific provisions" of all of the bills, he was actively engaged in "getting all the information" he could. More significantly, the president gave the first indication that he was warming to the idea of an independent aviation commission. In an apparent about-face from his position two years earlier, FDR wrote, "My general feeling is that . . . no administrative powers should be transferred to the Interstate Commerce Commission."[50]

As the president began to wade into the fray, other lawmakers increasingly looked to the administration for guidance. On May 26 Sam Rayburn wrote Roosevelt, enclosing a letter from Lea detailing the latter congressman's legislative plans and "urging the importance and necessity of administration interest in working out an aviation regulatory measure." Rayburn argued that "securing worthwhile legislation" was of the utmost importance; the matter, he wrote, necessitated immediate attention from both Congress and the White House. Less than a week later Roosevelt signaled a newfound willingness to work with Congress on exactly that issue. He instructed his secretary to "try to get Lea and [James] Mead," authors of the leading aviation bills in the House, "together and try to reconcile their two bills." FDR also made it clear that he remained opposed to vesting additional powers in the ICC. "The important thing," he wrote, is to prevent that body from gaining control of any "administrative duties."[51]

By July it appeared that legislation might emerge from Congress before the end of the session. Writing to the president at the end of the month, Lea emphasized that he "very much" hoped to see a new bill passed before Congress adjourned for the summer. In yet another vacillation, however, Roosevelt remained unwilling to commit. Replying to Lea on August 5, the president wrote, "I believe it would be desirable to postpone this matter until a later time when the various agencies of the Government concerned with this vital subject may have a better opportunity to work out a basic national program for aviation which will serve the needs of the country for some time to come."[52]

Roosevelt's hesitancy traced to several factors. Most importantly, he remained undecided on whether new legislation should create an independent aviation commission. Lea's proposal continued to split control over air commerce between the Post Office and the ICC, reflecting the president's apparent desire from two years earlier. In 1937, however, Roosevelt offered increasing opposition to ICC control. The administration also received criticism of Lea's proposal from the Commerce Department. In June, Director of Air Commerce Fred Fagg wrote to J. M. Johnson, assistant secretary of commerce, to express his concerns regarding Lea's bill. Fagg worried that the bill did not adequately clarify the powers granted to the ICC, Commerce Department, and Post Office. He also related that Lea's proposal to expand ICC regulatory powers would impinge on Commerce Department activities. Johnson concurred and forwarded Fagg's assessment to the White House with further commentary. Referencing his ongoing contact with Colonel James Roosevelt—the president's son and secretary—Johnson wrote that the bill was "objectionable" and failed to redress the regulatory and financial problems currently plaguing the air transport industry.[53]

The increasingly chaotic situation led Roosevelt to act decisively in an effort to establish some measure of control over the legislative landscape. In late July FDR wrote Second Assistant Postmaster General Harllee Branch, informing Branch that he hoped to establish a committee tasked with drafting a new aviation bill conforming to White House wishes. "It look [*sic*] now as if there will be no aviation legislation at this session," the president wrote, "I suggest that as soon as the session closes, the Interdepartmental Committee on Civil Aviation be expanded to cover the whole aviation field . . . and that the Committee charge itself with the preparation of a bill for the next session in January."[54] The Interdepartmental Committee traced its roots back to 1935, when representatives from the Post Office, State Department, and Treasury Department began examining the field of international air transport in an effort to clarify governmental policy and protect US aeronautical interests overseas. Roosevelt hoped that the group, already familiar with many aspects of federal policy, could easily expand its brief to the domestic context and make concrete legislative recommendations before Congress reconvened.

In less than a month, however, Roosevelt abandoned the plan. Demonstrating a desire to establish greater control over the drafting of new legislation, he moved to create an entirely new committee. The president highlighted that the group should focus exclusively on aviation legislation in an effort to streamline the drafting process and be as responsive as possible to White House desires. "I agree with your suggestion that a special commission, composed of representatives of the governmental agencies at present concerned with the various phases of aviation, and any others whose knowledge and advice may be helpful, be named," Branch wrote to the president in response to a request for counsel. The commission should,

Branch continued, "go into this whole question [of aviation regulation] and make recommendations to you" regarding the scope and content of federal oversight.[55]

By September, Roosevelt had his special commission, announcing the creation of the Interdepartmental Committee on Civil Aviation Legislation on September 15. Comprised of representatives of the War, Navy, Commerce, Post Office, and Treasury Departments, the president authorized the committee "to study aviation needs as related to future legislation, giving special attention to the bills introduced at the last session of Congress."[56] Tellingly, the White House saw to it that C. M. Hester was appointed to the group. Hester, a Treasury Department lawyer, was the central author of the administration's executive branch reorganization bill and enjoyed the president's full confidence. He headed the Interdepartmental Committee's Drafting Subcommittee and in coming months would serve as a key conduit between the White House, the committee, and Congress. Hester's relationship with the president's son and personal secretary, Lieutenant Colonel James Roosevelt—both personally and through the latter's secretary, James Rowe—was particularly significant; through the younger Roosevelt the solicitor provided the White House a steady stream of updates about the committee's activities and, after it finished its work, the legislative situation in Congress. James Roosevelt, in turn, funneled his father's influence through Hester, although the colonel also worked directly with interested parties when the need arose. Both Hester and Roosevelt, moreover, worked closely with Clarence Lea to reconcile the administration's bill with the representative's and shepherd it though Congress as all sides worked to iron out the myriad details associated with crafting a complicated piece of legislation.

As the committee began its work, they were confronted with a daunting task. The current state of federal policy encompassed a confused delegation of power between the ICC and Post Office and Commerce Departments. The airlines clamored for more airmail revenue and greater flexibility with regard to rates and routes and opposed "destructive" competitive bidding. Congress was inundated with legislative proposals dealing with everything from airmail rates to the totality of federal control. Many legislators looked to the White House for guidance, but FDR had been frustratingly unwilling to tip his hand. The Federal Aviation Commission report provided a potential model but to date had done little to unify opinion. There existed general support for an independent air commission in the industry and with key members of Congress, but the president's vacillations had forestalled efforts to create such an organization for the preceding two years.

Roosevelt demonstrated a keen interest in the committee's activities from the outset, although he continued to exhibit a frustrating lack of consistency in his policy recommendations. At an October 22, 1937, cabinet meeting, the president spoke with Secretary of Commerce Daniel Roper to share his thoughts on new legislation. FDR had recently spoken to Representative James Mead, who had introduced his own aviation bill to Congress during the previous session. Roper reported that the president was "impressed" with Mead's bill and that the dialogue had influenced FDR's thinking. In the wake of that conversation the president asked Roper to inform the Interdepartmental Committee of his desire that they embrace three objectives: placing all regulatory powers for aviation in the Commerce Department, all matters associated with the transport of airmail under Post Office control, and all matters associated with "rates, etc." in the hands of the ICC. This legislative model differed little from the system in place in basic structure and, while Roper expressed general approval, flew in the face of industry wishes for a comprehensive overhaul.[57]

Less than a month later, however, the committee transmitted a legislative proposal to James Roosevelt embracing a markedly different form. Summarized by C. M. Hester in a memorandum, the proposal apparently reflected a shift in the president's wishes. Hester told Roosevelt that the committee had acted in line with recommendations of the President's Committee on Administrative Management, specifically that organizations' emphasis on reorganizing regulatory commissions. The Interdepartmental Committee recommended that in addition to its regulatory function, the BAC take on added responsibilities for both safety and economic functions, including the issuance of certificates of convenience and necessity. Additionally, the committee proposed the establishment of an independent three-man Board of Air Commerce Appeals possessing final administrative authority over all nonexecutive questions. While housed in the Commerce Department, the bureau and the board would not be subject to the control of the commerce secretary except with regard to "'housekeeping' functions." In a subsequent meeting with Hester, James Roosevelt expressed approval of the proposal but suggested that he and the president desired that the proposed BAC have even more autonomy. Most importantly, Roosevelt told Hester, all decisions emerging from the Board of Air Commerce Appeals "should be final and not reviewable by the Secretary of Commerce."[58]

The Interdepartmental Committee responded to the president's growing support for an independent air authority with a new legislative proposal on November 26. The draft bill created a new Civil Aeronautics Board (CAB) that would exercise almost total control over both the regulation and oversight of civil aviation. Housed in the Commerce Department for administrative simplicity, the CAB would assume control over "all of the powers of the Secretary of Commerce with respect to air commerce and all of the powers of the Interstate Commerce Commission relating to the fixing of rates of airmail pay." While the Post Office would retain limited authority—control over "strictly postal functions"—the CAB would be empowered to "regulate completely the transportation of passengers and goods by air." The proposal provided for independent governmental regulation of airmail and passenger rates, "close and continuous governmental control of financial aid for air lines," federal oversight of airlines' financial structures, provisions for certificates of convenience and necessity for carriers, and governmental support for research and development.[59]

The draft bill spurred the administration to further action, as FDR at last seemed fully committed to making good on the FAC's promises of two years earlier. In early December, James Roosevelt met with congressional leaders to discuss the White House's legislative plans, and the president requested personal meetings with Pat McCarran and Clarence Lea to discuss the Interdepartmental Committee's proposal. Hester remained in close contact with the administration, penning a memo for James Roosevelt on December 13 with updates on the committee's activities and a request for the president to clarify his position on the structure of the proposed civil aviation commission. Colonel Roosevelt met with Hester and the rest of the committee that afternoon to transmit the president's wishes, the first in a series of conferences between the two parties over the course of subsequent months. By December 22 the committee proudly announced they had completed an updated draft of the bill that, while still in need of minor refinements, was well on the way to completion. J. M. Johnson, the committee's chairman, asked Roosevelt for feedback and reminded him that Hester and the Drafting Subcommittee were at the administration's disposal. Roosevelt discussed the proposal with the president, and by the end of the year it appeared that FDR stood firmly behind the Interdepartmental Committee's work.[60]

The dawn of 1938 saw James Roosevelt and C. M. Hester working feverishly to reconcile the leading congressional proposals—from McCarran in the Senate and Lea in the House—with the administration's bill. McCarran advocated creating an independent aviation commission, but his draft differed in a number of respects from the Interdepartmental Committee's draft; Lea's on the other hand, proposed vesting regulatory power over civil aviation in the ICC, a reflection of Lea's effort to bend to the president's wishes from the previous year. Lea, however, ultimately proved to be far more willing to support the administration's evolving interests. On January 7 Hester wrote James Roosevelt to report on conferences with both McCarran and Lea. While Hester was "encouraged" by his meeting with McCarran, the solicitor was far more positive regarding his discussion with Lea. The latter conference, Hester wrote, "was one of the most satisfactory I have ever had with any member of either House of Congress." So enthusiastic was Lea, in fact, that the congressman requested permission to distribute copies of the administration's proposal to members of the aviation industry for feedback and comment with the ultimate intention of substituting it for his own bill. Only three days later, J. M. Johnson happily reported that Lea had done just that, submitting to his committee a proposal that was "verbatim" the administration's bill. The resulting piece of legislation enjoyed the support of the White House and the aviation industry and appeared primed for an easy passage through Congress.[61]

Unfortunately, obstacles soon emerged in the bill's path. While Hester, Johnson, James Roosevelt, and Lea worked diligently to usher the bill out of committee, and FDR took an increasingly active role trying to build congressional support for the proposal, Senator McCarran remained frustratingly unwilling to reconcile his own bill with Lea's. During meetings and in correspondence with Hester, Lea, James Roosevelt, and the president, McCarran repeatedly expressed his desire to reach a consensus. He refused, however, to compromise on two key issues: he opposed granting the Post Office control over airmail schedules, and he opposed granting the new aviation commission the power to fix the rates charged by American carriers operating in foreign countries. Beginning in mid-January, supporters of Lea's bill met with McCarran and his representatives almost daily to try to reach a compromise. By January 23 it appeared that an agreement was close at hand. Hester informed James Roosevelt that following a long conference with representatives from Lea's and McCarran's offices, the senator was willing to go along with the majority of the administration's recommendations. The next day, however, Hester reported that McCarran had backtracked and remained unwilling to bend on either the Post Office or the foreign rate issue. By January 26 the president expressed a willingness to acquiesce to McCarran's wishes, although Hester counseled that he remain vague in his public pronouncements to allow continued room for negotiation.[62]

With apparent consensus among the administration, McCarran, and Lea, Hester worked feverishly through the month of February to finalize the new law. On February 10 he reported that while the Air Line Pilot's Association remained opposed to the bill, desiring that regulatory power be vested in the ICC, as that agency had demonstrated a history of supporting workers' interests, he was pleased that the airlines were firmly behind the proposal. The next day Hester spent more than eight hours with Lea and his staff making final changes to the latest draft, which he hoped would be ready the following week. Although it took a bit longer than Hester had anticipated, by the end of the month he was able to inform James Rowe that Lea was in the process of getting final approval from the airlines as he prepared to submit a finished draft.[63]

As Lea prepared to introduce the revised bill, however, McCarran dropped a bombshell. Rather than introducing legislation mirroring Lea's bill in the Senate, on March 3—the day before Lea introduced his bill in the House—McCarran instead unveiled an entirely new bill that, according to Hester and James Rowe, included "none of the White House recommendations." As Hester related to Rowe, the senator had apparently "thrown overboard" the aides who had worked with Lea and Hester to reconcile the administration, Senate, and House bills and instead "procured the assistance of two attorneys in the Interstate Commerce Commission," who quickly drafted an entirely new piece of legislation. Although McCarran announced in a press release that his bill was "in general conformity with the White House plans for aviation legislation," Hester was adamant that it reflected "very few, if any," of the president's desires.[64]

In the ensuing weeks the White House worked diligently with Lea to preempt McCarran's bill. On March 8 the president gave a press conference in which he downplayed the significance of McCarran's proposal and placed his support firmly behind Lea. Lea's bill, FDR told the press, enjoyed the full support of the administration, the aviation industry, and "interested Government agencies." Subsequently, administration officials worked with Sam Rayburn to speed Lea's bill through the House and secured a promise from Harry Truman that he would substitute Lea's bill for McCarran's in the Senate if McCarran refused to do so. Roosevelt also worked to ensure that prominent members of Congress would stand behind Lea's bill. On March 18 Hester reported that James Mead had engaged in a productive meeting with Lea and would endorse the legislation. The solicitor also responded to a request from the White House to meet with Kenneth McKellar and "get him in line on the civil aviation legislation." McKellar remained skeptical and asked Hester for further information, but he appeared willing to come around to the administration's view. Over the course of the next month, Hester, Rowe, and James Roosevelt continued to secure congressional allies, including Alben Barley (D-KY), Burton Wheeler (D-MT), and Royal Copeland (D-NY), who Hester called the administration's "ace in the hole" in reference to Copeland's willingness to block McCarran's legislation if need be.[65]

The president also engaged in a personal effort to ensure that his congressional allies clearly understood the administration's position. Through his son, FDR sent a series of confidential messages to Truman, Wheeler, and Lea, among others, with updates on the administration's internal policy discussions. The information, FDR hoped, would put the members of Congress "in a position to advise and consult with the President" as the legislative process unfolded. A week later the president penned a longer message to Lea outlining the significance with which he viewed the pending law. "It is imperative," FDR wrote, for Congress to enact new legislation during the current legislative session. "It is vital to this country that aeronautics should be placed on a healthy and stable basis," the president continued: "A new agency will be able to bring together in coherent form the present divided regulation in all phases of the industry." Citing the industry's pressing contemporary problems and the inadequacy of existing policy, Roosevelt urged Lea to redouble his efforts to ensure that a productive bill clear Congress as soon as possible.[66]

The administration's perseverance eventually paid off. McCarran bowed to White House pressure and returned to his earlier legislative draft, which moved quickly through the Senate. On April 15 Hester reported that Lea's bill had moved out of the congressman's subcommittee; he was hopeful that the bill would be reported favorably to the House the following week. Though some arm-twisting remained to be done, the Senate passed McCarran's bill on May 9, while the House approved Lea's nine days later. Minor differences in the two bills remained, but the interested parties were confident they could be resolved in conference. On June 1 Hester informed Rowe that the conference proceedings were moving forward smoothly, with both sides eager to reach a final agreement. The House agreed to the conference report on June 11, and the Senate followed suit on June 13. Ten days later, Franklin Roosevelt signed the Civil Aeronautics Act, formally establishing the regulatory foundation that would guide American aviation until deregulation in the late 1970s.[67]

In the end, Roosevelt's efforts were rewarded with a bill that reflected the culmination of his evolving thoughts on civil aviation policy and embodied a significant expansion of federal authority. The Civil Aeronautics Act created a new Civil Aeronautics Authority totally independent of the Commerce Department, Post Office, and ICC. The authority, comprised of a five-member board, including a chairman, vice-chairman, and administrator, held authority over all facets of civil aviation. Unifying control formerly held by the Commerce Department, the Post Office, and the ICC, the new organization was responsible for promoting aviation, fostering air commerce, establishing and maintaining airways, regulating air traffic, issuing certificates of convenience and necessity to air transport operators, setting airmail rates, granting airmail contracts, and determining air transport routes. The act also created a new three-member Air Safety Board that, while housed within the authority, had independent responsibility for accident investigation. Finally, the act removed the prohibition on federal airport development, for the first time allowing federal authorities to oversee and directly fund the construction and expansion of airfields.

The new law represented the culmination of more than twenty years of efforts to define the proper relationship between the government and commercial aviation. Although Roosevelt had entered office without a coherent vision for aviation policy, in the end he acted even more strongly than Hoover had to secure federal control over air transport. His evolving views on federal responsibility ultimately ensured that the new law would grant the federal government greater power to regulate and promote commercial flying than it had ever held before; his support for an independent regulatory body was particularly significant in this regard. The widespread agreement that aviation deserved independent oversight highlighted the rapid maturation of the industry, which was now poised to play an increasingly central role in Americans' lives. The Civil Aeronautics Act represented an unequivocal sign that the federal government was fully committed to the development of US aviation, a commitment that would be richly rewarded in the coming years and decades.

Policy makers, airline executives, and the press readily acknowledged the new law's significance. The June 27 edition of *Newsweek* hailed the act as a "Magna Carta of the Air," drawing attention to the comprehensive nature of the legislation and remarking that the newly created Civil Aeronautics Authority would certainly be "more air-minded" than its forebears. *Time* displayed a similar enthusiasm, in July telling its readers that "the new act was far better for all concerned than anything previously devised for air industry control." Few doubted, it seems, that the passage of the Civil Aeronautics Act represented a seminal moment in the development of American air commerce.[68]

With the question of civil aviation policy largely settled, Roosevelt increasingly turned his attention to the military. By 1938 the president looked at rising tensions in Europe with growing concern. The Munich conference of September of that year did little to assuage FDR's worries as he faced the reality that the United States' military remained ill prepared to defend the nation, let alone undertake a major conflict overseas. Military aviation was no exception; as a result of more than a decade of meager appropriations, the Army Air Corps and the navy struggled to field well-trained and equipped forces. The army's abject failure to fly the mail successfully in 1934 represented only the most visible example of the services' shortcomings.

Roosevelt was well aware of the challenges US military aviation faced; in fact, national defense figured prominently in Roosevelt's engagement with aviation policy from early in his presidency. Roosevelt had exhibited a prescient interest in aviation's military value during his tenure as assistant secretary of the navy, prefacing an ongoing focus on military aviation after he won the White House. He understood that aircraft were likely to play a central role in future wars and viewed the contemporary state of American military flying with concern. Faced with a steady diet of economic crises and a Congress disinclined to release additional funds for military expansion in the midst of the Great Depression, the president nonetheless maintained an emphasis on improving the quality and quantity of US military aviation. Like Herbert Hoover, Roosevelt saw important connections between civil and military flying—the most important being in regard to airframe and engine development, procurement, and pilot training—but FDR engaged the military context much more explicitly.

Ultimately, Roosevelt's commitment to developing military aeronautics represents one of the most consistent aspects of his larger aviation policy.[69]

Roosevelt's active engagement with military aviation began in the aftermath of the Black committee hearings. Spurred to action by the Federal Aviation Commission, in January of 1935 the president wrote the secretary of war to express his concerns regarding the worrying dearth of adequate military airframes. Referencing earlier correspondence in which he had pushed for the purchase of additional planes, FDR made it clear that while he understood that the current shortage reflected a lack of appropriations stretching back well before he took office, he remained frustrated and worried about contemporary circumstances. Lamenting the fact that in the present political and economic climate it would be "unwise" to press for additional monies, Roosevelt nonetheless looked for ways to increase procurement. "It is essential," he wrote, "that more complete plans be laid for increased production." While that goal remained out of reach at the moment, in the short term FDR recommended that "private manufacturers be speeded up on actual contract construction," since manufacturers were taking "far too long" to deliver aircraft. Looking forward, Roosevelt hoped that these measures would streamline the procurement process to the benefit of military and private contractors alike.[70]

The president's concerns about military aviation only grew in subsequent years. By late 1938 Roosevelt could look with pride on his accomplishments with regard to civil aviation, but an increasing clamor from military and civilian experts suggested that the military situation was less than optimistic. In December FDR received the most worrying news yet in the form of a memorandum from Joseph Ames, chairman of the NACA. Ames warned that at that time the United States was "rapidly falling behind, if it has not already fallen behind," European nations with regard to military aircraft production. In Ames's opinion this fact resulted from European governments' willingness to place emphasis on—and funds behind—their air forces. Noting many European nations' "tremendous increase in research facilities" in recent years, the chairman urged Roosevelt to approve funds for similar American facilities—specifically those at Langley Field. Doing so would require at least thirteen million dollars, a figure Ames considered well worth it, considering the dangers of further complacency.[71]

Ames found a sympathetic ear in the president, who in fact was already working along similar lines. FDR had looked on with concern as in the latter half of the 1930s a number of European nations—Germany, most prominently—had established and expanded pilot training programs for students. In Germany these initially took the form of local gliding clubs for high school–aged teens, but by the end of the decade they had transformed into a focused effort to create a deep well of trained pilots. Although the German efforts were purportedly civilian in nature, it took little imagination to perceive their potential military value. Roosevelt—who for the duration of his presidency had argued that virtually all aeronautical development had the potential to bolster national defense—responded by unveiling the Civilian Pilot Training Program (CPTP) in December 1938. Created by the Civil Aeronautics Act, the program provided government-funded pilot training at eleven colleges and universities throughout the country. On December 27 Roosevelt proudly announced that the program was designed to train twenty thousand pilots a year; he also suggested that while the CPTP was a civilian program, the skills were equally applicable to military flying. Ultimately, as a result of Roosevelt's ongoing support, more than four hundred thousand pilots received instruction under CPTP auspices—pilots who formed the backbone of the United States' air forces during World War II.[72]

By the summer of 1939 Roosevelt also began to advocate more aggressively for an expansion of US air forces. As he grew increasingly concerned with the deteriorating political situation in Europe, he turned to Charles Horner, president of the National Aeronautics Association, for assistance in building public support for military aviation. In an August letter FDR emphasized that his ongoing work to secure "great sums to increase the size and effectiveness of our military and naval air forces" lay at the center of his efforts to protect the country. "Few objectives are more important at the present time," FDR wrote, than the "continued progress of our [military] aviation." The president was worried, however, that the public did not share his concern. With the country still laboring under the Depression, a majority of Americans had little interest in European politics or increased military expenditures; Roosevelt hoped that Horner could enlist NAA resources to help sway public opinion. FDR requested that Horner implement an aggressive public relations campaign to educate the American people about aviation's centrality to American security. "If progress is to continue," the president argued, it was vital that the American people come to a "full realization of the importance of these efforts."[73]

After the German invasion of Poland in September 1939, Roosevelt's advocacy found a more receptive national audience. In May 1940 he famously called on Congress to approve funds to build fifty thousand planes a year and dramatically expand pilot training, and he increased his support for military aviation as the United States drew ever closer to involvement in the war. The ultimate success of US air forces in that conflict was due in no small part to Roosevelt's persistent focus on improving and expanding military aeronautics. His efforts in that realm stand as one of the most consistent and effective aspects of his aviation policy, highlighting the president's ongoing commitment to aeronautical development.

By the eve of US intervention in World War II, federal aviation policy had finally come of age. Although efforts to define the federal government's proper relationship to commercial flying stretched back to Herbert Hoover's tenure as commerce secretary, it was Franklin Roosevelt who brought that dream to fruition. Roosevelt's role in promoting the development of American aviation has often been overlooked in light of his apparent mishandling of the airmail scandal and his at times inconsistent focus on aeronautics. Those facts notwithstanding, his involvement with the tumultuous events of 1934, creation of the Federal Aviation Commission, crucial role in securing the passage of the Civil Aeronautics Act, and dedication to promoting military aeronautics signaled his ongoing commitment to the issue. Though he did not publicly express a powerfully coherent vision for aviation's future, as did his predecessor, in the end his accomplishments speak for themselves. Significantly, despite the marked differences between Hoover's and Roosevelt's larger economic philosophies, the two men demonstrated remarkable unanimity in their thinking on aviation. Both recognized aviation's importance to the country's future, consistently worked to promote commercial growth, emphasized the need for federal subsidies, focused on safety, and worked to expand federal regulation, oversight, and promotion. Additionally, both undertook those efforts in the difficult economic environment of the Great Depression, further highlighting their commitment to aeronautical development. Operating in a cultural environment that increasingly recognized aviation's economic value, Roosevelt was ultimately able to realize Hoover's dream of seeing commercial air transport reach maturity. When his signature formally enacted the Civil Aeronautics Act, Roosevelt put in place a policy that was to stand for more than four decades.

Another aspect of Roosevelt's aviation policy, however, remains virtually unknown. The president's dedication to public works resulted in the largest federal expenditures on aviation infrastructure in the nation's history, far eclipsing the efforts of the Bureau of Air Commerce. Through agencies like the Civil Works Administration, Public Works Administration, and Works Progress Administration the federal government spent millions of dollars to build and improve airports throughout the country. Those expenditures resulted in the creation of tremendous new infrastructure and in large part created the conditions for the possibility of the postwar commercial aviation boom. Little acknowledged, that history represents a central aspect of Roosevelt's commitment to promoting the continued development American aviation.

6

Laying Foundations

New Deal Public Works and Aviation Infrastructure

On a cold and blustery day in October of 1937, thousands of men, women, and children from Knoxville, Tennessee, traveled more than ten miles south of the city, their destination an area just north of the town of Maryville that, not long before, had been little more than forest and pastureland. Traffic increased steadily throughout the morning until about noon, by which time all of the local roads were gridlocked. Seven companies of National Guard troops, in addition to the entire motorcycle squad from the Knoxville police department, were required to manage the traffic and crowds. Though subject to hours of traffic snarls and a biting wind, the almost fifteen thousand Tennesseans who eventually arrived evidenced considerable excitement. They were in Blount County to attend the dedication of the new McGhee Tyson Airport.[1]

The festivities began late in the morning, when an experimental plane piloted by army lieutenant and University of Tennessee graduate John Sessums arrived. Shortly thereafter the famous air racer Al Williams spoke to the crowd via a local radio station while flying high over downtown Knoxville. He subsequently brought his bright orange plane low over the field before landing and addressing the crowd in person, calling the airport a "honey of a field" and praising the beauty of the nearby Smoky

Mountains, which, he stated, were "as picturesque as the Alps and the Rockies." Williams was followed by a flight of six National Guard planes, which collectively represented only a preview of the entertainment to come.[2]

By early afternoon the main event began. The Art Davis Air Circus treated the crowd to a smoke screen demonstration, skywriting, a series of parachute jumps, and, most thrillingly, a stuntman leaping from a plane at more than ten thousand feet in a wingsuit. After flying for nearly a mile around the field, the stuntman released his parachute and landed exactly in the middle of the new airport. A new Douglas twin-engine airliner—a plane the likes of which had never before been able to land in Knoxville—set down to the delight of the public. To cap off the demonstrations, Williams performed a series of acrobatic stunts and, in concert with the six National Guard pilots, simulated bombing runs on a "stucco-like" fort erected on the airfield.[3]

Although the crowd was undoubtedly interested primarily in the aerial stunts and celebrities, the day's events also included speeches and the formal dedication of the new field—carried live by local radio station WNOX. A Mr. Dempster, the Knoxville city manager, gave the dedication speech and unveiled a large portrait of McGhee Tyson, for whom the airport was named. Also making speeches were Colonel Harry S. Berry, the state WPA administrator, and Will Cheek, chairman of the State Aeronautics Committee. Highlighting the day's significance for Knoxville and East Tennessee in general, Berry proclaimed that the opening of the new airport "marked the most important date in our transportation history since the first locomotive came through here 80 years ago."[4]

Although Berry may have indulged in a bit of hyperbole, his assertion was not far from the mark. Before the opening of McGhee Tyson Airport, East Tennessee lacked the necessary facilities to allow large, modern airliners like the Boeing 247 and Douglas DC-2 and DC-3 to operate in the region. Similar circumstances were endemic to the nation in the late 1930s, as a new generation of airliners entered service at a time when existing airfield infrastructure proved increasingly obsolete. In Knoxville, as in hundreds of towns and cities around the country, New Deal public works programs provided the solution. McGhee Tyson Airport was made possible by the appropriation of almost six hundred thousand dollars in federal funds by the Works Progress Administration (WPA), a pattern repeated across the country.[5] These programs represent one of the New Deal's enduring legacies and highlight Franklin Roosevelt's commitment to promoting aeronautical progress.

During the Great Depression, Roosevelt's sponsorship of New Deal public works efforts had at least as significant an effect on the development of American aeronautics as did his efforts in the legislative arena. Roosevelt and key advisors like Harold Ickes and Harry Hopkins used New Deal agencies such as the Civil Works Administration (CWA), Public Works Administration (PWA), and WPA to reshape aviation infrastructure around the country, in the process constructing the literal foundations for future commercial growth. Between 1933 and 1939 New Deal public works agencies expended hundreds of millions of dollars on aviation-related projects, in the process building or improving almost one thousand airfields throughout the country. In so doing, Roosevelt and his supporters addressed glaring weaknesses in existing airport infrastructure while simultaneously opening the door to a dramatic expansion of governmental responsibility. Significantly, the disbursement of these monies mandated local buy-in; towns and cities had to submit formal requests for federal funds and provide matching contributions. New Deal public works spending on aviation infrastructure reflected a unique synergy between American air-mindedness and expanding federal efforts to support aeronautical development. Hundreds of towns and cities clamored for access to federal funds to improve their local airports, while New Dealers strove to distribute federal capital to the projects with the greatest potential to advance American aviation. These efforts represent one of the most significant, and certainly one of the most overlooked, elements of Franklin Roosevelt's aviation policy. They mandate a reevaluation of that policy but also highlight the enduring legacy of New Deal public works spending.

From the beginning of his presidency, federally sponsored public works activities represented a key facet of Franklin Roosevelt's New Deal. In an effort to jump-start the moribund economy and create employment opportunities for Americans, Roosevelt and his fellow New Dealers oversaw the creation of a wide-ranging public works agenda. Under the auspices of organizations such as the CWA, PWA, and WPA, the Roosevelt administration expended billions of dollars to support the creation of public buildings, roads, bridges, dams, and airports. According to historian Jason Scott

Smith, between 1933 and 1939 the federal government disbursed more than two-thirds of its emergency expenditures on public works programs, an increase of 1,650 percent over the four-year period preceding the Depression.[6]

Traditionally, historians have dismissed these programs as unsuccessful efforts to end the unemployment crisis and break the Depression's grip. In this view, at best these programs served as well-meaning efforts that failed in their fundamental task; at worst they were corrupt, wasteful "boondoggles" that served to prop up the existing economic order. In recent years scholars such as Jason Scott Smith, Robert Leighninger, and Nick Taylor have sought to reassess public works programs' legacy by drawing attention to their productive capacity. In Smith's words, agencies like the PWA and WPA provided an "extraordinarily successful method of state-sponsored economic development" as they promoted the dual goals of work relief and infrastructure creation while transforming the landscape and redefining government's relationship to the people.[7]

During its tenure the PWA, relying on private contractors and focusing for the most part on large-scale construction projects such as Boulder Dam, disbursed funds in 3,068 of the nation's 3,071 counties. Following its creation in 1935, the WPA provided direct employment while focusing on lighter construction. It was responsible for building seventy-eight thousand bridges, improving almost forty thousand public buildings, building 480 airports, and improving 470 others. The WPA also created a number of subsidiary organizations, such as the Federal Writers' Project and the National Youth Administration. Among other efforts, WPA employees recorded oral histories of surviving former slaves, painted murals around the country, and employed thousands of young people while providing them with job training. These programs created physical reminders of the New Deal's lasting influence on American life and, as Smith suggests, "wrought in concrete and steel a tangible representation of [New Deal] political philosophy."[8]

Aviation-related public works activities offer perhaps the clearest example of these programs' ability to promote economic development. Their efforts addressed glaring weaknesses in contemporary airport infrastructure while opening the door to a dramatic expansion of government responsibility. When Franklin Roosevelt assumed the presidency, the majority of American airports were little more than level grass fields with a windsock, a hangar or two, and possibly a lighted beacon. Although the Commerce Department worked steadily to improve navigation and radio aids for pilots and construct emergency landing fields along major airmail routes in the years after passage of the Air Commerce Act and establishment of the Aeronautics Branch of the Department of Commerce in 1926, by the early 1930s the majority of US airports remained largely unimproved.

This unfortunate situation emerged from the intersection of federal policy, local interests, and economic realities. Federal policy reflected the legacy of Herbert Hoover's vision for American aeronautics. With regard to airports, Hoover emphasized that aviation should adhere to the precedent set by federal shipping policy—the so-called dock concept: the federal government assumed responsibility for constructing and maintaining shipping lanes and harbors, but not piers or docks. Transferring that philosophy to aeronautics, the 1926 Civil Aeronautics Act mandated that the federal government undertake the construction of airways, navigational aids, and emergency landing fields but forbade the government from building, owning, or operating nonmilitary airfields. As a result, federal unwillingness to subsidize airport construction—and indeed federal inability after the passage of the Air Commerce Act—resulted in haphazard development throughout the 1920s and early 1930s.

Further complicating matters, while the Air Commerce Act clearly defined airfields as a local responsibility, it did little to delineate the nature of that local control. As a result, by the mid-1920s a variety of public and private interests—municipalities, private individuals, and private organizations, among others—controlled airports around the country. In fact, the Air Commerce Act largely served to formalize existing practices. In the early 1920s neither the Post Office nor the military had sufficient funds to undertake widespread airfield construction. As a result, they turned to local governments. Emphasizing the value of airports to growing towns and cities, both the Post Office and the military lobbied urban centers to construct airfields, leading to a steady increase in facilities around the country.[9]

Gradually, the increasing standardization of commercial flying driven by federal regulation and technological development increased support for municipal ownership. Advocates for public ownership pointed to the leading role the federal government embraced in licensing, safety regulation, and infrastructure creation, arguing that municipal control should begin where federal control ended. Further, proponents contended that public ownership of airports represented the only way to ensure that all users would be treated fairly, as interested parties worried that private owners might be tempted to sell airport property if a more profitable use presented itself—something public control would protect against. Finally, in many cases airports proved to be unprofitable enterprises, a significant problem for private ownership but less of a concern for local governments that increasingly came to view airfields as a municipal asset: attracting air service, promoting modernization, and serving as a visible example of a town or city's air-mindedness.[10]

As a result, by the mid-1930s the template for America's airports was largely in place. Airfields would serve as public utilities, embracing standardized operating principles and promoting both local and national interests. That template, however, predominantly applied to unimproved fields lacking a majority of the services crucial to modern commercial operations.

Airports' lack of improvement became an increasingly acute problem as commercial operations matured in the early 1930s. As passenger services expanded and newer, larger, and faster aircraft came into service, grass fields and a lack of adequate terminal space proved increasingly inadequate to meet the growing needs of airlines and passengers alike. As early as 1930, scholars began to call attention to the unacceptable state of America's airfields. Writing in the *Annals of the American Academy of Political and Social Science*, Austin MacDonald emphasized that a majority of American airports "fall considerably short of any reasonable standard of adequacy." Most lacked adequate lighting, drainage, hangers, repair facilities, and transport links to their associated population centers. Many, in fact, were "only one or two stages removed from cow pastures."[11] By the time Franklin Roosevelt assumed the presidency, it had become abundantly clear that virtually all of America's airports would need significant improvements to handle growing passenger traffic and larger, heavier aircraft. The weight and speed of new aircraft like the Boeing 247 and Douglas DC-3 necessitated paved, reinforced runways that would not become waterlogged after heavy rains or throw up clouds of dust during droughts. Airlines needed larger hangars for these planes, while growing passenger traffic mandated larger terminals and more organized ticketing and boarding procedures. Additionally, as radio, navigation, and landing aids continued to improve, airports found themselves needing ever more infrastructure to stay abreast of current developments. In short, the rapid development of commercial aviation and the increasing importance of passenger operations mandated that airports rapidly improve their facilities or risk missing out on airline service.

Unfortunately, the financial upheaval brought on by the Great Depression meant that at the time when municipal governments had the greatest need to fund airport improvements, they were the least able to do so. The economic downturn hamstrung municipalities unable to fund basic governmental services, to say nothing of paved runways, airport perimeter lighting, and new terminal buildings. As a result, airport development lagged far behind the rapid gains aircraft manufacturers and airlines made during the same period. By the mid-1930s hundreds of American towns and cities found their ability to provide commercial service limited by obsolete airports, while hundreds of others lacked fields at all.

This context set the stage for the tremendous gains New Deal public works programs brought to American airports. FDR's willingness to abandon the dock concept—and its attendant limitations on federal aid—signaled a new federal willingness to support desperately needed infrastructure development. While the strictures imposed by the Air Commerce Act limited public works agencies' freedom of action—for example, the WPA expended tremendous funds to pay for labor but could not appropriate monies for materials—these agencies nonetheless wrought fundamental changes to American airport infrastructure.

New Deal agencies—especially the WPA's Airways and Airports Division—operated in close collaboration with municipalities to maximize the utility of federal investment. Between 1933 and 1939 federal officials focused on funding aviation-related projects that offered the maximum benefit to both local communities and the nation at large. Localities had to apply for federal dollars and substantiate the utility of the proposed work. WPA administrators carefully weighed applications and demonstrated a willingness to reject trivial or overbudgeted requests. Public works funding thus provided a vital resource for communities unable to undertake airport improvements on their own—a crucial resource in the midst of the Depression. Further, the physical legacy of WPA investment highlights the gains New Deal public works brought to American aviation during a period of rapid aeronautical development, challenging interpretations of these programs as mere make-work endeavors.

New Deal public works' aviation-related activities must be seen as integral to Franklin Roosevelt's aviation policy and a fundamental element of the New Deal's legacy. Public works projects modernized America's airports and created the literal foundation for the postwar boom in commercial aviation. Through airport expansion—the construction of paved runways, new terminals, new and larger hangars, and paved ramps and the installation of perimeter lighting, runway lighting, and spotlights—and the construction of entirely new airports, these agencies put thousands of Americans to work while fashioning the physical foundations that made possible widespread commercial passenger service in large, modern airliners. These agencies' actions serve as concrete evidence of the president's lasting commitment to promoting American aeronautical development.

From the outset, public works formed a central element of Franklin Roosevelt's aggressive New Deal political agenda. Knowing even before his election that his response to the social and economic conditions created by the Depression would define the early years of his presidency, Roosevelt moved quickly to enact a dynamic legislative program. That program altered radically the relationship between the American government and the people, in the process redefining government's responsibility to its citizens. Within that larger context, public works formed a key element of Roosevelt's strategy to mitigate the harshest effects of the Depression. According to Jason Scott Smith, programs such as the PWA and WPA "emerged at the intersection of economic development and unemployment," promoting the dual goals of work relief and infrastructure creation.[12] In so doing, they built on a tradition of using government-funded building programs to allay high levels of unemployment stretching back to the early nineteenth century.

Upon assuming the presidency, Roosevelt immediately moved to increase public works expenditures. His efforts began with the passage of the National Industrial Recovery Act (NIRA) in June of 1933. Title II of the NIRA provided for the creation of the PWA with an appropriation of $3.3 billion. Those monies—the equivalent of almost $60 billion today—represented almost 6 percent of the US gross domestic product that year and more than 165 percent of the government's revenues. Roosevelt and his aides—notably Harold Ickes, secretary of the interior and subsequent director of the PWA, and Francis Perkins, secretary of labor—hoped that the funds would be sufficient to relieve unemployment while simultaneously improving the nation's infrastructure.[13]

In a July 1933 press release, Ickes provided philosophical justification for the president's public works agenda, arguing that the goal of the newly announced program was "to employ as much labor as possible in order to speed up the return of prosperity." To that end he argued that federal employment on public works projects would benefit all of society, not merely those receiving a government check. Ickes suggested that "by employing as many people as possible at a living wage," federal money would increase purchasing power, stimulate commerce, and result in "an ascending economic spiral."[14]

For Ickes, the goal of creating economic growth mandated that the PWA expend funds only on projects with a demonstrable value beyond the immediate employment they might offer—that is, projects that "contribute something of value to the community and not merely be a makeshift to supply work." In a speech to the American Conference of Mayors in September 1933, Ickes expanded on that theme, suggesting that PWA programs offered "the greatest opportunity for municipal improvements in the history of the country." These statements succinctly encapsulate the dual goals of New Deal public works. Although Ickes later received criticism for his parsimonious disbursement of PWA funds, his early articulation of Roosevelt's agenda clearly established the ideological foundation for these New Deal programs.[15]

New Deal public works activities soon expanded far beyond the initial dictates of the NIRA. The preliminary PWA appropriation formed the beginning of what ultimately became a series of massive New Deal expenditures on public works. In 1935 Roosevelt created the WPA with an initial appropriation of $4.88 billion, and both the PWA and the WPA received additional funds during their respective tenures. Roosevelt also advocated for the creation of the CWA and the Civilian Conservation Corps, though these programs proved far less costly—and thus exerted less influence—than either the PWA or WPA.[16] Collectively, these programs signaled the ongoing centrality of public works to Roosevelt's New Deal. The agencies disbursed billions of taxpayer dollars to stimulate employment and improve the American landscape. Projects such as the Hoover Dam, the Appalachian Trail, roads, bridges, airports, public buildings, and countless other improvements came to fruition under the auspices of New Deal public works. Admittedly, these programs did not pull the United States out of the Depression. They did, however, fundamentally change the American landscape and served to redefine the relationship between the American government and the people. As such, public works must be seen as an integral element of Roosevelt's New Deal agenda—not merely as an attempt to promote employment, but as an effort to promote the creation of valuable infrastructure.

Nowhere were those dual goals more apparent than in New Deal efforts to construct airports and other aviation-related infrastructure. Largely through the efforts of the WPA's Airways and Airports Division—which funded improvement programs for virtually every American airport—public works expenditures revolutionized the American air transport network, laying the groundwork for the modern air commerce system and creating the conditions for the possibility of dynamic growth in the years after World War II. These efforts stand as a preeminent example of Roosevelt's efforts to support the growth of American commercial aviation and highlight his willingness to embrace a dynamic model of economic development.

Even before the WPA's establishment in 1935, members of the Roosevelt administration identified airports as sites that would benefit from public works expenditures. As early as 1933 the CWA embarked on an ambitious program to improve airports around the country. In an October 1934 memo, CWA director Harry Hopkins reflected on the goals of that effort. Hopkins stated that in the fall of 1933 the CWA airport program embraced improvement efforts "on a very elaborate and extensive scale." The program invited communities to acquire land for the creation of new facilities or improvement of existing ones in return for federal support for construction. More than two thousand did so, a figure almost equal to the number of the country's recognized airports at the start of the program. CWA efforts, like those of their WPA successors, mandated local buy-in, basing appropriations on communities' willingness and ability to contribute to the process. The immediate positive response suggested widespread public support for aeronautical development and highlights the collaborative nature of New Deal public works policy with regard to aviation. In fact, the CWA effort appears to have created the template that guided subsequent WPA activities.[17]

For the duration of the airport program, CWA administrators worked closely with the Commerce Department to ascertain the most beneficial way to disburse federal funds. Hopkins related that CWA administrators collaborated with the BAC on a study "to determine a plan likely to give the best results from an aviation standpoint considering the needs and requirements of our national defense branches, the probable extension of commercial air transport, and the necessity for emergency facilities." The result of that study was a renewed federal focus on airport safety, clearly reflected in the CWA request that participating communities confine expenditures to projects that "would result in the preparation of the best possible landing fields" designed to "directly add to the safety of commercial air transport."[18]

Though it lasted less than six months, the CWA program was remarkably successful. During its tenure the CWA disbursed more than $9 million to fund two thousand aviation projects, half of which achieved completion. Although this fell short of Commerce Department officials' desire to construct an airport in every American population center with more than five thousand residents, in Hopkins's opinion the CWA effort "resulted in the greatest contribution to the safety and convenience of air transport during the history of its development." The program also demonstrated communities' and states' enthusiastic support for—and willingness to play an active role in—aviation infrastructure development. So enthusiastic were they, in fact, that as the program wound down, the *New York Times* reported that administration officials found themselves overwhelmed with local and state protests over the program's termination. While the CWA was unable to redress all—or even most—of the United States' aviation infrastructure deficiencies, the airport program provided evidence that public works could bring material benefit to airports; moreover, its effectiveness established a template that Hopkins would use moving forward.[19]

The influence of the short-lived CWA program soon spread far beyond Hopkins's office. In late 1934 reference to that program appeared in testimony before Roosevelt's Federal Aviation Commission. John Geisse, head of the BAC's Development Section, spoke at length about the CWA program's value while emphasizing the need to continue infrastructure improvements. Geisse's opinions echoed the conclusions of other federal officials, including Secretary of Commerce Daniel Roper, but Geisse's responsibilities in the BAC provided him with a privileged position from which to comment on the intersection of public works and aeronautics. Tellingly, Geisse's testimony provided further justification for federal action while prefacing the expansion of Roosevelt's aviation-related public works efforts in the coming years.

Geisse emphasized the material benefit public works expenditures could bring to communities, the nation, and the aviation industry. Arguing that federal expenditures were "in the interests of every man, woman and child in the United States," he suggested that public works projects had value both "as a stimulus to recovery and as an aid to national defense." Geisse suggested that the CWA program should serve as a template, emphasizing the value of cooperation between federal and local government.

Like Hopkins, Geisse highlighted the immediate and enthusiastic local response to CWA efforts, relating that his office "was absolutely swamped with requests for assistance." In Geisse's opinion, had the program continued it would have resulted in every American community of substance having its own airport.[20]

Unfortunately, the CWA program ended before that goal could be realized. As a result, Geisse focused on the pressing need for additional airfield construction. He reported that more than one thousand American cities with populations of five thousand or more lacked landing facilities, in addition to more than fifteen thousand communities with populations under five thousand. More worryingly, he reported that the majority of airports in America's larger cities were "most inaccessible." For Geisse, public works represented the best way to address the urgent need for improved aviation infrastructure during difficult economic times. Federal expenditures would "accomplish much in eliminating this unfortunate condition," he testified, and "permit the airplane to attain the utility of which it is capable."[21]

Geisse also emphasized the benefits that expanded public works expenditures on aviation could offer the nation at large. While he argued that public works projects would provide immediate material benefit to the aviation industry and national defense, he also suggested that federal spending on aviation had great potential to stimulate economic development. Aviation-related expenditures, he claimed, had the potential to encourage employment far more than spending on public parks, public buildings, and the like. Geisse reported that "airplane manufacturers . . . have been able to make sales in the vicinity of the C.W.A. airport projects that they could not possibly have made without this activity." That "induced expenditure" for new aircraft created employment opportunities "additional to [those] occasioned directly and indirectly by the Federal expenditure." Public works spending on aviation infrastructure thus had the potential to sustain an entire industry while simultaneously furthering larger goals.[22]

Indeed, for Geisse, federal support for aeronautics represented a foundational investment in America's future—specifically an avenue through which the government could promote national development. Reminding the Federal Aviation Commission that their mission was to concern themselves "with the future of aviation, not the present," Geisse called upon commission members to "consider the utility of the airplane not as it is today but rather what it may reasonably expect to become five or ten years hence." In his estimation "the provision of landing facilities at close intervals. . . together with the development of safer and more economical airplanes will have a profound effect on our inclination to purchase an airplane." Geisse thus envisioned a truly air-minded nation, a nation with a dense network of commercial air transport, and a nation in which a significant minority of citizens actually owned a plane.[23]

Geisse's testimony demonstrates an acute understanding of the ramifications of aviation-related public works beyond airport boundaries. While highlighting these projects' immediate material benefits, he focused just as strongly on how an ongoing public works agenda had the potential to revolutionize American life. Like Hopkins, Geisse saw public works not merely in terms of immediate employment, but rather in terms of what that employment could create. His identification of the CWA program's material value and the potential of similar projects to revolutionize American aviation stands as a testament to the expanding influence of public works ideology—specifically, the central place of public works in plans for aeronautical development.

Federal activities accelerated dramatically following Roosevelt's creation of the WPA in the spring of 1935. Roosevelt tasked the WPA with providing direct employment—largely to unskilled laborers—on building projects around the country. Unlike the PWA, which operated through private contractors, the WPA focused on maximizing the number of workers on government payrolls, leading many observers to criticize Hopkins and other WPA administrators for promoting make-work projects emphasizing employment over productivity.[24] The WPA's ability to foster valuable infrastructure creation and promote economic development, however, challenges that conclusion, particularly with regard to aviation-related expenditures.

From the outset, WPA activities reflected the influence of the CWA airport program that preceded it even as the new organization embraced a more expansive agenda. Administration officials began work with the explicit objective of realizing the unfulfilled goals the CWA and Aeronautics Branch had identified two years earlier. The WPA also established a close working relationship with the BAC that helped guide its aeronautical efforts moving forward. In early October 1935 the BAC's director, Eugene Vidal, appointed seven regional and thirteen district supervisors to oversee what the *New York Times* dubbed the WPA's "airport program." Vidal tasked those officials—all experienced engineers and pilots—with providing WPA state administrators technical advice, evaluating aviation-related proposals, and aiding in ongoing development programs. At the national level, WPA administrators used BAC airport guidelines as a basis for project evaluation and forwarded all aviation-related requests to the board for technical review before engaging in a "stringent" internal engineering review. This relationship continued to inform WPA activities as they expanded, ensuring the quality and relevance of WPA aeronautics projects.[25]

The WPA's airport program hit the ground running, with expenditures immediately dwarfing those of the CWA. In September 1935, Airways and Airports Division technical supervisor L. L. Odell reported that as of September 14 the WPA had approved work on 459 projects, encompassing total federal appropriations of $57.5 million. That figure represented more than 600 percent of total CWA expenditures for airport construction, giving a sense of the scale of WPA efforts, which ultimately totaled more than $400 million. Odell, however, provided those figures to demonstrate how far short appropriations fell of the goals set by the BAC. Odell related that the CWA/BAC program had identified 1,229 first-priority work projects, necessitating the allocation of $80.4 million in federal funds. He suggested, however, that the BAC had undervalued the cost of many of those ventures. In Odell's opinion, the completion of all 1,229 projects would require the disbursement of $76.5 million above and beyond BAC estimates. Despite the enormity of this sum, Odell "respectfully suggested that WPA funds in the total amount . . . be earmarked for allocation to Airway and Airport work" in order to "meet the requirements of the Bureau of Air Commerce program."[26]

By the spring of 1936, WPA administrators had accepted that they would be unable to fully realize the goals established by the BAC program. The scope of that program and the limitations on WPA appropriations imposed by the agency's mandate to promote employment and inability to pay for skilled labor and materials confirmed that the WPA could not serve as the BAC's construction arm. Many proposed projects emerged from localities with little or no need for additional employment, for instance, and others necessitated materials, rather than labor, for completion. Nonetheless, the Airways and Airports Division staff maintained a clear focus on the larger goal of aeronautical development. According to a WPA press release, as of February 15 the agency had released funds for 410 airport and airway projects. Those projects, 325 of which were already under construction, would employ fifty thousand men and involved funds totaling $21,090,965. The same document also provided an update on the number of Washington-approved aviation-related projects; to date, Roosevelt had signed off on more than 1,400, encompassing total allocations of $110,172,828.[27]

According to Hopkins, those approvals reflected a concerted effort by WPA administrators to work with other federal agencies to maximize the value of WPA expenditures. The director explained, "The WPA airways and airports program illustrates the co-ordinated effort required in the creation of works of national value through employment of labor formerly on relief." WPA staff, he related, worked closely with other federal agencies, including the Departments of Treasury, War, Navy, Commerce, and the Post Office to maximize the value of WPA public works. The Airways and Airports Division, moreover, continued to work in concert with the BAC to ensure the utility of aeronautical projects. "Arrangement has been made with . . . Commerce," Hopkins emphasized, "for the inspection of all WPA airway and airport projects as to their aeronautical fitness."[28]

Speaking at a BAC-sponsored National Airport Conference almost two years later, WPA chief engineer F. C. Harrington expanded on Hopkins's point. Addressing representatives from the Aeronautical Chamber of Commerce, Air Transport Association, Airline Pilots Association, National Aeronautic Association, Treasury Department, US Conference of Mayors, and War Department, Harrington emphasized that the WPA continued to do its utmost to fund only the most worthwhile aviation infrastructure projects. While granting that the WPA's lack of ability to expend funds on materials or skilled labor limited the administration's activities, Harrington nonetheless argued that "within this limitation the Works Progress Administration endeavors to produce a maximum in permanent public improvements which are beneficial to the local communities and to the nation as a whole." Ultimately, the WPA chief engineer concluded that he and other senior WPA administrators regarded the "airport program . . . as perhaps the most worth while program that we have carried out."[29]

Harrington's, Hopkins's, and Odell's focus on funding meaningful projects clearly challenges the WPA's make-work stereotype. As had the CWA, the Airways and Airports Division took its lead from the BAC, the government agency with direct responsibility over aeronautics. That relationship suggests that the WPA formed a part of a larger governmental effort to promote the continued development of American flying. Although the strictures imposed by the WPA's enabling legislation made it impossible to achieve all of the BAC's goals, WPA administrators did the best they could within those limits.

Both the CWA and WPA airport building programs highlight the Roosevelt administration's abandonment of the "dock" concept. Using public works funds for airport construction flew in the face of Hoover's view that governmental responsibility should end at the airport boundary. Although this new federal willingness to fund aviation-related construction certainly had its roots in the dire economic conditions of the 1930s, it remains significant that Roosevelt and Hopkins did not hesitate to allocate federal funds for airport construction. In fact, this move may have precipitated a legislative change. The Civil Aeronautics Act subsequently removed proscriptions on federal funding for airports. The bill included a proviso authorizing an immediate federal survey of the nation's airports and established a federal airport aid program to support airfield development with an initial appropriation of $12,000,000, and subsequently allowed the government to take the lead in funding a national air traffic control system and encouraging an ongoing federal push for airfield improvement.[30]

Roosevelt's embrace of expanded federal activism, moreover, reinforced the central role public works programs would play in federal efforts. When the Civil Aeronautics Authority—created by the Civil Aeronautics Act—completed its airport survey and presented a proposal for a national airport program to Congress in the spring of 1939, authority officials suggested that a substantial percentage of the necessary funds come from WPA coffers. The WPA also made key contributions to national defense efforts between 1940 and 1943. Working closely with the army and navy, WPA officials oversaw a wide-ranging effort to construct strategic airfields that played an important role in wartime air transport. These contributions once again highlight New Deal agencies' central place in the narrative of American aviation infrastructure development as they exemplified the changing federal relationship with aeronautics.[31]

As state administrators released funds on more and more projects, both WPA employees and the American public began to appreciate the gains the Airways and Airports Division brought US towns and cities. In the fall of 1937 the WPA's Washington office sent a party of observers on a three-week airport inspection trip around the country, eventually encompassing more than eleven thousand miles of travel and visits to thirty states. Designed to evaluate the work WPA activities had accomplished to date, members' interactions with local officials and the general public offer insight into Americans' opinions of that work. A. B. McMullen, chief of the administration's Airport Section Safety and Planning Division, reported that he "found the highest praise for the work the WPA has done, particularly on airports." That praise, however, did not necessarily reflect comprehensive knowledge of WPA activities. W. Sumpter Smith, the WPA's principal aeronautical engineer, wrote that he "was surprised at the fact . . . that the great majority of the local businessmen . . . had practically no idea of the actual workings of the WPA . . . or just what they were actually accomplishing." Despite that ignorance, Smith indicated that "these businessmen were amazed to know the extent of actual worthwhile permanent physical facilities" being constructed with WPA funds.[32]

Public appreciation for WPA projects sprung in large part from Americans' support for aeronautical development. McMullen wrote that his most significant impression from the trip "was the keen interest in aviation demonstrated by the public officials, business men and influential citizens wherever we went." The public clearly understood the government's central role in development efforts. "In all sections of the country," McMullen related, Americans highlighted the "necessity for a well planned long-term program of airport and airway development with the Federal Government," specifically, "a nationwide system of airports adequate to permit the continual growth and safe operation of air transportation in the United States." Media reports and public actions confirm Americans' thoroughgoing interest in development. Reporting on the WPA's "big airport program," the *New York Times* pointed to "the large volume of projects sponsored by public bodies throughout the country" as powerful evidence of Americans' "widespread interest in aviation."[33]

The *Times* and papers throughout the country provided readers with a steady stream of articles lauding airport construction; in Knoxville, Tennessee, the *News Sentinel* published more than thirteen hundred pieces on airports and related topics between 1927 and 1938. In that city WPA workers had to erect a fence around ongoing airport construction to hold back the thousands of locals flocking to see the new field, and the city council found itself forced to open the new terminal building on Sundays to satisfy citizens' desire to tour the facility. In Knoxville and elsewhere, tens—and in large cities, hundreds—of thousands flocked to airport dedication ceremonies featuring addresses from leading local and state dignitaries. These examples provide telling evidence of contemporary American "air-mindedness" and emphasize local governments' and the American public's shared hopes for continued development.[34]

Americans' continued passion for aviation is not surprising, but it is significant. By the late 1930s the pioneering days of flying were, for the most part, in the past. While aerial triumphs such as Lindbergh's trans-Atlantic flight dominated the public consciousness in the late 1920s, the passage of a decade witnessed the maturation of the industry and, consequently, the loss of much of the danger and glamour associated with flying. Those circumstances notwithstanding, however, the American public maintained a keen interest in aeronautical development. McMullen's observations confirm that the "winged gospel" was still alive and well in many parts of the country, in spite of eight years of economic misfortune. That fact certainly bolstered the Airways and Airports Division's popularity, but McMullen's report also points to a more focused interest in the continued development of American aviation. Although public works represented only one part of a much larger edifice, Americans could point with pride to the improvements the WPA wrought. In the context of the Depression, these gains offered hope for the future far beyond the immediate employment created by the projects.

While WPA administrators exhibited pride in the accomplishments of public works programs, they also recognized the continued need for federal guidance and funding. McMullen wrote that as a result of WPA actions, "airport construction has advanced at least 15 years." In his judgment, "present day transport planes could not be economically operated had it not been for the new airports constructed and the improvements and enlargements made on existing airports by . . . Work Relief agencies." Progress to date, however, merely emphasized the need for additional federal action. US airports, McMullen reported, "are still far behind the development of the airplane and the air transport requirements of [the present day]."[35] New aircraft like the DC-3 and the continued development of radio communications and air traffic control accelerated the rate of change and highlighted the need for even faster infrastructure construction to keep pace.

For both McMullen and Smith, that context dictated the need for a coherent development plan for US airports. In his report Smith emphasized the "absolute necessity" of "a national plan for the logical development of a Federal Airways System." Such a plan, he argued, demanded a construction program to expand airport infrastructure and create uniform standards and layouts for airports and other ground-based facilities. He explained that such a program would require constructing and/or improving more than one thousand airports above and beyond those already benefiting from WPA investment, a task he considered the baseline requirement for "an adequate national airways system [able] to accommodate flying equipment already in use or actually under construction." Smith estimated that a plan of that magnitude would cost more than three hundred million dollars.[36]

McMullen also supported an expanded program of infrastructure development, though he did not articulate a plan as specific as Smith's. In his letter McMullen emphasized the need to "make a modern airport usable 24 hours a day, 12 months a year." That necessity, coupled with the rapid enlargement of transport aircraft, made paving, lighting, and other associated infrastructure "absolutely necessary" for the successful operation of flying fields. McMullen estimated the cost of his program at 285 million dollars—strikingly close to Smith's valuation.[37]

Unfortunately, these types of comprehensive development programs lay outside the WPA's purview, a fact both men conceded. McMullen acknowledged that WPA efforts would achieve more lasting results "if more funds were available for materials and equipment," but the Safety and Planning Section chief had no illusions about the WPA's ability to meet those needs. McMullen recognized that the WPA's mission inherently limited appropriations for purposes other than employment, undermining his desire to see the agency expand its aviation-related activities. Bearing those limitations in mind, McMullen nonetheless remained focused on using federal monies to realize a mature air transport system, recommending "an annual appropriation for airport construction be made available to and administered by some Federal agency."[38]

Smith expressed an even clearer understanding of the limitations imposed by work relief programs. "It is obvious," he wrote, "that a relief program should be concerned primarily with work only at those locations where needy unemployed persons are eligible for relief. . . . Funds available for non-labor purposes will very likely be inadequate for any high-type construction." From these facts Smith drew the obvious conclusion, recording, "I do not believe it practicable for a relief organization, such as the WPA, to carry out a nation-wide airport program if preference is to be given to the necessity for aviation facilities rather than to the requirement for relief." Like McMullen, he suggested the need for a federal airport program administered by "some federal agency," within which the WPA would operate as a source of labor where conditions permitted.[39]

Far from overseeing a make-work program, both Smith and McMullen were frustrated by the WPA's inability to bring plans for comprehensive improvements in aviation infrastructure to fruition. At the same time, however, both men clearly recognized that the WPA's primary responsibility was to provide work relief, not promote a national airways program. Balancing these two goals, Smith and McMullen highlighted the progress WPA funds had brought about to date and the potential for further gains while emphasizing the need for a different federal agency to take the lead in promoting a national program of airway development.

Significantly, both men understood WPA airways construction as one aspect of a larger effort to develop American aeronautics. Their depictions of local leaders' enthusiasm only furthered the view that, at least with regard to the WPA's aviation-related work, all concerned parties embraced public works not only for their contributions to local employment, but also as a way to promote aeronautical progress. As such, it appears that public works had the potential to fulfill the dual goals of putting Americans to work while offering an avenue for valuable infrastructure improvements. Reflecting on the lengthy inspection trip, McMullen summarized Airways and Airports Division activities to date. "In general," he wrote, "the airport program conducted by the WPA is popular throughout the United States and the permanent improvements made on airports, which are the foundation of all aviation, have done a great deal to counteract or silence critics of the Works Progress."[40] Though not without difficulties, from McMullen's perspective, at least, WPA actions were a rousing success.

Observing WPA activities at the local level largely confirms McMullen's assessment. The WPA's wide-ranging aviation activities transformed US airports and related infrastructure. While airport construction lay at the heart of the Airways and Airports Division's mission, WPA monies funded everything from a campaign to paint navigational information on prominent rooftops to new weather forecasting models. Local governments, business leaders, and the public at large demonstrated overwhelming support for these activities, viewing both the jobs WPA projects brought and the resulting infrastructure as key facets of local and regional economic development. The WPA's contributions to cities such as Chicago, Knoxville, Newark, San Diego, and Saint Louis, moreover, confirm the Airways and Airports Division's focus on funding projects of value.

In Chicago, local and civic leaders looked to the WPA to help fund an aggressive airport expansion project. In 1936 the inadequacy of the city's existing field prompted Edgar Gorrell, president of the Air Transport Association of America, to warn the city that airlines would be forced to "cut Chicago off their main travel lines" barring significant improvements. In response, in 1937 Chicago applied to the WPA for more than $2.4 million to expand the municipal airfield. Chicago subsequently requested additional funds to construct a light lane for an instrument approach system. These projects employed more than four thousand, achieving completion by the fall of 1939 and, according to Mayor Edward Kelley, creating "one of the finest [airports] in the country devoted to commercial purposes."[41]

Like Chicago, Newark applied to the WPA for funds to improve an already active municipal airport—the busiest airport in the United States in the prewar era. By the mid-1930s Newark desperately needed improvements to maintain its level of service. While Newark city officials had a history of using public works monies to improve the airport even before the WPA's establishment in 1935—the city received more than one million dollars from the PWA to build a new terminal building in 1934—they hoped that the WPA would fund a raft of improvements. Ultimately, Newark applied for almost four million dollars in WPA monies to fund airport expansion and construct new hangars. With total expenditures rising to more than five million dollars, the Newark project was a qualified success. Although the construction improved the airport's ability to accommodate the increasing demands of planes and passengers, in the end the construction of LaGuardia Field in New York—completed in October 1939 and largely funded by WPA grants—signaled the beginning of the end for Newark's preeminence in the New York area.[42]

WPA work in San Diego and Saint Louis reveals a similar pattern. Lindbergh Field served both the city of San Diego and the military in the vicinity with land- and sea-based facilities. Between September 1937 and January 1939 the city applied for almost $600,000 in WPA funds to elongate and pave runways, improve drainage, construct a new wharf for seaplanes, and build several new hangars. Thanks to that construction, Lindbergh Field served as an important wartime transport center, offering facilities for ground-based planes and seaplanes and addressing both civilian and military needs. In Saint Louis, public works funded much more modest improvements to Lambert Field. An appropriation of slightly less than $110,000 funded runway extension and drainage, and additional requests financed a new hangar and radio towers.[43]

The WPA also embraced a number of nonairport projects. In California the WPA financed an air marking program. State officials applied for funds to paint "508 roof markers in 508 towns as an aid to air navigation." The *San Diego Evening Tribune* reported that ten-foot-high directional signs, designed to make air travel safer, would be painted on barns, factories, and mountains. Quaint by modern standards, this project formed a valuable safety aid for both private and commercial pilots and expanded a program initiated by the Commerce Department more than ten years earlier. The WPA weather bureau also engaged in an ambitious five-year-long weather study designed to help meteorologists accurately forecast conditions in the upper atmosphere. WPA employees took hourly surface readings at 260 airports around the country over a five-year period and used balloons to measure high-level air currents at 120 sites. The study, the *New York Times* reported, was the "only one of its type in the United States," representing tremendous value for commercial flying and national defense.[44]

Beyond providing insight into the material benefits these projects encompassed, examining the mechanics of Airways and Airports Division activities reveals the dynamics shaping WPA actions. Most prominently, WPA engagement at the local and regional levels confirms the close working relationship between the administration and the BAC and both organizations' focus on creating valuable infrastructure. In 1937 A. B. McMullen wrote Earl C. Popp, the BAC's western regional supervisor, in reference to San Diego's application for WPA funds. McMullen noted that while his superiors in the administration's Project Control Division supported San Diego's application, they awaited BAC review and approval as a precondition to any release of funds. Clarifying his instructions to Popp, McMullen emphasized that his superiors required "complete working plans be prepared and submitted to and approved by the Bureau of Air Commerce and the Chief Regional Engineer" before the WPA state administrator authorized any operations. In Chicago the WPA's Engineering Division recommended the approval of that city's application for more than $2.4 million in federal funds, "subject to approval of plans and specifications by the Bureau of Air

Commerce and the Regional Engineer–WPA." Subsequently, the regional engineer raised concerns about the proposed work, forcing local authorities to modify their proposal until it met with WPA and BAC approval.[45]

WPA and BAC administrators often tabled or rejected wasteful or unnecessary applications outright. Chicago's application for $8.5 million to fund a new island airport received close scrutiny, as WPA administrator Harry Goldberg expressed concern that the project did not accord with administration goals. Goldberg highlighted the fact that "other airports proposed in the same general location" would offer similar benefits "for a smaller or no expenditure of government money," concluding that Chicago's plan ran "counter to the provision of the spirit and provisions of the Work Relief Act." He also emphasized the central role the BAC played in the decision, reminding his superiors that "final decisions rest first, upon the Department [*sic*] of Air Commerce."[46]

Even more striking are WPA and BAC assessments of several Saint Louis proposals. Correspondence between airport engineer W. M. Aldous and John Wynne, chief of the bureau's Airport Section, shows that Saint Louis had a history of presenting hastily prepared and inadequately researched proposals—a fact the bureau did not look well upon. Late in 1936 Aldous reported that the WPA had rejected a September 1935 proposal to reconstruct the banks of a creek and that approved proposals from the summer and fall of 1936 were far over budget. In reference to an October 1936 proposal, Aldous wrote, "It is just as well . . . that it was rejected as the quantities [of materials] involved are sheerest guesswork." Summing up Saint Louis's efforts to secure public works appropriations to date, he concluded that the city's proposals were "classified as purely relief . . . the estimates as submitted on all past projects represented just guesses." The engineer therefore recommended that the WPA allocate the funds for "desirable work" rather than the make-work projects Saint Louis proposed. Aldous's concerns, however, did not result in significant change to Saint Louis officials' behavior. In 1939 B. M. Harloe, WPA chief engineer, warned the Missouri state WPA administrator that city officials needed to submit plans for "suitable public projects representing permanent improvements," not merely make-work ventures. Harloe emphasized that the WPA "may not properly recommend the approval of applications which require disproportionate expenditures of Federal funds . . . for work whose permanent value is not commensurate with the expenditures required."[47]

Coordination between the WPA and BAC also resulted in more constructive outcomes. In Newark the bureau pushed the WPA to undertake additional construction with the goal of improving safety. Writing to WPA assistant administrator F. C. Harrington, John Wynne noted that "the Department of Commerce has been trying for some time to interest the City of Newark in installing . . . [a] new airway traffic control unit." According to Wynne, Newark had been unwilling to pay for the project, and, as a result, Wynne hoped Harrington would include it "in the present enormous investment plan now going on at Newark Airport." Highlighting the significance of the air traffic control unit, Wynne argued, "From a safety viewpoint, the Department of Commerce is more interested in the unit than any item of improvement for the new airport."[48]

The WPA's focus on work relief did have the potential to restrict administration activities. In Newark, WPA-funded construction on a hangar stalled when engineers realized that work on the building's large sliding doors could not be completed with the existing workforce. Fred Childs, chief engineer for the WPA state division of operations, wrote that completing the hangar necessitated "skilled craftsmen be engaged to perform special construction work." He suggested that "it would be most desirable . . . to carefully consider the practicability of having all special work performed under private contracts."[49] That, of course, would mean that funds for such contracts would not come from WPA appropriations, forcing the city to pay for them itself or look to another government agency such as the PWA.

In some cases, local funding limitations restricted WPA activities. Because the WPA did not provide funds for materials, that responsibility fell upon local communities. Although theoretically the WPA's procurement of local matching funds would provide for necessary materials and, if necessary, skilled labor, in reality those strictures could limit WPA actions. Additionally, its focus on work relief meant that the administration could embark only on work in areas containing sufficient numbers of needy workers. This precluded the administration from undertaking important projects in sparsely populated areas or areas with low unemployment.

The WPA's inability to undertake construction on private land could also limit and disrupt operations. Chicago struggled with that stricture during a 1937 airport expansion program that aimed to double the size of its municipal field. As part of that effort, the city purchased a large tract of land from the Chicago and Western Indiana Railroad. Unfortunately, the railroad maintained a right-of-way for tracks bisecting the enlarged airport property. That strip of private property prevented WPA workers from extending two runways, threatening to undermine the entire project. Eventually the city reached a compromise, acquiring a right-of-way for the railroad around the new field at an estimated cost of more than eight hundred thousand dollars to be borne by the city.[50] Although not a common barrier to airport improvements nationally, this issue, like those above, demonstrates the sometimes difficult nature of public works agencies' efforts to promote America's air transport network.

A detailed examination of one community's history of engagement with New Deal public works further underlines the multifaceted factors shaping infrastructure development while confirming the support WPA activities enjoyed from municipal governments, the public, and the business community. Knoxville, Tennessee, offers a representative example; there, despite the city council's fiscal conservatism, public and private actors embraced WPA-funded development with open arms. Knoxville's desire to take advantage of New Deal largesse stretched back to 1933, when the city applied for ten thousand dollars in CWA funds to improve the city's small municipal airport. Knoxville had purchased the field in the fall of 1929 but almost immediately found it to be inadequate; despite sustained efforts from the city manager, city council, chamber of commerce, and leading businessmen to bring an airline to Knoxville, the field lacked the size and facilities to host commercial service. City applications to both the Reconstruction Finance Corporation and CWA yielded limited federal aid, but the resulting work left the field well short of airline and Commerce Department requirements. In 1934 American Airlines finally inaugurated airmail service to the city, but did so at a competing private airport. American's service was plagued by difficulties from the outset, however. Their chosen field was so short that aircraft could not land without a steady wind; as a result, American's planes often bypassed Knoxville, to the great frustration of local leaders.[51]

Even worse, Post Office Department officials informed Knoxville that the field was not suitable for modern passenger liners. In a letter to the Knoxville postmaster, Second Assistant Postmaster General Harllee Branch defined the stakes in no uncertain terms: "If your community expects to continue to receive air mail service," Branch wrote, "the airport will have to be placed in suitable condition for the use of the type of planes which will be used on the transcontinental route." City officials responded by looking to establish a new municipal field outside the city limits. Following a survey by representatives from American Airlines and the BAC that strongly encouraged the city to construct a new, larger airport on a rural site, the city council created an airport committee to investigate that possibility. Unfortunately, Knoxville lacked the funds to complete such a project, leaving the city at an impasse.[52]

As it did in hundreds of other towns and cities, the WPA offered a path forward. In June 1935 newly appointed state WPA administrator Harry S. Berry made public his desire to give airport projects high priority; Knoxville was at the top of his list. Berry fast-tracked a WPA survey of possible sites and by late August encouraged the city to file an application for WPA funds. Less than two weeks later the city did so, requesting almost half a million federal dollars. By the end of September the city council approved the new site, and in early November Knoxville learned that the WPA's Washington office had formally released $470,000 for the project.[53]

The city, however, had yet to purchase the land upon which the new field was to be built. In a dramatic turn of events, during a December 10 city council meeting a small but powerful group of fiscal conservatives refused to authorize the necessary forty thousand dollars, unleashing a firestorm of criticism that offers some of clearest evidence of the widespread support the WPA airport project enjoyed. The day after the meeting, the *Knoxville News Sentinel*'s editors penned an editorial pillorying the city council's decision. Arguing that the council should "correct at the earliest possible moment the error made last night," editors argued that the city government "owed it to the progress of Knoxville" to fund the new airport. "The city cannot afford to isolate itself from aeronautical progress," they wrote; ignoring the opportunity WPA funds offered was shortsighted and foolish.[54]

The following day even more anger was unleashed. Under a front-page headline proclaiming, "'Don't Muff Chance to Get First Class Airport' Business Leaders Beg Council," the paper ran a series of quotes from leading local businessmen urging the council to reconsider its decision. Representative were the comments of Howell Davis, president of a local cement company. "I don't see how Knoxville can do without an adequate airport if it is to keep up with the march of progress," Davis wrote. "It would be a shame if the Council passed up this opportunity." The director of the local chamber of commerce had stronger words for the city government. Clarence Holland wrote, "I have been working for a Class A airport for this city since 1928 and will continue to do so. I hope that the Council . . . will see its way clear to put this proposition through."[55]

For years, the chamber of commerce and the business community had provided consistent support for airport development in Knoxville. The chamber highlighted airport development in annual agendas, sponsored the dedication ceremonies for Knoxville's first municipal airport that included a week-long air tour that flew leading Knoxville businessmen around the state, and went so far as to run a series of ads in the *News Sentinel* urging the municipal government to purchase or build an adequate field.[56] That advocacy extended to WPA activities. Although business leaders undoubtedly saw the WPA's airport work as a means to an end, they nonetheless served as powerful advocates for public works spending, viewing WPA-enabled airport development as key to local and regional economic development.

Ultimately, public pressure forced the city council to reverse course. In a special session on December 14, 1935, the council passed an emergency ordinance to appropriate the necessary funds. With the cash in hand, the city manager purchased the relevant land, and WPA crews began construction in the spring of 1936. By the summer the project was well underway as the administration funded comprehensive activities, including clearing, grading, installing drainage, paving, lighting, laying brickwork, and a host of other incidental jobs.[57]

As work on the airport proceeded, Knoxville residents increasingly appreciated the scope of WPA activities. By the fall of 1936 the airport employed hundreds of WPA workers, and the WPA provided jobs for almost four thousand individuals on more than fifty projects in the Knoxville area. In early 1937 the *News Sentinel* offered clear evidence of Knoxville residents' appreciation for the WPA's contributions to the local economy. In a full-page spread, the paper published numerous photos of WPA projects and lauded the benefits the administration brought to the region. Far from conforming to the popular boondoggling stereotype, author Al Manola argued, WPA projects brought "real value to the city." As one of the most visible—and popular—WPA projects in the area, the new airport represented a point of pride for the paper and the larger Knoxville community. The paper provided readers with consistently laudatory coverage, including regular construction updates and large photo collections. Knoxville residents demonstrated their enthusiasm through their eagerness to visit the construction site. Though it lay more than nine miles from the center of town, and the round-trip drive could take well over an hour, thousands of Knoxvillians flocked to the field, eventually forcing WPA crews to erect a fence to hold back the crowds.[58]

Nowhere was Knoxville's enthusiasm for the new airport more evident than during the field's triumphant dedication, which served as a powerful confirmation of local and regional support. The enthusiasm with which state and local officials, the business community, and the public embraced the new field, moreover, highlights the success and popularity of the WPA's airport program. McGhee Tyson Airport benefited from almost six hundred thousand dollars in federal funds, without which the city would have been unable to fund a new airport. That new field brought commercial passenger service to Knoxville—American Airlines DC-2 aircraft began landing in Knoxville in July 1937—allowing east Tennessee to benefit from the emerging national air transport network. McGhee Tyson Airport continues to serve the region today, emphasizing the critical role New Deal public works programs played in creating foundational aviation infrastructure throughout the country. Public support for the WPA project, moreover, suggests that not only did the administration's airport program challenge the popular "make-work" stereotype, but it also represented an important probusiness element of the larger public works edifice. These factors confirm that the Airways and Airports Division was uniquely able to realize the WPA's dual goals of employment and economic development.[59]

Between 1933 and 1939 America's aviation infrastructure witnessed revolutionary changes. Largely through the efforts of New Deal public works agencies, America's airports were modernized with the construction of concrete runways, lighting systems, taxiways, terminals, hangars and control towers. These changes came at a crucial period in American aeronautical development and at a time of dire need for many American workers. Rapidly advancing technology resulted in the creation of new, larger transport aircraft and an expanding air transport network precisely at a time when communities found themselves unable to assume the cost of new airport construction. In that context New Deal public works achieved the dual goal of putting Americans to work and promoting the development of US aviation infrastructure.

The history of these agencies' activities, however—particularly those of the WPA's Airways and Airports Division—remains largely unknown. In many ways it appears that Airways and Airports Division's activities offer the clearest and most successful example of the achievement of some measure of success in practice by New Deal public works policy. The construction or improvement of more than nine hundred airports around the country, as well as programs such as the air marking campaign in California, created conditions for the possibility of the postwar commercial air transport boom. Although perhaps not the ideal way to make over America's aviation infrastructure, WPA activities demonstrate that administrators consistently worked to encourage projects with the maximum value for localities and the nation. Far from promoting a make-work program, the WPA worked closely with the BAC and local communities to encourage construction projects that would have a lasting value for American aeronautics.

These public works projects must occupy a prominent place in any discussion of aeronautical development during the 1930s. Franklin Roosevelt's promotion of public works as a source of employment and an avenue through which to encourage infrastructure improvements found great success with American aviation. The activities of these New Deal agencies also set a precedent for federal work on airports—a fact not lost on the president. In no small part due to the effectiveness of public works airport construction projects, the Civil Aeronautics Act removed the legal barriers preventing federal work on airfields and set the stage for greater governmental responsibility in the postwar period. Along with his establishment of the FAC and his consistent drive to shape the Civil Aeronautics Act, the president's creation of the CWA, PWA, and WPA offers the clearest evidence of Roosevelt's efforts to promote the development of American aviation. Although they failed to bring the United States out of the Depression, the actions of these public works agencies created the foundation of the modern American air transport network: the airways and airports we still use to this day.

7

Conclusion

To the Jet Age and Beyond

More than three-quarters of a century have passed since the passage of the Civil Aeronautics Act. In that time American commercial aviation has experienced a host of revolutionary changes—entering the jet age, embracing the hub-based system created by deregulation, and facing the challenges of coping with terrorist threats in the post–September 11 world. Due in no small part to those developments, Americans' collective relationship with commercial flying has undergone a fundamental change. In recent decades flying increasingly has become a necessary evil, something to be endured rather than celebrated. Americans bemoan high fares, checked-baggage fees, the lack of inflight meals, seemingly incomprehensible routing, diminutive seats, and endemic delays. At the airport, passengers must tolerate long lines at security checkpoints, full-body scanners, and the necessity of segregating liquids—in containers of three ounces or less—into a clear plastic bag. To pass through security everyone must remove his or her shoes, keys, cell phone, belt, and jacket. Arriving on time seems a minor miracle, particularly if the checked baggage does too.

These prevailing conditions offer a sharp contrast to Americans' continued love affair with aviation. Perhaps because our contemporary experiences with flight lack glamour, daring, and romance, those characteristics dominate our cultural memory. The bookshelves at Barnes & Noble and the pages of Amazon.com abound with aviation-related material, from glossy photo books of aircraft to memoirs of fighter aces and record-setting pilots. Hollywood continues to churn out films dramatizing the world aloft; *Memphis Belle* (1990), *The Aviator* (2004), *Flyboys* (2006), and *Red Tails* (2012) represent only a few of the many productions in this genre. Die-cast airplanes, plastic and wood models, and remote control aircraft take center stage in toy and hobby shops around the country, while air shows draw large crowds for both contemporary and historic demonstrations. In New York's Hudson River Valley the Old Rhinebeck Aerodrome has created a living museum. The aerodrome offers visitors a ticket to the past in the form of a 1920s airfield, complete with a grass field, hangars, tools, workshops, and, of course, the largest collection of airworthy vintage aircraft in the nation. Every summer the field plays host to air shows, drawing tens of thousands from across the country.

Tellingly, the interwar period forms an ongoing focal point of Americans' fascination with flight. From the Smithsonian National Air and Space Museum's Golden Age of Flight exhibit to the film *Amelia* (2009), which offers a romanticized view of Amelia Earhart's life and aerial exploits, this era continues to captivate. The reasons are not hard to pinpoint. Those years encompassed perhaps the most glamorous and dynamic period in American aviation history. Rapid technological advances resulted in flight higher, farther, and faster than ever before. For the first time aircraft could cross oceans, reach dizzying speeds, and claw their way into the stratosphere. Simultaneously, that period gave rise to some of the most accomplished and charismatic figures in American aviation history. Charles Lindbergh stands apart from his peers, but others, such as Amelia Earhart, Wiley Post, Roscoe Turner, Jacqueline Cochran, Jimmy Doolittle, and Howard Hughes, became household names as they pushed the boundaries of what humans and the machines they created could accomplish. Americans enthusiastically embraced these pilots, lionizing their efforts to fly farther, faster, and higher as aviation dominated media coverage and events like the National Air Races drew hundreds of thousands of spectators from throughout the country.

Most popular representations of the interwar period put forward an easily comprehensible, progressive narrative. In these views America and Americans are triumphant, recovering from the embarrassment created by the nation's aviation-related shortfalls during World War I to lead the world in aeronautical development and personal accomplishment. American ingenuity and technological expertise quickly combined to produce aircraft that were the envy of the world. Aerial heroes from the period embodied core American values: hard work, perseverance, triumphing over seemingly impossible odds. Their exploits exemplify Americans' desires for daring, glamour, and adventure.

This dominant cultural narrative, however, relegates the federal government's central role in promoting aeronautical development to the shadows. Although governmental efforts to implement legislation, build infrastructure, and regulate and promote American flying lack the glamour of air racing or transoceanic flights, they were a necessary precondition for aviation's progress. Largely overlooked by the public, efforts by policy makers such as Herbert Hoover, William MacCracken, Walter Brown, Hugo Black, Franklin Roosevelt, and Harry Hopkins must occupy a central place in any analysis of interwar aeronautical development.

The coherence and continuity of federal aviation policy during the interwar period is remarkable. Hoover's initial vision emerged at a time when aviation was a glorified sideshow, lacking any firm commercial foundations. That vision's perseverance through the Great Depression and the transition from Republican to Democratic leadership indicates its dynamism but also showcases policy makers' continuing commitment to making aviation a central aspect of American life. Policy makers eschewed the statist models embraced by European nations while crafting policies that protected the embryonic airline industry from damaging market forces. Their willingness to regulate *for* an industry, create financial viability through informal airmail subsidies, engage in aggressive promotion efforts, and, eventually, directly fund airport construction created the foundational conditions that allowed US commercial flying to mature. These actions represent one of the preeminent examples of the government successfully fostering the growth of a commercial enterprise.

The essential continuity of federal policy, moreover, suggests the need to reevaluate prevailing assumptions about the relationship between Hoover's associationalism and FDR's New Deal. At least with regard to aviation, both administrations exhibited a fundamental agreement regarding the core aspects of federal policy: (informal) subsidization, regulation, safety, infrastructure creation, and promotion. Both associationalists and New Dealers, it seems, deemed aviation's continued development important enough to warrant significant federal assistance. Additionally, both groups saw airmail subsidies as a way to walk a tightrope between the destructive potential of a truly free market and the specter of nationalization. This basic agreement highlights important aspects of continuity between these two economic models while once again emphasizing Americans' overwhelming interest in fostering aeronautical development.

Hoover and Roosevelt's policies, however, were not identical, and their differences hold insight for scholars of the interwar period. Hoover's focus on employing existing regulatory structures—epitomized in his adherence to the dock concept—exposes the limitations of his associationalist vision. Although Hoover oversaw a remarkable expansion of federal power with regard to aviation, that expansion occurred within an existing policy framework. Roosevelt, however, quickly demonstrated that the New Deal knew no such limits. Most significantly, his embrace of public works signaled Roosevelt's commitment to radically expanding the federal government's responsibility for the industry. The president's support for the Civil Aeronautics Act furthered this trend, breaking away from existing bureaucratic structures and establishing aviation as an industry worthy of an independent government agency.

It is doubtful, however, that any of Hoover's or Roosevelt's policies could have been sustained without the widespread American enthusiasm for flying. Although early in the period Americans undoubtedly associated aviation with danger and heroism rather than commerce, throughout the era they displayed a passionate interest in flying. That passion created an environment conducive to the development of federal policy. Federal policy, moreover, played an important role in altering Americans' perceptions of flying by making aviation safer and more ubiquitous. By 1938 consistent federal activism facilitated aviation's emergence as a legitimate contender in the transportation field.

In the decades since 1938 American commercial aviation grew to play an ever more important role in American life. Its dynamic expansion, moreover, offers powerful evidence of the fundamental soundness of the policy framework created in the 1920s and '30s. The postwar boom, the rise of jet aircraft, and commercial flying's increasing centrality to Americans' lives in the decades following World War II serve as concrete reminders of that success. The upheaval affecting the air transport industry in the wake of deregulation offers perhaps the most compelling evidence for the wisdom of policies crafted during the interwar period. In recent years the changes wrought by deregulation have combined with concerns about terrorism and an increasing focus on environmental issues to profoundly alter our collective relationship with commercial flying. Today, the majority of Americans take flying for granted except when their flights are delayed or their luggage lost. Though we have lost much of our enthusiasm for commercial aviation, contemporary conditions demonstrate the extent to which the vision crafted by early policy makers has been realized.[1]

Commercial flying began a period of exponential growth with America's entrance into World War II. At the time Congress passed the 1938 Civil Aeronautics Act, which created the regulatory foundation that would guide commercial operations until the late 1970s, America was still mired in the Great Depression, and flying remained the province of the well-to-do. The war swept aside those limits and by 1945 created a profoundly different environment ripe for airline expansion.

World War II promoted commercial growth through pilot training, infrastructure creation, airframe manufacturing, and economic development. Building on the legislative victory of the Civil Aeronautics Act, Roosevelt's Civilian Pilot Training Program turned out an estimated four hundred thousand graduates by 1944.[2] These pilots formed the backbone of the US Army Air Forces pilot pool during the war, offering the military an easily accessible and generally well trained pool of fliers and freeing up military resources for advanced training and other functions. While the CPTP greatly aided the war effort, it ultimately had at least as significant an effect on commercial flying. Like the flight training programs that trained scores of barnstormers-to-be during World War I, the CPTP created a large contingent of well-qualified pilots who would fill out airline ranks in the postwar years.

The war also supported the expansion of infrastructure. Wartime needs precipitated the construction of a new wave of airfields, above and beyond those already created by New Deal public works. Many of these were built under the auspices of the WPA as a continuation of the prewar program. Between 1939 and 1943, in fact, the agency expended upwards of three billion dollars to construct airfields for military use. The Army Corps of Engineers also contributed to the process, building over five hundred new fields through the Development of Landing Areas for National Defense (DLAND) program. After the war's conclusion, the federal government turned approximately half of the WPA and DLAND fields over to civilian control, creating hundreds of new opportunities for localities to gain access to the national air transport network.[3]

Wartime conditions also provided commercial aviation with more immediate benefits. As historian Carl Solberg writes, "When at last the United States went to war, all the airlines went to war" as well. Following formal US intervention, the military took control of 200 of the nation's 360 commercial airliners, contracting them to fly missions for military purposes. By preexisting agreement, airlines kept their private identity and profit-making function but served military ends. General Henry "Hap" Arnold formalized this state of affairs by creating the Military Air Transport Command, which for the duration of the war operated national and international air routes and oversaw the ferrying of men and equipment overseas.[4]

New, larger aircraft also came into service during the war, accelerating a process that began in the late 1930s at least in part as a result of federal efforts to promote increased passenger volume. In the years immediately before the conflict, Douglas, Lockheed, and Boeing had all begun development of larger, four-engined commercial airliners. These planes—most notably the Douglas DC-4 and the Lockheed Constellation—entered service shortly after the war began and were immediately pressed into military service. Wartime necessity mandated the rapid development and manufacture of these aircraft that, for the first time, could cross the country nonstop and even span oceans. Military orders accelerated production dramatically, filling the coffers of manufacturers and bringing thousands of new aircraft into service.

Aeronautical technology leapt ahead during wartime as well. Huge military budgets allowed manufacturers to invest in new and unproven technologies at government expense. The rapid development of military aircraft resulted in concomitant gains for their civilian counterparts. Engine turbochargers and turbo-superchargers came into widespread use, and manufacturers perfected cabin pressurization, with the result that aircraft flew higher, faster, and farther than ever before. Airframe and engine manufacturers thus entered the postwar era eager to apply these new technologies to the next generation of passenger aircraft.[5]

Collectively, these developments put American commercial aviation in a position to realize dramatic gains in the immediate postwar era. The country had hundreds of new airports, thousands of qualified pilots, and scores of war surplus aircraft ready to serve the needs of the traveling public. Additionally, the military's decision to appropriate airlines' fleets into government service provided a constant stream of revenue during the wartime years and ensured that the vast majority of flights were full. In 1944, for example, over 90 percent of seats were filled on domestic routes, a significantly higher percentage than in the years before the war.[6] Airframe and engine manufacturers also ended the war with coffers bursting from wartime contracts and new technologies ready to be put to use in the next generation of airliners. Finally, the war pulled the United States out of the Depression, ushering in a new era of prosperity that opened the possibility of air travel to a larger proportion of the traveling public.

After war's end, US commercial carriers made good on that potential. Passenger traffic—which had begun to trend upwards in the period immediately before the war—grew exponentially, from 6.7 million in 1945 to 12.5 million a year later. Between 1943 and 1950 passenger numbers for scheduled domestic airlines grew more than sixfold. Much of this growth reflected wartime developments, but it also highlighted changing economic realities. Bucking the postwar inflationary trend, the average price of an airline ticket fell by one-third between 1940 and 1946. That fact, coupled with postwar prosperity, meant that airlines could, for the first time, compete directly against the railroads. While Pullman service accounted for six times more passenger miles than did airlines in 1941, five years later that advantage had shrunk by half. By 1951 America's railroads found themselves relegated to second place. In that year airline passenger miles surpassed those of the railroads for the first time—a gap that would widen markedly in subsequent years. In 1958 more passengers crossed the Atlantic on aircraft than on ships, signaling the death knell for the cruise lines that had dominated transatlantic transport for more than a century.[7]

Commercial growth occurred under the watchful eye of the CAB, which oversaw route allocation on all interstate airline travel, monitored ticket prices and airmail subsidies, and approved all new routes and air carriers. The body embraced the pre–Civil Aeronautics Act duties of the Post Office, Interstate Commerce Commission, and Bureau of Air Commerce, in the process further consolidating federal control over commercial development stretching back to the Coolidge administration. Under CAB direction, the postwar years witnessed the steady expansion of airline service across the country, largely at the hands of the prewar "big four" airlines: United, American, TWA, and Eastern. Though some new carriers, such as Delta, experienced growth during that era, for the most part the CAB stifled insurgents' attempts to upset the status quo.[8]

The airline passenger experience also experienced significant change during the era. Wartime technological development and profitability spurred the creation of a new generation of aircraft that revolutionized air travel. Representing the pinnacle of piston-engined airline development, aircraft such as the Douglas DC-7 and Lockheed Super Constellation introduced passengers to pressurized cockpits, allowing aircraft to fly above low-level turbulence and minimize discomfort during ascents and descents. These same aircraft were also capable of longer-range operation at higher speeds, for the first time permitting nonstop transcontinental operations in both directions and enabling nonstop transatlantic service. Simultaneously, these planes' operating efficiency built upon the profitability of the DC-3 and unquestionably made carrying passengers a lucrative undertaking. These aircraft were so successful—and so superior to European designs—that aviation historian R. E. G. Davies claims that the "years after 1945 were an era of complete American dominance in the supply of civil transport aircraft."[9]

The postwar era also brought dramatic changes in international air travel. Pan American, which before the war had been the "chosen instrument" of the United States overseas, lost its monopoly on international routes. Carriers like TWA began to compete for the lucrative transatlantic run, and other airlines inaugurated service across the Pacific and to Central and South America. The United States also concluded a number of international agreements governing the air transport arena. Most notably, the United States joined the International Air Transport Association (IATA), which functioned as a kind of CAB-writ-large in the international arena. The IATA oversaw safety standards, coordinated schedules for international routes, and served as a rate-fixing organization to limit competition.[10]

Ironically, although the years following World War II in many ways represented the pinnacle of US commercial dominance, the period also saw commercial aviation cede its technological edge to the military. Wartime research and development—much of it funded by the government—paved the way for the creation of what President Dwight Eisenhower termed the military industrial complex. In the context of rising Cold War tensions and large military budgets, the postwar years encompassed a dynamic period of aeronautical progress. Military test pilots like Chuck Yeager became the era's aerial heroes, replacing figures such as Charles Lindbergh, Amelia Earhart, and Roscoe Turner. The Air Force's test center at what would become Edwards Air Force Base in California became ground zero for new achievements, from the breaking of the sound barrier to the origins of the space program. Military development of technologies like jet engines, rocketry, guided missiles, and flight at sustained supersonic speeds far surpassed the advances civilian aircraft realized during the era, although many military-led advancements eventually trickled down into the civilian sector.[11]

Fundamentally, the postwar period reflected the continuing strength and vitality of Hoover's regulatory and promotional programs. Although technology advanced and passenger traffic grew dramatically, the foundational policies crafted by Hoover and his allies in the early 1920s remained more than adequate to the task of guiding the sustained growth of American air transport. The Civil Aeronautics Administration (CAA) grounded a federal regulatory apparatus that remained true to Hoover's desire to promote safety, oversight, and infrastructure creation. The CAA's expanding postwar role—largely through introducing radio navigation aids and instrument landing systems—highlighted the continued relevance of that vision. Similarly, the CAB's oversight of rates and routes proved integral to the continued development of rational, structured growth, in the process confirming the efficacy of Hoover's and Brown's actions during the late 1920s and early 1930s. Indeed, the extent to which these foundational policies remained relevant to a rapidly evolving commercial industry is astounding. Not until the late 1970s did the government move away from this model, a decision that would have profoundly damaging consequences for American commercial flying.[12]

The seeds of that change emerged with the introduction of jet aircraft in the late 1950s. The launch of new jet airliners such as the Boeing 707 and Douglas DC-8 initiated a period of rapid technological development that ultimately proved harmful for the airlines. Commercial jets burst onto the scene in 1949 when the British first flew their Comet—though that aircraft ultimately proved to be a disaster for the British air transport industry. US manufacturers followed suit, and the Boeing and Douglas aircraft undertook their first flights in 1957 and 1958, respectively. These aircraft achieved significantly higher speeds than their piston-engined counterparts; could fly even higher, thus avoiding turbulence; and were much quieter and vibrated less than propeller-driven aircraft. Jets were also glamorous, and passengers soon demonstrated a marked enthusiasm for the new planes.

Pan American Airways formally opened the jet age for US airlines in 1955 with an order for twenty Boeing 707s, and the other large US carriers soon followed suit.[13]

Airlines' embrace of jet aircraft, however, adversely affected their bottom lines. Jets entered service before older piston-engined aircraft had reached the end of their useful lives. Fundamentally, airlines purchased new jet aircraft before they had paid off the previous generation of planes, planes that were still new enough to provide valuable—and profitable—service. This situation, according to R. E. G. Davies, was unique to aviation, sharply distinguishing it from other transportation forms in which technological development never outpaced commercial growth. As a result, by the early 1960s airlines struggled to fund jet purchases while simultaneously paying off their piston-engined fleet—a situation that placed the carriers in increasingly precarious financial straits.[14]

Airlines' embrace of jets also had profound implications for other aspects of America's air transport network. As C. E. Woolman, president of Delta Airlines, noted in 1956, "We are buying airplanes that haven't been fully designed, with millions of dollars we don't have. . . . We are going to operate them off airports that are too small, in an air traffic control system that is too slow, and we must fill them with more passengers than we have ever carried before." At the dawn of the jet age only fourteen US airports could support jetliners, so, at least initially, airlines were sharply limited in the routes on which they could use jets. Increasing passenger numbers quickly overwhelmed the ticketing and boarding systems in contemporary airports. Chicago showed the way into the future with the opening of O'Hare Airport in 1955—the first airport to employ the now commonplace organizational scheme of terminals radiating out from a central hub as well as the use of moving jetways to board passengers—but for decades airlines and passengers alike struggled with outdated ticketing, boarding, and luggage handling operations.[15]

Jet capabilities also forced the government to address serious shortcomings in its regulatory apparatus. A 1950 Commerce Department reorganization moved the CAA—which had formerly occupied an administrative position directly under the commerce secretary—to the office of an undersecretary, relegating the agency to a subservient status. During Dwight Eisenhower's presidency the agency also suffered budget cuts in the president's economy-minded efforts. As a result of these circumstances the CAA struggled to cope with the tremendous changes affecting the industry. The

CAA's shortcomings—most notably its lack of ability to exercise positive control over wide swaths of US airspace—were painfully exposed in June 1956 when two airliners collided in midair over the Grand Canyon in Arizona. In the wake of the disaster the CAA received a new influx of federal dollars, and under the leadership of a new director, James Pyle, aggressively moved to modernize its operations. The agency embraced a radar-based air traffic control system, clarified flight rules, and expanded its positive control over the nation's airways. Although much work remained to be done, by 1958 the CAA was well on the way to creating a regulatory apparatus fit for the jet age. In that year the Federal Aviation Act moved the CAA's function to a new regulatory body totally separate from the Commerce Department: the Federal Aviation Agency (FAA). The act granted the new agency a broader mandate that transferred responsibility for air safety regulation from the CAB to the FAA and encompassed expanded control over a joint civil-military system of air navigation and air traffic control.[16]

The introduction of jet aircraft also suggested the next logical step for commercial flying: supersonic travel. American efforts to construct a supersonic transport (SST) represented the apogee of federal engagement with commercial aviation while simultaneously exposing a growing opposition to federal oversight that would eventually lead to deregulation. The process began in 1961, when President John F. Kennedy authorized the FAA to undertake a series of feasibility studies to assess the viability of constructing a supersonic airliner. At the president's behest, the FAA would oversee the development of an American SST, for the first time placing a federal agency in charge of the development of a commercial aircraft. From the beginning, federal officials recognized that the government would have to subsidize the construction of such an aircraft. Initially, Kennedy stated that the government would carry up to 75 percent of the development cost, a figure that rose to more than 90 percent in subsequent years. Federal willingness to assume financial responsibility for the research and development of the SST represented a significant expansion of federal power into the commercial sector and defined a new, activist role for the FAA.[17]

In 1967 Boeing won the right to begin construction of the new SST, promising to deliver a prototype no later than 1973. Almost immediately, however, the project met with significant and sustained public criticism. Initially, criticism focused on the noise pollution that SST sonic booms would create. As early as 1970 the FAA responded with an order restricting supersonic operations to overwater routes. This limited the SST's appeal, making it unlikely that airlines would use the aircraft for transcontinental service. Simultaneously, the project began to draw fire from environmental groups concerned that exhaust gasses from the high-altitude flights would harm the ozone layer. By 1971 criticism reached a level sufficient for Congress to vote down additional appropriations for the project, effectively ending the American SST program.[18]

The end of American effort to create a supersonic airliner signaled the end of an era. From the mid-1920s until the early 1970s the United States led the world in aeronautical development. From the early airmail network to the DC-3 to the postwar aviation boom, American aircraft manufacturers and airlines remained at the forefront of technological and commercial progress. By the early 1970s, however, it appeared that the consensus no longer applied to airline travel. A 1971 public opinion poll demonstrated that 85 percent of Americans opposed the continued development of an SST—an opinion that did not necessarily reflect disenchantment with commercial flying in general, but did suggest a shift in Americans' relationship with aeronautics.[19] No longer, it seems, did Americans prioritize technological development over environmental concerns. This changing relationship doomed the SST project and prefaced the end of the political consensus that had governed federal engagement with commercial aviation since the 1920s.

Americans' flagging enthusiasm for federally supported commercial growth laid the groundwork for the passage of the Airline Deregulation Act of 1978. That act shattered the consensus that had driven the growth of American commercial aviation for the preceding fifty-three years. The push for deregulation was led by small airlines that did not share in the bounty CAB oversight offered to large carriers. As they had in 1932, these carriers allied themselves with congressional Democrats who argued that the government had an obligation to protect commercial competition. These forces were opposed by large, well-established airlines happy with a status quo that had brought them stable and profitable operations for more than half a century. Led by Senator Edward Kennedy (D-MA) and President Jimmy Carter, the proponents of deregulation ultimately won the day, supported by an American public who believed that the end of federal oversight would bring lower fares. By the end of 1981 domestic airlines would have total freedom in choosing their routes—a freedom that extended to ticket pricing a year later. By 1984 the CAB was no more.[20]

The Airline Deregulation Act formally closed the book on Herbert Hoover's vision for American air commerce. The bill liberalized the playing field for airlines, in the process removing the government's ability to shape commercial growth by controlling rates and routes. Although federal officials did maintain their responsibilities for air traffic control, navigational aids, licensing, and safety, 1978 signaled the end of the consensus that had facilitated US airlines' rise to world dominance. In many ways the end of that consensus represented an admission that commercial aviation had reached a new level of maturity. Flying was now an integral part of America's transportation network. In 1980 nearly three hundred million passengers flew America's airways, a far cry from the tiny numbers of the pre–World War II era.[21] It remained clear, however, that airlines remained fragile commercial operations. Federal subsidies and the CAB-imposed structure had hidden that fact for the most part, but escalating aircraft costs and rising energy prices highlighted the fact that American commercial aviation's foundation was built on shifting financial sands.

In the wake of deregulation, airlines experienced a series of upheavals. A succession of mergers and acquisitions rocked the industry as many carriers found themselves unable to compete in the newly liberalized economic climate. Shockingly, Pan Am, for over half a century the most glamorous and dynamic airline in the world, fell victim to the prevailing conditions, shuttering operations in 1991. Surviving operations increasingly embraced a hub-and-spoke route structure that limited costs and maximized aircraft use. Airlines also offered travelers lower fares—as much as 30 percent lower, by some estimates—as carriers engaged in increasingly cutthroat competition for passengers. As a result of these changes, passenger numbers continued to grow, but many airlines found themselves in dire financial straits. The fragility of the contemporary industry profoundly reflects these conditions, as airlines struggle to avoid bankruptcy amid high energy costs, continuing worries about carbon emissions, and security concerns.[22]

Airlines' contemporary focus on reducing services and implementing seemingly unending fees highlight just how thin profit margins remain. As low-cost carriers come and go on a seemingly yearly basis, established airlines have increasingly banded together through mergers and the formation of alliance systems to streamline operations while finding new ways to bolster their bottom lines. Carriers charge for checked bags, in-flight food, even window and aisle seats. They routinely overbook flights to ensure that they can fill all available seats, forcing airlines to bump passengers from reservations sometimes confirmed and paid for weeks or months in advance. While passengers fly more cheaply than was possible during the era before deregulation, contemporary conditions present an ongoing challenge to carriers and passengers alike.

Not surprisingly, the public's relationship with commercial flying has experienced a significant shift in recent decades. No longer do we thrill at the thought of taking to the skies. The hub-and-spoke system creates frustrating flight routings, while delays at major hubs often wreak havoc on the entire system. In the wake of the events of September 11, 2001—which represented only the most recent of a string of hijackings that trace their origins to the late 1960s—security concerns form an increasingly prominent facet of airline travel. Checkpoints, screening, bag checks, and worries about safety define the experience for many passengers already frustrated by fees and delays. Those facts reflect commercial aviation's centrality to modern American life but also highlight the difference between contemporary attitudes and those of the preceding three-quarters of a century. Today Americans complain about airport noise, protest airline carbon emissions, and express outrage over security hassles, whereas their forbears thrilled at the opening of a new local airport.[23]

Passenger frustrations and contemporary challenges notwithstanding, few argue for a return to the policies of the past. Today, the public and airlines alike have come to terms with the new order in which the federal government retains control over licensing, safety, crash investigation, and air traffic control while allowing market forces to govern rates and routes. The challenges and opportunities of the contemporary context, however, reinforce just how valuable federal control was during the early years of air transport when safety was more a dream than a reality and profit from passenger carriage alone was simply unrealistic. The government's ability to affect positive change for the airline industry, moreover, suggests that the state can—at least in certain circumstances—provide valuable guidance and assistance to industry and the larger economy. In today's environment of crumbling infrastructure and byzantine regulations we should remind ourselves that government can be a force for good.

While banality and frustration dominate the contemporary air travel experience, those very characteristics serve as reminder of just how far commercial flying has come from its halting beginnings. Perhaps because air travel occupies an ambivalent place in the lives of contemporary Americans, interest in aeronautics—particularly the "golden age" between the world wars—remains high. The ongoing popularity of the Smithsonian Institution's National Air and Space Museum offers the clearest evidence of Americans' continued love affair with flying. In 2009 more than seven million visited the museum on the National Mall, and over a million more frequented its annex near Dulles Airport, making it one of the most visited museums in the world.[24]

In 2016 the Smithsonian announced plans for an almost one billion dollar makeover for the museum in an effort to update galleries and keep abreast of demand.[25] Visitors experience galleries devoted to World War I, World War II, *Pioneers of Flight*, and the *Golden Age of Flight* as well as an exhibition entitled *America by Air*, which focuses specifically on commercial air transport. The museum holds Charles Lindbergh's *Spirit of St. Louis*, the X-1 in which Chuck Yeager broke the sound barrier in 1947, a Douglas World Cruiser from the first around-the-world flight, and the X-15, the fastest aircraft ever to fly, along with myriad other treasures. Those planes' prominent place on the National Mall, and the public's ongoing desire to see and revere them, confirm the enduring passion this country has for aeronautics.

The popularity of the *Golden Age of Flight* and *America by Air* exhibits, not to mention the prominent place Lindbergh's *Spirit of St. Louis* occupies in the museum's atrium, serves as an ongoing reminder that Americans retain a special reverence for interwar flying. Air travel's contemporary ubiquity has only furthered engagement with a period of dynamic growth, individual heroism, and commercial success. In our enthusiasm for the glamorous aspects of aviation history, however, we should not lose sight of the complex and often contentious nature of aeronautical development between the world wars, the period that witnessed the birth of America's modern air transport system. Owing much to the work of a visionary band of advocates, commercial aviation grew from humble beginnings to span the country, oceans, and eventually the world. That growth occurred largely as a result of focused federal actions. From the halting efforts to craft regulatory legislation in the early 1920s to the activities of the WPA's Airways and Airports Division, federal officials and federal dollars underwrote a coherent program of aeronautical development. Without that federal engagement, our modern transportation infrastructure would undoubtedly look far different. In fact, airlines' contemporary fragility and the intense competition engendered by deregulation serve as constant reminders of just how crucial federal engagement was to the nascent interwar industry. Often overlooked, the evolution of federal aviation policy should rightly occupy a prominent place in the narrative of America's developmental path in the twentieth century.

Notes

Introduction

1. Eugene F. Provenzo Jr., "The St. Petersburg–Tampa Airboat Line," *Florida Historical Quarterly* 58, no. 1 (July 1979), 72–77.

2. William M. Leary, *Aerial Pioneers: The U.S. Airmail Service, 1918–1927*, 10–34.

3. Ibid., 30–34.

4. Ibid., 33–50.

5. "Aero Mail a Success," *Washington Post*, May 16, 1918; "First Air Mail in Washington in 200 Minutes," *New York Times*, May 16, 1918.

6. Leary, *Aerial Pioneers*, 40.

7. Benjamin B. Lipsner, *The Airmail: From Jennies to Jets*, 35.

8. Reminiscences of Leroy Ponce de Arce (1960), 12, Oral History Collection, Aviation Section, Columbia University.

9. Leary, *Aerial Pioneers*, 35.

10. Reminiscences of Ben Odell Howard (1960), 25, and Reminiscences of Ellen Church (1960), 18, Oral History Collection, Aviation Section, Columbia University.

11. Robert J. Dilger, *American Transportation Policy*, 5–6.

12. Ibid., 8.

13. Ibid., 8–9.

14. "New York's Auto Imports Increase," *New York Times*, July 14, 1913.

15. Dilger, *American Transportation Policy*, 10–11.

16. See Gabriel Kolko, *The Triumph of Conservatism: A Reinterpretation of American History, 1900–1916*.

17. William Manchester, *The Glory and the Dream: A Narrative History of America, 1932–1972*, 8; Mark Rose, Bruce Seely, and Paul Barrett, *The Best Transportation System in the World: Railroads, Trucks, Airlines, and American Public Policy in the Twentieth Century*, 28–36.

18. Series such as the Smithsonian History of Flight and Bantam Air and Space provide the most prominent examples of a whole genre of aeronautical literature. Written primarily for aviation enthusiasts, these works chiefly rely on interviews and anecdotal evidence to examine specific planes, pilots, or themes. Martin Caidin is

perhaps the best known writer in this genre with more than thirty publications to his credit on subjects ranging from the P-38 fighter plane to a history of Alaskan bush pilots. Within the realm of popular literature there also exist a significant number of works—many of them penned by historians—devoted to military aviation. Many of these focus on World War II, but biographies and books about particular aircraft also predominate. See, for example, Walter J. Boyne, *Beyond the Wild Blue: A History of the U.S. Air Force*; *Clash of Wings: World War II in the Air* (New York: Simon and Schuster, 1994); Eric Bergerud, *Fire in the Sky: The Air War in the South Pacific* (Boulder: Westview Press, 2000); James J. Hudson, *Hostile Skies: A Combat History of the American Air Service in World War I*; John C. McManus, *Deadly Sky: The American Combat Airman in World War II*; Mark K. Wells, *Courage and Air Warfare: The Allied Aircrew Experience in the Second World War* (London: Frank Cass, 1995); Richard J. Overy, *The Air War, 1939–1945*; Roger A. Freeman, *The Mighty Eighth: A History of the Units, Men, and Machines of the U.S. 8th Air Force* (London: Cassell & Co., 2000); *Zemke's Wolfpack: The True Story of Hub Zemke and the 56th Fighter Group—Top Aces over Europe in World War II* (New York: Pocket Books, 1988); Edward Jablonski, *Flying Fortress: The Illustrated Biography of the B-17s and the Men Who Flew Them* (New York: Doubleday, 1965); and Norman Fortier, *An Ace of the Eighth: An American Fighter Pilot's Air War in Europe* (New York: Ballantine Books, 2003).

19. Henry Ladd Smith, *Airways: The History of Commercial Aviation in the United States*; R. E. G. Davies, *A History of the World's Airlines*; R. E. G. Davies, *Airlines of the United States since 1914*; Carl Solberg, *Conquest of the Skies: A History of Commercial Aviation in America*; Roger E. Bilstein, *Flight in America: From the Wrights to the Astronauts*; T. A. Heppenheimer, *Turbulent Skies: The History of Commercial Aviation*. A subgenre examining the histories of specific airlines also exists. See *Pedigree of Champions: Boeing since 1916*; Robert Daley, *An American Saga: Juan Trippe and His Pan American Empire*; David W. Lewis and Wesley Phillips Newton, *Delta: History of an Airline*; and Crosby Maynard, *Flight Plan for Tomorrow: The Douglas Story*.

20. David Courtwright, *Sky As Frontier: Adventure, Aviation and Empire*. A number of other scholars focus on the enduring connections between aviation and culture, though the majority of these works touch only briefly—if at all—on the United States. Most prominently, Robert Wohl's series Aviation and the Western Imagination (Yale University Press) offers powerful insight into the widespread prevalence of aeronautical themes in European and American culture, although he focuses the majority of his analysis on European subject matter. Also of relevance, Lawrence Goldstein's *The Flying Machine and Modern Literature* demonstrates that flying appears prominently in western literature from Da Vinci to Norman Mailer, while Peter Fritzsche's *A Nation of Fliers: German Aviation and the Popular Imagination* suggests that America is not the only nation with powerful cultural connections to aeronautics. Finally, edited collections from Dominick Pisano and Roger Launius

and Janet Daly Bednarek offer insight into some broader aviation-related themes. Both *The Airplane in American Culture* and *Reconsidering a Century of Flight* embrace an explicitly American context, and both works present readers with numerous essays offering insight into a variety of aviation-related themes. These include public perception, race, gender, and art, but ultimately suggest little in the way of connections between culture and technological development or political actions.

21. Nick A. Komons, *Bonfires to Beacons: Federal Civil Aviation Policy under the Air Commerce Act*; F. Robert van der Linden, *Airlines and Airmail: The Post Office and the Birth of the Commercial Aviation Industry*.

In the last few decades a growing body of scholarship has engaged myriad other aspects of interwar aviation. Though these works do not—and do not claim to—offer a comprehensive take on interwar policy, they provide valuable insight into aspects of that larger narrative. David Lee's excellent essay, "Herbert Hoover and Commercial Aviation Policy," *Business History Review* 58, no. 1 (Spring 1984): 78–102, highlights Hoover's motivations both as secretary of commerce and as president. Lee offers persuasive analysis that Hoover's associationalist economic philosophy guided his aviation policy, and that his intense interest in new technologies such as aviation and radio led him to take an active role in promoting new industries he felt had value for the nation. Lee also provides valuable insight into Senator Hugo Black's 1933–34 investigation into US Post Office airmail contracts with his essay "Senator Black's Investigation of the Airmail, 1933–1934," *The Historian* 53, no. 3 (Spring 1991): 423–42. Alan P. Dobson echoes Lee's focus on the executive in *FDR and Civil Aviation: Flying Strong, Flying Free*. Dobson argues that Roosevelt played a decisive role in the development of national and international commercial flying, leaving a legacy that greatly influenced the post–World War II era. While Dobson provides a worthwhile glimpse into FDR's engagement with commercial flying, *FDR and Civil Aviation* does little to connect Roosevelt's policies with those of his forebear and fails to address the New Deal's role in promoting creation of aviation infrastructure. Also of relevance are Janet Daily Bednarek's *America's Airports: Airfield Development, 1918–1947*, Stuart Banner's *Who Owns the Sky? The Struggle to Control Airspace from the Wright Brothers On*, and Jenifer Van Vleck's *Empire of the Air: Aviation and the American Ascendency*. These works offer valuable analyses of specific topics—airports, legal issues, and the connections between aviation and American globalism, respectively—but deal only tangentially with the larger context of federal policy.

22. Joan Hoff Wilson, *Herbert Hoover: Forgotten Progressive*, 56–69; Ellis Hawley, *The New Deal and the Problem of Monopoly: A Study in Economic Ambivalence*, 2nd ed.; Thomas K. McGraw, ed., *Regulation in Perspective: Historical Essays*; Robert D. Leighninger Jr., *Long-Range Public Investment: The Forgotten Legacy of the New Deal*; Jason Scott Smith, *Building New Deal Liberalism: The Political Economy of Public Works, 1933–1956*. Significantly, William Leuchtenburg's seminal work *Franklin D. Roosevelt and the New Deal* is notable only for almost entirely overlooking aviation, an omission shared by Paul Conkin's *The New Deal*, 3rd ed.

Chapter 1

1. “Hoover to Pick Air Board,” June 21, 1921, Box 39, Herbert Hoover Papers as Secretary of Commerce, Herbert Hoover Presidential Library, West Branch, Iowa (hereafter cited as Hoover Commerce Papers).

2. “Notes for Meeting with the Air Craft Men,” July 16, 1921, Box 39, Hoover Commerce Papers.

3. Joan Hoff Wilson, *Herbert Hoover: Forgotten Progressive*, 56–69. For more information on Hoover’s attempts to apply the associative state to specific industries, see Ellis Hawley, “Three Facets of the Hooverian Associationalism: Lumber, Aviation, and Movies, 1921–1930,” published in Thomas McGraw’s *Regulation in Perspective: Historical Essays*.

4. David Courtwright, *Sky As Frontier: Adventure, Aviation and Empire*, 3–70.

5. Reminiscences of Dean Smith (1960), 4–5, Oral History Collection, Aviation Section, Columbia University.

6. Francis D. Walton, “Is It Safe to Fly?” *The Nation*, October 22, 1930, 438–39; Kenneth Brown Collings, “Flying Is Still Dangerous,” *Reader’s Digest*, July 1934, 40–42; Courtwright, *Sky As Frontier*, 52.

7. Joseph J. Corn, *The Winged Gospel: America’s Romance with Aviation, 1900–1950*, 27.

8. R. E. G. Davies, *A History of the World’s Airlines*, 40.

9. Ibid., 41. See also William M. Leary Jr., “At the Dawn of Commercial Aviation: Inglis M. Uppercru and Aeromarine Airways,” *Business History Review* 53, no. 2 (Summer 1979): 167–90.

10. “New York’s Auto Imports Increase,” *New York Times*, July 14, 1913.

11. Memorandum for Secretary Hoover: Air Navigation Committee, April 5, 1921, and Air Navigation Committee, April 8, 1921, Box 39, Hoover Commerce Papers.

12. Charles Walcott to Herbert Hoover, March 23, 1921, Box 39, Hoover Commerce Papers.

13. C. F. Riddin to Herbert Hoover, June 22, 1921, Box 39, Hoover Commerce Papers.

14. Herbert Hoover to Frederick C. Hicks, December 30, 1921, quoted in Nick Komons, *Bonfires to Beacons: Federal Civil Aviation Policy under the Air Commerce Act, 1926–1938*, 22.

15. For a comprehensive treatment of legal issues related to aviation, see Stuart Banner, *Who Owns the Sky? The Struggle to Control Airspace from the Wright Brothers On*.

16. Reminiscences of Gill Robb Wilson (1960), 23–24, Oral History Collection, Aviation Section, Columbia University.

17. For further information, see Komons, *Bonfires to Beacons*, 35–64.

18. Reminiscences of Dean Smith (1960), 16, Oral History Collection, Aviation Section, Columbia University.

19. Ibid., 14–15.

20. Courtwright, *Sky as Frontier*, 59; Reminiscences of Dean Smith (1960), 21.

21. Komons, *Bonfires to Beacons*, 23.

22. F. Robert van der Linden, *Airlines and Airmail: The Post Office and the Birth of the Commercial Aviation Industry*, 8.

23. Ibid.

24. Statement of Secretary Hoover on Commercial Aviation, September 24, 1925, and Speech to SF [San Francisco] Chamber of Commerce, September 1926, Box 40, Hoover Commerce Papers.

25. Statement of Secretary Hoover on Commercial Aviation, September 24, 1925, and Speech to SF Chamber of Commerce, September 1926.

26. Speech to SF Chamber of Commerce, September 1926.

27. Komons, *Bonfires to Beacons*, 72.

28. Speech to SF Chamber of Commerce, September 1926.

29. Ibid.

30. Statement of Secretary Hoover on Commercial Aviation, September 24, 1925, and Speech to SF Chamber of Commerce, September 1926.

31. Speech to SF Chamber of Commerce, September 1926.

32. Ibid.

33. Ibid.

34. Ibid.; "Hoover Foresees a Greater Air Service," released for publication in *New York Times*, June 26, 1927, Box 40, Hoover Commerce Papers.

35. Statement of Postmaster General Harry S. New before the Air Service Inquiry Board, October 13, 1925, Box 41, Hoover Commerce Papers.

36. Ibid.

37. Ibid.

38. Ibid.

39. Paul Henderson, "The Air Mail: Its Commercial Future," *Aero Digest*, March 1925, 128–29.

40. US President's Aircraft Board, *Hearings*, Washington, DC, 1925, 1471, quoted in Komons, *Bonfires to Beacons*, 29.

41. Komons, *Bonfires to Beacons*, 66–67.

42. van der Linden, *Airlines and Airmail*, 10.

43. For more information, see Banner, *Who Owns the Sky?* 102–34, and Komons, *Bonfires to Beacons*, 27–28.

Chapter 2

1. "Douglas World Cruiser *Chicago*," Long Description, Smithsonian National Air and Space Museum, Object Collection, accessed July 8, 2014, https://airandspace.si.edu/collection-objects/douglas-world-cruiser-chicago.

2. Nick Komons, *Bonfires to Beacons: Federal Civil Aviation Policy under the Air Commerce Act, 1926–1938*, 70–74.

3. Ibid., 72–73; "Aviation By Investigation," Address by William MacCracken to the Law Club, December 11, 1925, Box 52, William MacCracken Jr. Papers, Herbert Hoover Presidential Library, West Branch, Iowa.

4. "Aviation By Investigation"; Komons, *Bonfires to Beacons*, 72.

5. "Aviation By Investigation."

6. Ibid.

7. Komons, *Bonfires to Beacons*, 75–78.

8. "Aviation By Investigation."

9. Statement of Secretary Hoover on Commercial Aviation, September 24, 1925, Box 39, Hoover Commerce Papers.

10. Department of Commerce Memo re: Civil Aviation Report by Joint Committee of the Commerce Department and American Engineering Council, January 24, 1926, Box 40, Hoover Commerce Papers; "Aviation By Investigation."

11. "Aviation By Investigation."

12. Ibid.

13. Komons, *Bonfires to Beacons*, 78–81.

14. Ibid., 46–58.

15. "Notes for Meeting with the Air Craft Men," July 16, 1921, Box 39, Hoover Commerce Papers; Komons, *Bonfires to Beacons*, 46.

16. Komons, *Bonfires to Beacons*, 48–50.

17. "Aviation By Investigation"; Komons, *Bonfires to Beacons*, 50–51.

18. Herbert Hoover to Maurice C. Clearly, June 25, 1921, Box 39, Hoover Commerce Papers.

19. Komons, *Bonfires to Beacons*, 54–55.

20. Ibid., 55–57.

21. Godfrey Cabot to William MacCracken, November 1, 1922; Samuel Bradley to William MacCracken, November 22, 1922; and Howard Coffin and B. H. Mulvihill to William MacCracken, June 13, 1923, Box 36, National Aeronautics Association Archives, National Air and Space Archives, National Air and Space Museum, Smithsonian Institution, Suitland, MD (hereafter cited as NAA Archives).

22. Samuel Bradley to William MacCracken, January 22, 1923, and William MacCracken to Samuel Bradley, January 23, 1923, Box 36, NAA Archives.

23. Howard Coffin to B. H. Mulvihill, July 31, 1923; William MacCracken to Howard Coffin, August 7, 1923; Howard Coffin to William MacCracken, September 20, 1923; and William MacCracken to Samuel Winslow, December 3, 1923, Box 36, NAA Archives.

24. B. H. Mulvihill to William MacCracken, April 11, 1923, and William MacCracken to Howard Coffin, August 7, 1923, Box 36, NAA Archives.

25. William MacCracken to George Bogert, December 13, 1923, Box 36, NAA Archives.

26. Howard Coffin to William MacCracken, September 20, 1923, and William MacCracken to Samuel Winslow, December 3, 1923, Box 36, NAA Archives.

27. Komons, *Bonfires to Beacons*, 63.

28. H. Victory to W. F. Durand, December 18, 1925, and Charles Walcott to Senator Hiram Bingham, December 12, 1925, Box 1, Record Group 255, Records of the National Aeronautics and Space Administration, National Archives and Records Administration, College Park, MD.

29. Report of Special Subcommittee of National Advisory Committee for Aeronautics on the Encouragement and Regulation of Aircraft in Commerce, April 22, 1926, Box 1, RG 255, NARA; Komons, *Bonfires to Beacons*, 82–83.

30. Hiram Bingham to Charles D. Walcott, April 15, 1926, Box 1, RG 255, NARA.

31. Minutes of Meeting of Special Subcommittee on the Encouragement and Regulation of Aircraft in Commerce, April 22, 1926, and Report of Special Subcommittee of National Advisory Committee for Aeronautics.

32. Report of Special Subcommittee of National Advisory Committee for Aeronautics.

33. "Information Bulletin Number One," Department of Commerce, Aeronautics Branch, Information Division, September 1926, Box 121, Hoover Commerce Papers.

34. Lester D. Gardner, "The Development of Civil Aeronautics in America," prepared for the Fourth International Congress of Aerial Navigation, October 1, 1927, Box 40, Hoover Commerce Papers, 22.

35. "Information Bulletin Number One."

36. Ibid.

37. Gardner, "Development of Civil Aeronautics," 22.

38. Ibid., 23.

39. Ibid.

40. Ibid., 25–30.

41. Ibid., 32.

42. Ibid., 31.

Chapter 3

1. Byrd's claim has been challenged by a number of scientists and scholars. It appears doubtful that he actually flew over the North Pole.

2. Reminiscences of Harold M. Bixby (1960), 27, Oral History Collection, Aviation Section, Columbia University.

3. Ibid., 24–27.

4. Russell Owen, "Flight to Paris Lures Noted Pilots of the Air," *New York Times*, March 20, 1927, XX5.

5. "Aviation Leaders Praise Lindbergh," *New York Times*, May 22, 1927, 5; "Orville Wright Lauds Lindbergh's Flight," *New York Times*, May 23, 1927, 2.

6. "Mayor Welcomes Flier at City Hall," *New York Times*, June 14, 1927, 2.

7. Joseph Corn, *The Winged Gospel: America's Romance with Aviation, 1900–1950*, 17.

8. Ernest K. Gann, "Thirty-Three Hours That Changed the World," *Saturday Review*, April 16, 1977, 8.

9. "Losses & Profits," *Time*, March 31, 1930, 51; Reminiscences of Admiral Emory S. Land (1960), 38, Oral History Collection, Aviation Section, Columbia University; David Courtwright, *Sky as Frontier: Adventure, Aviation and Empire*, 82.

10. Courtwright, *Sky as Frontier*, 82–83.

11. Ibid., 82; Roger Bilstein, *Flight in America: From the Wrights to the Astronauts*, 57; "10,472,024 Miles Flown on Nation's Airways, with 52,934 Passengers, 1928 Report Shows," *New York Times*, March 11, 1929, 21; Nick A. Komons, *Bonfires to Beacons: Federal Civil Aviation Policy under the Air Commerce Act, 1926–1938*, 99–100.

12. "Hoover Foresees a Greater Air Service," released for publication in *New York Times* June 26, 1927, Box 40, Hoover Commerce Papers.

13. Clarence M. Young, Untitled Report for the President, August 22, 1930, and Theodore G. Joslin, Secretary to the President, to Clarence M. Young, May 5, 1931, Box 56, President's Subject File, Herbert Hoover Presidential Library, West Branch, Iowa.

14. Untitled Report for the President, March 5, 1931, and Luther K. Bell, General Manager Aeronautical Chamber of Commerce of America, Inc., to Theodore G. Joslin, Secretary to the President, July 6, 1931, Box 56, ibid.

15. Herbert Hoover to the Honorable Secretary of Commerce, March 23, 1929, Box 57, ibid.

16. Remembrances of Clarence M. Young as told to Raymond Henle, 21, Herbert Hoover Presidential Library, West Branch, Iowa.

17. F. Robert van der Linden, *Airlines and Airmail: The Post Office and the Birth of the Commercial Aviation Industry*, 63–65.

18. Ibid., 63.

19. A. G. Patterson undated memorandum for Mr. Harllee Branch, Box 116; Berry Brothers Informational Bulletin, February 21, 1930, Box 112; and Statement by Mr. Fulton Lewis Jr. Regarding Post Office Department Administration of the Foreign and Domestic Air Mail Subsidies, 4–10, Box 119, all in Record Group 46, Records of the Senate Special Committee to Investigate Ocean Mail and Air Mail Contracts, National Archives and Records Administration, Washington, DC.

20. Commercial Aviation and the Air Mail, Address by Postmaster General Walter F. Brown before the Cleveland Chamber of Commerce, January 14, 1930, Accession II, Box 742, Folder 2, Pan American Airways Papers, University of Miami Special Collections, Miami, Florida; Statement by Mr. Fulton Lewis Jr., 3–4. For more information, see Komons, *Bonfires to Beacons*, 192–95.

21. In fact, following the stock market crash in October of 1929, the majority of major airlines found their stock dangerously devalued. For example, the stock of North American Aviation fell from a high of 19¾ to a low of 4, and United Aircraft stock fell from 109½ to less than 45. Further, after the economic downturn virtually all of the major carriers quickly began to hemorrhage their cash reserves. See van der Linden, *Airlines and Airmail*, 106.

22. Post Office Press Release, May 27, 1929, Box 117, RG 46, NARA.

23. Ibid.

24. Statement by Mr. Fulton Lewis Jr., 22.

25. Post Office Press Release, May 27, 1929.

26. Ibid.

27. Post Office Press Release, September 11, 1929, Box 117, RG 46, NARA; Commercial Aviation and the Air Mail, January 14, 1930.

28. Commercial Aviation and the Air Mail, January 14, 1930.
29. R. E. G. Davies, *A History of the World's Airlines*, 124.
30. Statement by Mr. Fulton Lewis Jr., 20.
31. Post Office Press Release, May 10, 1929, Box 117, RG 46, NARA.
32. Statement by Mr. Fulton Lewis Jr., 16.
33. Commercial Aviation and the Air Mail, January 14, 1930.
34. Ibid.
35. Ibid.
36. "Hoover Foresees a Greater Air Service," released for publication in *New York Times*, June 26, 1927, Box 40, Hoover Commerce Papers.
37. Commercial Aviation and the Air Mail, January 14, 1930.
38. Post Office Press Release, February 16, 1931, Box 117, RG 46, NARA; van der Linden, *Airlines and Airmail*, 106–36.
39. van der Linden, *Airlines and Airmail*, 152.
40. Post Office Press Release, May 19, 1930, Box 117, RG 46, NARA.
41. W. Irving Glover memorandum for Earl Wadsworth, May 15, 1930, Box 120, RG 46, NARA.
42. Southern Air Transport "Meeting of the Executive Committee," May 1, 1930, Box 120; Earl B. Wadsworth, Post Office Department Memorandum, May 20, 1930, Box 130; and Statement of C. E. Woolman to Post Office Investigators C. Fleming and V. V. Sugg, Monroe, Louisiana, February 21, 1934, Box 117, all in RG 46, NARA.
43. Wadsworth, Post Office Department Memorandum, May 20, 1930.
44. Hainer Hinshaw to Colonel L. H. Brittin, January 17, 1930, Box 156, RG 46, NARA, and Earl B. Wadsworth, Post Office Department Memorandum, May 20, 1930.
45. Undated Northwest Airways memo, Box 156, RG 46, NARA; Statement of C. E. Woolman, February 21, 1934; Testimony of C. E. Woolman in *Investigation of Air Mail and Ocean Mail Contracts: Hearings before a Special Committee on Investigation of Air Mail and Ocean Mail Contracts*, US Senate, 73rd Cong., 2nd sess., Part 4 (Washington, DC: Government Printing Office, 1934), 1597–1608.
46. William MacCracken to Walter F. Brown, June 4, 1930, and Hainer Hinshaw to Walter Brown in Earl Wadsworth, Personal Notes at "Spoils Conference," June 4, 1930, Box 130, RG 46, NARA.
47. Statement of C. E. Woolman, February 21, 1934; Earl B. Wadsworth, Post Office Department Memorandum, June 5, 1930, Box 130, RG 46, NARA; van der Linden, *Airlines and Airmail*, 167–68.
48. Van der Linden, *Airlines and Airmail*, 187–90.
49. Statement of Walter F. Brown to the Senate Special Committee, February 1934, Box 123, RG 46, NARA, 1, 4. See also Testimony of Walter F. Brown, in *Investigation of Air Mail and Ocean Mail Contracts*, 2349–681; 2741–42.
50. Statement of Walter F. Brown to the Senate Special Committee, 4–5.
51. Ibid., 5.

Chapter 4

1. Benjamin D. Foulois and C. V. Glines, *From the Wright Brothers to the Astronauts: The Memoirs of Major General Benjamin D. Foulois*, 244.

2. Charles Lindbergh telegram to Franklin Roosevelt, February 11, 1934, and Stephen Early, Secretary to the President, untitled memo, February 12, 1934, Official File (OF) 19, Franklin D. Roosevelt Papers as President, Franklin D. Roosevelt Presidential Library, Hyde Park, New York (hereafter cited as President's OF).

3. Foulois and Glines, *Wright Brothers to Astronauts*, 244–48; "Army's First Week," *Time*, March 5, 1934, 46–47; "Air Mail: Climax of Cancellation Drama Reached as New Bids from Commercial Carriers Are Opened," *Newsweek*, April 28, 1934, 26.

4. John F. Shiner, "The Coming of the GHQ Air Force, 1925–1935," in *Winged Shield, Winged Sword: A History of the United Stated Air Force*, ed. Bernard C. Nalty, 1:125–27.

5. The majority of historians interpret Black's actions as a sharp break from the Republican past. See, for example, R. E. G. Davies, *A History of the World's Airlines*, 129–33; Ellis Hawley, *The New Deal and the Problem of Monopoly: A Study in Economic Ambivalence*, 2nd ed., 240–44; and F. Robert van der Linden, *Airlines and Airmail: The Post Office and the Birth of the Commercial Aviation Industry*, 260–91.

6. Nick Komons, *Bonfires to Beacons: Federal Civil Aviation Policy under the Air Commerce Act, 1926–1938*, 222.

7. Ibid., 223.

8. Paul Henderson to C. M. Keys, August 28, 1931, Box 126; C. M. Keys to Paul Henderson, August 31, 1931, Box 126; and Statement by Mr. Fulton Lewis Jr. Regarding Post Office Department Administration of the Foreign and Domestic Air Mail Subsidies, Box 119, all in RG 46, NARA.

9. P. G. Johnson to Frederick Rentschler, August 3, 1931, Box 126, and L. H. Brittin to Mr. Lilly February 16, 1933, Box 157, RG 46, NARA.

10. Statement by Mr. Fulton Lewis Jr., Box 119; Hainer Hinshaw to William Lawson, November 24, 1931, Box 125; Paul Henderson to C. M. Keys, August 28, 1931, Box 126; and C. M. Keys to Paul Henderson, August 31, 1931, Box 126, all in RG 46, NARA; Komons, *Bonfires to Beacons*, 249–50; van der Linden, *Airlines and Airmail*, 260–61.

11. 72 Cong. Rec. 1239–40 (1930), quoted in Howard Ball, *Hugo L. Black: Cold Steel Warrior*, 79. See also ibid., 71, 80.

12. S. Res. 349, 72nd Cong., 2nd sess., approved February 25, 1933, copy in Box 116, RG 46, NARA.

13. Black's mention of fraud in the Coolidge administration referred to a bid for an airmail route between Pueblo, Colorado, and Cheyenne, Wyoming, tendered by Harry New in 1925—a bid unrelated to Brown's actions five years later. "The Truth about Air Mail Contracts," Address by Senator Hugo Black to Congress, April 25 and 26, 1934, 2–4, Box 118, RG 46, NARA.

14. Questionnaire for Airmail Contract Carriers, undated, Box 116, RG 46, NARA.

15. Senator Hugo Black Discusses "Aviation and Air Mail Contracts," transcript, CBS, February 16, 1934, Box 477, Hugo Black Collection, Manuscript Division,

Library of Congress (hereafter cited as Hugo Black Papers); "Truth about Air Mail Contracts."

16. Hainer Hinshaw memorandum to P. G. Johnson, June 1, 1933, Box 125, RG 46, NARA.

17. Ibid.

18. "Subsidy Suspended," *Time*, February 13, 1933, 47; "Mail Subsidy Inquiry Approved," *New York Times*, February 16, 1933, 4; "Moves to Prevent Airmail Changes," *New York Times*, February 1, 1933, 9; "Senate Wipes Out Sum for Air Mail," *New York Times*, February 2, 1933, 2; "Brown Protests Ban on Air Mail Funds," *New York Times*, February 4, 1933, 14; "Will Seek to End Airmail Subsidies," *New York Times*, February 18, 1933, 31; Lauran D. Lyman, "Air Leaders Are Hopeful," *New York Times*, February 19, 1933, XX7.

19. Black, "Aviation and Air Mail Contracts," CBS, February 16, 1934.

20. "Truth about Air Mail Contracts"; van der Linden, *Airlines and Airmail*, 268.

21. Testimony of Thomas H. McKee, *Investigation of Air Mail and Ocean Mail Contracts: Hearings before a Special Committee on Investigation of Air Mail and Ocean Mail Contracts*, US Senate, 73rd Cong., 2nd sess., Part 4 (1934), 1443–48.

22. Testimony of Erle P. Halliburton, ibid., 1488–93; Testimony of Theodore Taney, ibid., 1611–28; Testimony of Maj. William B. Robertson, ibid., 1719–38.

23. Testimony of Paul Henderson, ibid., 1457–88; Testimony of Hainer Hinshaw, ibid., 1578–95.

24. Statement of Mr. Fulton Lewis Jr.

25. Ibid., 50.

26. C. M. Keys to Hugo Black, January 11, 1934, Box 126, RG 46, NARA; Statement of C. E. Woolman to Post Office Investigators C. Fleming and V. V. Sugg, Monroe, Louisiana, February 21, 1934, Box 117, RG 46, NARA; van der Linden, *Airlines and Airmail*, 268–71; A. Scott Berg, *Lindbergh*, 190.

27. Testimony of Frederick B. Rentschler, *Investigation of Air Mail and Ocean Mail Contracts: Hearings before a Special Committee on Investigation of Air Mail and Ocean Mail Contracts*, US Senate, 73rd Cong., 2nd sess., Part 4 (1934), 1800–1802; Frederick Rentschler to A. G. Patterson, December 1, 1933, Box 129, RG 46, NARA.

28. "Truth about Air Mail Contracts"; van der Linden, *Airlines and Airmail*, 268–71.

29. "The Mail," *Time*, February 19, 1934, 30; *The Nation*, February 7, 1934, 154; Paul Y. Anderson, "So They Found the Body," *The Nation*, February 21, 1934, 219.

30. "Air Mail Inquiry Next," *New York Times*, January 3, 1934, 8; "Brown Is Pictured As Fusing Air Lines, *New York Times*, January 12, 1934, 3; "200 Are Questioned in Air-Mail Inquiry," *New York Times*, January 14, 1934, 29; Lauren D. Lyman, "Spotlight on Air Mail," *New York Times*, January 21, 1934, XX6; "Conferences in 1930 of Vast Air Mail Network Revealed in Official Memoranda," *New York Times*, February 15, 1934, 10; "Black Denounced Air-Mail Grants," *New York Times*, February 17, 1934, 7.

31. Foulois and Glines, *Wright Brothers to Astronauts*, 235–40; Komons, *Bonfires to Beacons*, 254–56.

32. Executive Order 6591, February 9, 1934, President's OF 19; Foulois and Glines, *Wright Brothers to Astronauts*, 238–39.

33. Foulois and Glines, *Wright Brothers to Astronauts*, 237.

34. Ibid., 242; Shiner, "Coming of the GHQ," 122–23.

35. Foulois and Glines, *Wright Brothers to Astronauts*, 240–42; Shiner, "Coming of the GHQ," 124; Reminiscences of General Benjamin Foulois (1960), 50, Oral History Collection, Aviation Section, Columbia University.

36. Foulois and Glines, *Wright Brothers to Astronauts*, 242–43; Shiner, "Coming of the GHQ," 124–25.

37. Reminiscences of Joseph Atkinson (1960), 24, and Reminiscences of General Elwood Quesada (1960), 24, Oral History Collection, Aviation Section, Columbia University.

38. James Farley to Hon. Hugo L. Black, February 14, 1934, Box 117, RG 46, NARA.

39. Statement of Walter F. Brown to the Senate Special Committee, February 1934, Box 123, RG 46, NARA; "Says Hoover Stood by Air-Mail Policy," *New York Times*, February 23, 1934, 10.

40. "Truth about Air Mail Contracts."

41. Ibid., 6, 10–25.

42. Ibid., 6, 10–12.

43. Ibid., 12–38.

44. Ibid., 10–38.

45. Franklin D. Roosevelt to Hugo Black, March 7, 1934, archivist's cross-reference, Box 477, Hugo Black Papers; cross reference, President's Personal File 607, Franklin D. Roosevelt Presidential Library, Hyde Park, New York.

46. Ibid.; "Turnback," *Time*, March 19, 1934, 53–54.

47. Traditionally, scholars have largely embraced the view that Black's actions were a referendum on Republican policies. See van der Linden, *Airlines and Airmail*, 260; Davies, *History of the World's Airlines*, 129; Komons, *Bonfires to Beacons*, 251–69.

48. Black, "Aviation and Air Mail Contracts," CBS, February 16, 1934.

49. Ibid.; "Truth about Air Mail Contracts."

50. Black, "Aviation and Air Mail Contracts," CBS, February 16, 1934.

51. Franklin D. Roosevelt to Senator Hugo Black, June 19, 1935, and James Farley to Senator Hugo Black, January 13, 1936, Box 83, Hugo Black Papers.

52. Paul H. Brattain to Senator Hugo Black, October 29, 1935; Marion Rushton to Hugo Black, May 29, 1935; Hugo Black to Marion Rushton, May 31, 1935; Edward Bern to Senator Hugo Black, October 15, 1935; Hugo Black to Edward Bern, October 19, 1935; and Request of Senator H. L. Black for a list of magazine articles on the air mail investigations, March 14, 1934, all in Box 83, Hugo Black Papers.

53. David L. Behncke to Senator Hugo Black, July 6, 1935; David L. Behncke to Senator Hugo Black, February 7, 1935; Senator Hugo Black to F. W. Wittemore, February 9, 1935; David L. Behncke to Senator Hugo Black, February 14, 1935; David L. Behncke to Senator Hugo Black, February 16, 1935; Senator Hugo Black to David Behncke, February 20, 1935; F. W. Wittemore to Senator Hugo Black, February 18,

1935; David Behncke to Senator Hugo Black, February 21, 1935; John F. Malone to Senator Hugo Black, February 21, 1935; Hugo Black to John F. Malone, February 26, 1935; David Behncke to Senator Hugo Black, February 27, 1935; David Behncke to Senator Hugo Black, March 1, 1935; Hugo Black to David Behncke, April 4, 1935; and David Behncke to Senator Hugo Black, April 13, 1935, all in Box 83, Hugo Black Papers.

54. David Behncke to Senator Hugo Black, May 9, 1935; Hugo Black to David Behncke, May 13, 1935; Edward G. Hamilton to Senator Hugo Black, May 15, 1935; David Behncke to Senator Hugo Black, May 16, 1935; David Behncke to Senator Hugo Black, May 20, 1935; Hugo Black to David L. Behncke, April 20, 1935; David Behncke to Senator Hugo Black, April 17, 1935; Hugo Black to Francis Biddle, April 20, 1935; Benedict Wolf to Senator Hugo Black, April 23, 1935; and David Behncke to Senator Hugo Black, April 24, 1935, all in Box 83, Hugo Black Papers; David Behncke telegram to Senator Hugo Black, June 6, 1934, Box 112, RG 46, NARA.

55. Paul Thomas to Hugo Black, March 6, 1936; Hugo Black to Paul Thomas, March 16, 1936; J. Lee Smith to Hugo Black, March 5, 1936; and Hugo Black to J. Lee Smith, March 9, 1936, all in Box 83, Hugo Black Papers.

Chapter 5

1. R. E. G. Davies, *A History of the World's Airlines*, 11–20, 93–122.

2. Ibid., 30–31.

3. Ibid., 23–98.

4. Article for September Number of *Flying*, September 1915, Box 40, Franklin D. Roosevelt Papers Relating to Family, Business, and Personal Affairs, Franklin D. Roosevelt Presidential Library, Hyde Park, New York.

5. "War at Sea and Its Weapons: A Description of the Purpose of a Navy and the Use of Its Different Ships," Article I, "General Introduction—Scouts and Aircraft," September 27, 1915, Box 40, ibid. See also Robert van der Linden, *Airlines and Airmail: The Post Office and the Birth of the Commercial Aviation Industry*, 1; William E. Leuchtenburg, *Franklin D. Roosevelt and the New Deal: 1932–1940*, 8; and Roger Bilstein, *Flight in America: From the Wrights to the Astronauts*, 173.

6. van der Linden, *Airlines and Airmail*, 263.

7. For more information on Roosevelt's style, see Paul K. Conkin, *The New Deal*, 3rd ed., 1–20, and Leuchtenburg, *Franklin D. Roosevelt*, 12–13, 328–29.

8. For more information on Roosevelt's commitment to military aviation, see Bilstein, *Flight in America*, 128–31, and Michael S. Sherry, *The Rise of American Airpower: The Creation of Armageddon*, 49.

9. Charles Lindbergh telegram to Franklin Roosevelt, February 11, 1934, President's OF 19; "Action on Airmail Unfair, Lindbergh Tells President," *New York Times*, February 12, 1934.

10. Report for Harllee Branch, Second Assistant Postmaster General, April 12, 1943, Box 177, RG 46, NARA.

11. Thomas Mann Randolph Meikleham telegram to President Franklin D.

Roosevelt, February 13, 1934; Maurice Goodman telegram to Stephen T. Early, February 13, 1934; Emma E. Dillon to Franklin Roosevelt, February 14, 1934; Myles F. Lasker to Stephen Early, February 13, 1934; Russell Edwards to Stephen Early, February 13, 1934; and Sallie Stockard to Stephen Early, February 13, 1934, all in President's OF 19; "Air Mail: Flyer-Heroes in Washington Present Their Side of the Case as Eleventh Army Pilot Dies," *Newsweek*, March 24, 1934, 10.

12. Report for Harllee Branch, April 12, 1934; Harry W. Musselwhite to Franklin Roosevelt, February 10, 1934, President's OF 19.

13. Croll Hunter to Franklin Roosevelt (copy to James Farley), February 15, 1934, President's OF 19.

14. E. F. Gillespie to Franklin Roosevelt, n.d., and Frank E. Patrick to Mr. Chester H. Rowell, Editor, *San Francisco Chronicle* (copy to President Roosevelt), n.d., President's OF 19.

15. Brigadier General William Mitchell to Hugo Black, March 11, 1934, President's OF 19. Mitchell's political ties to both the Democratic Party and Franklin Roosevelt also deserve mention, however. By the early 1930s Mitchell—who was court-martialed under a Republican administration—had become a fervent Democratic supporter. He assisted Roosevelt's presidential campaign in 1932, going so far as to serve as a delegate at the 1932 Democratic National Convention in Chicago and campaigning for Roosevelt in Virginia and Maryland after the latter had secured the party's nomination. Mitchell's actions may have been motivated by a desire to secure a post in the new administration, and he maintained ties with Roosevelt through the first several years of his presidency. Regardless, after his election Roosevelt endeavored to distance himself from the former general, whose rabid focus on promoting American airpower made him a problematic political ally. Taking these facts into account, it seems that Mitchell's engagement with the airmail scandal may also have been a reflection of his efforts to stay in Roosevelt's good graces. For more information, see James J. Cooke, *Billy Mitchell*, 261–71.

16. "Army's First Week," *Time*, March 5, 1934, 46–47; "Air Mail: Climax of Cancellation Drama Reached as New Bids from Commercial Carriers Are Opened," *Newsweek*, April 28, 1934, 26.

17. Archivist's cross-reference, President's Personal File 607, Franklin D. Roosevelt Papers as President, Franklin D. Roosevelt Presidential Library, Hyde Park, New York; Franklin Roosevelt to Hugo Black, March 7, 1934, Box 477, Hugo Black Papers.

18. Roosevelt to Black, March 7, 1934.

19. "Turnback," *Time*, March 19, 1934, 53–54.

20. Statement by Ernest R. Breech, President, North American Aviation, Inc., commenting on President Roosevelt's letter dated March 7, 1934, to Chairman Mead of the House Post Office and Post Roads Committee and Senators McKellar and Black, undated, and Statement by Richard W. Robbins, President, Transcontinental and Western Air, Inc., commenting on President Roosevelt's letter dated March 7, 1934, to Chairman Mead of the House Post Office and Post Roads Committee and Senators McKellar and Black, March 9, 1934, President's OF 19.

21. Statement by Ernest R. Breech, President, North American Aviation, Inc. com-

menting on President Roosevelt's letter dated March 7, 1934, to Chairman Mead of the House Post Office and Post Roads Committee and Senators McKellar and Black, undated, and Statement of Captain Eddie Rickenbacker, Vice President of North American Aviation, Inc., before the Senate Committee on Post Office and Post Roads on Senate Bill S. 3012 to Revise Air-Mail Laws, March 17, 1934, President's OF 19.

22. Franklin Roosevelt to Hugo Black, March 7, 1934, Box 477, Hugo Black Papers. Note that Roosevelt's focus on breaking up aviation holding companies broadly parallels his focus on efforts to stem the influence of electrical power trusts. See Ellis W. Hawley, *The New Deal and the Problem of Monopoly: A Study in Economic Ambivalence*, 2nd ed., 325–43.

23. L. H. Brittin to E. T. Clark, June 11, 1930, Box 156, RG 46, NARA. Historian Ellis Hawley has played a key role in contextualizing New Dealers' aviation policy. In *The New Deal and the Problem of Monopoly*, Hawley argues that Roosevelt and other New Dealers addressed aviation as a "public utility"—an inherently monopolistic industry providing essential public service, desiring governmental regulation to protect its special status. In the depressed economic atmosphere of the 1930s, he suggests, aviation executives looked to the government to protect them from the harshest aspects of the economic climate, citing the fragile status of the emerging industry and aviation's value to national defense as evidence of their need for federal assistance. Within this context, Hawley contends, Roosevelt initially worked to promote competition and demolish the "cartels" created by aviation holding corporations. In this view the Airmail Act of 1934 represented a short-lived effort to promote competition, an effort ultimately undone by the passage of the Civil Aeronautics Act in 1938. Hawley's analysis, however, overlooks the complexities inherent in contemporary aviation policy. He largely ignores Roosevelt's role in crafting both the 1934 legislation and the Civil Aeronautics Act of 1938 and fails to identify any continuity in the president's actions. Further, his analysis largely disregards both Hoover's key role in creating and promoting a coherent aviation policy and the reality of aviation's difference from other transportation models; Hawley fails to account for aviation's truly nascent status in the early 1930s, equating aviation executives with railroad tycoons and power monopolies. Ultimately, this analysis presents an overly simplistic and in many ways misleading interpretation of Roosevelt's engagement with aviation policy and obscures the significance of the president's actions vis-à-vis the Airmail Act of 1934 and subsequent policy developments. See Hawley, *New Deal and Problem*, 226–27, 240–44.

24. A significant point of divergence with New Deal policy vis-à-vis utilities, where FDR did embrace nationalization in the form of the Tennessee Valley Authority. See Hawley, *New Deal and Problem*, 325–43.

25. Franklin Roosevelt to Hugo Black, March 7, 1934, Box 477, Hugo Black Papers. Historians have given Roosevelt little credit for his role in facilitating a productive end to the airmail scandal—in fact, usually depicting this result as something of an accident. According to Robert van der Linden, in the end, Farley, Roosevelt, and the Democrats "unwittingly . . . validated Walter Brown's program." Van der Linden and others point to the supposedly partisan origins of the Black Special Committee

as evidence that Roosevelt and the Democrats remained focused on political issues rather than acting out of a genuine desire to shape aviation. Roosevelt's lack of a coherent, publicly stated aviation policy has also led to charges that his actions sprang from political expediency. The widespread unpopularity of his decision to cancel private contracts and have the army fly the mail has only furthered perceptions that the president lacked awareness of the complexities of military and civilian aviation. Finally, FDR's opposition to some of Walter F. Brown's policies has led to the conclusion that Roosevelt failed to appreciate the value of the preceding administration's aviation strategy. In sum, existing scholarship paints Roosevelt as acting for selfish political reasons, reacting to a scandal through which the president sought to score political points, rather than from any genuine desire to promote aviation. In this view the fact that Roosevelt was able to bring about a functional end to the airmail scandal represented something of a happy accident. See van der Linden, *Airlines and Airmail*, 235–91 (quote on 286). Also reflecting this analysis are Davies, *History of the World's Airlines*, 128–30, and Nick Komons, *Bonfires to Beacons: Federal Civil Aviation Policy under the Air Commerce Act, 1926–1938*, 254–69.

26. White House Memo, undated, President's Personal File 39, Franklin D. Roosevelt Papers as President, Roosevelt Presidential Library; Komons, *Bonfires to Beacons*, 348–51; and Solberg, *Conquest of the Skies*, 198–99.

27. White House Memo: Aviation Commission, President's OF 249b.

28. Clark Howell to Franklin Roosevelt, July 25, 1934, President's OF 249b.

29. List of Witnesses to Whom Air Transport Questionnaire Was Sent, Box 6, Record Group 197, Records of the Civil Aeronautics Board, National Archives and Records Administration, College Park, MD.

30. Rex Martin testimony before the Federal Aviation Commission, September 25, 1934, Box 14, RG 197, NARA.

31. Harllee Branch testimony before the Federal Aviation Commission, September 25, 1934, Box 14, RG 197, NARA.

32. Eddie Rickenbacker testimony before the Federal Aviation Commission, October 3, 1934, Box 14; Ernest Breech testimony before the Federal Aviation Commission, October 4, 1934, Box 15; W. A. Patterson testimony before the Federal Aviation Commission, October 8, 1934, Box 15, all in RG 197, NARA.

33. Hiram Bingham testimony before the Federal Aviation Commission, October 1, 1934, Box 14, RG 197, NARA.

34. Daniel Roper testimony before the Federal Aviation Commission, September 24, 1934, Box 14, RG 197, NARA.

35. Lester Seymour testimony before the Federal Aviation Commission, October 4, 1934, and W. A. Patterson testimony before the Federal Aviation Commission, October 8, 1934, Box 15, RG 197, NARA.

36. Charles Lindbergh testimony before the Federal Aviation Commission, October 16, 1934, Box 15, RG 197, NARA.

37. Daniel Roper testimony before the Federal Aviation Commission, September 24, 1934, Box 14, and Dr. Karl Compton testimony before the Federal Aviation Commission, October 22, 1934, Box 16, RG 197, NARA.

38. Eddie Rickenbacker testimony before the Federal Aviation Commission, October 3, 1934, and Daniel Roper testimony before the Federal Aviation Commission, September 24, 1934, Box 14, RG 197, NARA.

39. "Airlines: U.S. Report Shows All Types of Air Traffic Soaring," *Newsweek*, March 28, 1936, 43; "Aviation Comes of Age," *Life*, August 22, 1938, 44.

40. *Report of the Federal Aviation Commission*, January 1935, 9–13, Box 19, RG 197, NARA.

41. Ibid., 39.

42. Ibid., 14–35.

43. Clark Howell to Franklin Roosevelt, January 16, 1935, President's OF 249b.

44. Komons, *Bonfires to Beacons*, 348–52, 361–69.

45. Pat McCarran to Clarence Lea, February 26, 1938, Box 4, and Report by the Air Commerce Planning Committee of the Business Advisory Council for the Department of Commerce, October 20, 1937, Box 3, James Roosevelt Papers, Franklin D. Roosevelt Presidential Library, Hyde Park, New York (hereafter cited as James Roosevelt Papers).

46. Komons, *Bonfires to Beacons*, 351.

47. Report by the Air Commerce Planning Committee.

48. C. M. Hester to James Roosevelt, December 30, 1937, Box 3, James Roosevelt Papers.

49. Franklin Roosevelt, "Memo for Mac," February 10, 1937, President's OF 2955.

50. Komons, *Bonfires to Beacons*, 357; Franklin Roosevelt to Harry Truman, May 29, 1937, President's OF 2955.

51. Sam Rayburn to Franklin Roosevelt, May 26, 1937, and Franklin Roosevelt, White House Memo, May 31, 1937, President's OF 2955.

52. Clarence Lea to Franklin Roosevelt, July 30, 1937, and Franklin Roosevelt to Clarence Lea, August 5, 1937, President's OF 2955.

53. Fred Fagg memo to Assistant Secretary Johnson, June 3, 1937, and James Johnson to James Roosevelt, June 3, 1937, Box 41, James Roosevelt Papers.

54. Franklin Roosevelt memorandum for Harllee Branch, July 31, 1937, President's OF 2955.

55. Harllee Branch to Franklin Roosevelt, August 17, 1937, President's OF 2955.

56. Franklin Roosevelt memo to Mr. McIntyre Re: Secretary of Commerce, September 15, 1937, archivist's cross-reference, President's OF 2955.

57. Daniel Roper memorandum for Colonel Johnson, October 22, 1937, Box 3, James Roosevelt Papers.

58. C. M. Hester memorandum for James Roosevelt, November 15, 1937, and C. M. Hester memorandum for James Roosevelt, November 16, 1937, Box 3, James Roosevelt Papers.

59. J. M. Johnson to James Roosevelt, memorandum and "Summary of a Proposed Bill to Promote and Regulate Civil Aeronautics," November 26, 1937, Box 3, James Roosevelt Papers; Comparison of Report of the President's Aviation Committee with H.R. 7273 (submitted by Mr. Lea), undated, President's OF 2955.

60. C. M. Hester memorandum for James Roosevelt, December 13, 1937; J. M.

Johnson to James Roosevelt, December 22, 1937; C. M. Hester to James Roosevelt, December 23, 1937; and James Roosevelt to C. M. Hester, December 27, 1937, all in Box 3, James Roosevelt Papers.

61. Clarence Lea to James Roosevelt, January 6, 1938; C. M. Hester to James Roosevelt, January 7, 1938; and J. M. Johnson to James Roosevelt, January 11, 1938, all in Box 3, James Roosevelt Papers.

62. "Memorandum for Representative Rayburn," undated; "Memorandum for Mr. James Roosevelt," January 17, 1938; C. M. Hester to James Roosevelt, January 18, 1938; C. M. Hester to James Roosevelt, January 22, 1938; C. M. Hester to James Roosevelt, January 23, 1938; C. M. Hester to James Roosevelt, January 24, 1938; C. M. Hester memorandum for James Roosevelt, January 25, 1938; and J. M. Johnson to James Roosevelt, January 26, 1938, all in Box 3, James Roosevelt Papers.

63. C. M. Hester memorandum for James Rowe, Assistant to James Roosevelt, February 10, 1938, and C. M. Hester to James Roosevelt, February 12, 1938, Box 4, James Roosevelt Papers.

64. James Rowe memorandum for James Roosevelt, March 3, 1938; Senator Pat McCarran Press Release, "Broad Powers to Regulate Commercial and Civil Aviation Given to Independent Authority in New Senate Draft of Bill," March 3, 1938; and C. M. Hester memorandum for James Rowe, March 3, 1938, all in Box 4, James Roosevelt Papers.

65. James Rowe memorandum for James Roosevelt, March 8, 1938; C. M. Hester memorandum for James Rowe, March 8, 1938; C. M. Hester memorandum for James Rowe, March 18, 1938; C. M. Hester memorandum for Kenneth McKellar, March 18, 1938; and C. M. Hester to James Rowe, April 12, 1938, all in Box 4, James Roosevelt Papers.

66. James Roosevelt confidential letter to Burton Wheeler, April 5, 1938; James Roosevelt confidential letter to Harry Truman, April 5, 1938; James Roosevelt confidential letter to Clarence Lea, April 5, 1938; and Franklin Roosevelt to Clarence Lea, April 12, 1938, all in Box 30, James Roosevelt Papers.

67. C. M. Hester memorandum to James Rowe, Assistant to James Roosevelt, April 15, 1938, and C. M. Hester memorandum to James Rowe, June 1, 1938, Box 4, James Roosevelt Papers.

68. "A Magna Carta of the Air: New Control Setup Welcomed by Growing Industry," *Newsweek*, June 27, 1938, 39; "Civil Aeronautics Authority," *Time*, July 18, 1938, 35.

69. See "War at Sea and Its Weapons: A Description of the Purpose of a Navy and the Use of Its Different Ships"—Article I, "General Introduction—Scouts and Aircraft," September 27, 1915, Box 40, Franklin D. Roosevelt Papers Relating to Family, Business, and Personal Affairs, Franklin D. Roosevelt Presidential Library, Hyde Park, New York; Bilstein, *Flight in America*, 128–31; and Sherry, *Rise of American Airpower*, 49, 59–61.

70. Franklin Roosevelt memorandum for the Secretary of War, January 15, 1935, President's OF 249.

71. Dr. Joseph Ames to Franklin Roosevelt, December 30, 1938, President's OF 249.

72. Alan P. Dobson, *FDR and Civil Aviation: Flying Strong, Flying Free*, 119–20.

73. Franklin Roosevelt to Charles Horner, August 30, 1939, President's Personal File 3843, Franklin D. Roosevelt Papers as President, Roosevelt Presidential Library.

Chapter 6

1. "12,000 or More See Dedication of New Airport," *Knoxville News-Sentinel*, October 15, 1937, copy in Box 38, Record Group 69, Records of the Works Progress Administration, National Archives and Records Administration, College Park, MD.

2. Ibid.

3. Ibid.

4. Ibid.

5. Report by H. S. Sanders, WPA Regional Engineer, December 2, 1937, Box 38, RG 69, NARA.

6. Jason Scott Smith, *Building New Deal Liberalism: The Political Economy of Public Works, 1933–1956*, 1.

7. Barton J. Bernstein, "The New Deal: The Conservative Achievements of Liberal Reform," in *Towards a New Past: Dissenting Essays in American History*; William Leuchtenburg, *Franklin D. Roosevelt and the New Deal, 1932–1940*, 125, 130; Arthur Schlesinger Jr. *The Age of Roosevelt: The Coming of the New Deal*, 282–96; and Howard Zinn, "The Limits of the New Deal," in *The Politics of History*, 133–34; Smith, *Building New Deal Liberalism*, 19, 22; Robert D. Leighninger Jr., *Long-Range Public Investment: The Forgotten Legacy of the New Deal*, Nick Taylor, *American Made: The Enduring Legacy of the WPA: When FDR Put the Nation to Work*.

8. Smith, *Building New Deal Liberalism*, 2, 19, 208, 258. For more information on New Deal public works, see Taylor, *American Made*; Leuchtenburg, *Franklin D. Roosevelt*, 118–42; Schlesinger, *Age of Roosevelt*; and Gerald D. Nash, *The Great Depression and World War II: Organizing America, 1933–1945*, 33–36.

9. Janet R. Daly Bednarek, *America's Airports: Airfield Development, 1918–1947*, 6.

10. Ibid., 42.

11. Austin F. MacDonald, "Airport Problems of American Cities," *Annals of the American Academy of Political and Social Science*, Vol. 151, *Postwar Progress in Child Welfare* (September 1930): 226.

12. Smith, *Building New Deal Liberalism*, 22.

13. Ibid., 2, 31.

14. Department of the Interior memorandum to the Press, Interview with Harold L. Ickes, Secretary of the Interior, by Walter Trumbull, July 3, 1933, Box 1, Record Group 135, Records of the Public Works Administration, National Archives and Records Administration, College Park, MD. Significantly, Ickes worked to establish quotas for African Americans on PWA work rolls. The building trades had long been an almost exclusive bastion of white male workers, and Ickes's efforts represent one

of the first organized attempts by the federal government to actively promote equality in a racially exclusive labor market. See Smith, *Building New Deal Liberalism*, 38.

15. Ibid.; Harold L. Ickes, Secretary of the Interior, Speech to the Conference of Mayors at A Century of Progress Exposition in Chicago, Illinois, September 23, 1933, Box 1, RG 135, NARA. Unfortunately, the vast majority of PWA records were destroyed before being transferred to the National Archives and Records Administration. As a result, no specific project files remain from the period before 1940. As other records indicate—including references in Federal Aviation Commission testimony, passing statements in the records of the PWA's Investigations Division, and references in WPA project files—the PWA did fund a number of aviation-related projects. The exact number, specific expenditures, and nature of those allocations, however, remain unclear. Nonetheless, subsequent public works agencies' aviation-related allocations suggest the influence of Ickes's rationale.

16. The CWA functioned as a short-term relief program in the winter of 1933–34, while the CCC put unemployed men ages eighteen to twenty-four to work on projects related to conservation and the protection of natural resources between 1933 and 1942.

17. Memorandum, October 29, 1934, Box 51, Airway and Airport Projects Folder, Harry L. Hopkins Papers, Franklin D. Roosevelt Presidential Library, Hyde Park, New York (hereafter cited as Hopkins Papers). At the time, Hopkins was serving as the head of the Federal Emergency Relief Agency (FERA). In November of 1933 Roosevelt authorized him to establish the machinery of the CWA. Roosevelt later appointed Hopkins to head the WPA, a post he held until he became secretary of commerce in December 1938. Hopkins reported that at the start of the program there were 2,028 airports in existence in the United States. That number referred to all types of fields, including government, army, navy, municipal, emergency, and private.

18. Memorandum, October 29, 1934, Box 51, Airway and Airport Projects Folder, Hopkins Papers.

19. "$101,000,000 Spent on New Airports," *New York Times*, February 27, 1938, 14; Memorandum, October 29, 1934, Box 51, Airway and Airport Projects Folder, Hopkins Papers; Bonnie Fox Schwartz, *The Civil Works Administration, 1933–1934: The Business of Emergency Employment in the New Deal*, 183; "Plan to Salvage 1,450 CWA Airports," *New York Times*, April 12, 1934, 3.

20. John Geisse, Testimony before the Federal Aviation Commission, October 18, 1934, Box 15, RG 197, NARA.

21. Ibid.

22. Ibid.

23. Ibid.

24. Exemplifying this interpretation is William Leuchtenburg's analysis. He describes Harry Hopkins's central goal as "putting to work as many men as he could who were currently on relief." Roosevelt's decision to allocate more authority—and more federal dollars—to Hopkins's WPA than to the more parsimonious Ickes's PWA, in Leuchtenburg's words, represented a "regrettable" decision. See Leuchtenburg, *Franklin D. Roosevelt*, 125.

25. Oliver McKee Jr., "More New Airports: WPA's Expansion Program Aims to Keep Pace with Growing Air Transport," *New York Times*, October 6, 1935, 169; *Final Report of the* WPA *Program*, 1935–43, 51. See also "Airport Projects Pushed by WPA," *New York Times*, August 16, 1936, 22; "Big Aviation Gains Seen by Vidal," *New York Times*, December 25, 1936, 8; "Airport Projects by WPA Reach 940," *New York Times*, August 15, 1937, 5; "Work Begins Today on Queens Airport," *New York Times*, September 9, 1937, 25.

26. L. L. Odell, Works Progress Administration Division of Airways and Airports Memorandum, September 24, 1935, Box 5, Record Group 237, Records of the Federal Aviation Administration and Preceding Agencies, National Archives and Records Administration, College Park, MD; *Final Report of the* WPA *Program*, 122.

27. Works Progress Administration, Press Release, March 29, 1936, Airway and Airport Projects Folder, Hopkins Papers. The discrepancy between these numbers and the ones from L. L. Odell listed above reflect the complex nature of the WPA appropriations process. States and localities applied to the WPA to fund specific projects. The president had to approve all requests, which then had to be cleared by the administration's Washington, DC, office. At that point projects were "approved," but funds could not yet be released. After approval, the Washington office referred applications to WPA state administrators, who provided further review, and only then released funds for construction. State administrators made their determinations on the basis of localities' and states' employment needs, as well as the potential for projects to promote infrastructure. Thus, a project could be "approved" but have the release of its funds pending for some time. Further complicating matters, these WPA figures reflect only federal allocations, not state and local contributions.

28. Ibid.

29. Statement by Lieutenant Colonel F. C. Harrington, Proceedings of the National Airport Conference, December 6 and 7, 1937, page 75, Box 3, James Roosevelt Papers.

30. See Komons, *Bonfires to Beacons*, 372–73, and Bednarek, *America's Airports*, 98–99.

31. "CAA Gives 3 Plans for Airport System," *New York Times*, March 25, 1939, 4; *Final Report of the* WPA *Program*, 51, 84; "Defense Projects Get WPA's Priority," *New York Times*, June 7, 1940, 14; "WPA to Increase Work on Defense," *New York Times*, June 15, 1940, 8; "WPA Construction As a Defense Aid," *New York Times*, July 7, 1940, 4; "Defense Projects Expanded by WPA," *New York Times*, November 11, 1940, 19; Harvey E. Valentine, "Work Begun on Airports," *New York Times*, April 20, 1941, XX8; "Large WPA Fund Spent on Defense," *New York Times*, July 15, 1941, 15; "Pre-Crisis WPA Aid in Defense Hailed," *New York Times*, October 19, 1941, 25.

32. A. B. McMullen to Corrington Gill, Assistant Administrator, Works Progress Administration, November 23, 1937, Box 6, and W. Sumpter Smith memorandum for Corrington Gill, Assistant Administrator, Works Progress Administration, November 25, 1937, Box 5, RG 237, NARA.

33. McMullen to Gill, November 23, 1937, Box 6, RG 237, NARA; "Big Airport Program On," *New York Times*, February 9, 1936, XX7.

34. Hodges Briscoe to Mr. McDaniel, August 25, 1937, Hodges Briscoe Collection (one box), Calvin M. McClung Historical Collection, East Tennessee History Center, Knoxville Tennessee; "Strenuous WPA Work 'Spoils' Crawford's Arm, Elbow, and Trip," *Knoxville News Sentinel*, September 13, 1936, A-4; "Gen. Knox Open Letter to City Manager Dempster," *Knoxville News Sentinel*, September 24, 1937, 13; "Airport Buys Fence," *Knoxville News Sentinel*, September 30, 1937, 4; "12,000 or More See Dedication of New Airport," *Knoxville News Sentinel*, October 15, 1937, 1; "40,000 Attend Airport Dedication," *Nashville Tennessean*, November 2, 1936, 1; "325,000 See Mayor Dedicate Airport to World Service," *New York Times*, October 16, 1939, 1.

35. McMullen to Gill, November 23, 1937.

36. W. Sumpter Smith memorandum for Corrington Gill, Assistant Administrator, Works Progress Administration, November 25, 1937, Box 5, RG 237, NARA.

37. McMullen to Gill, November 23, 1937.

38. Ibid.

39. W. Sumpter Smith memorandum for Corrington Gill, Assistant Administrator, Works Progress Administration, November 25, 1937, Box 5, RG 237, NARA.

40. McMullen to Gill, November 23, 1937.

41. "Mayor Certain Present Airport Can Be Enlarged," *Chicago Daily News*, December 4, 1936; WPA Result of Engineering Review, November 29, 1937; WPA Project Update, Data As Reported 3-1-38; Edward Kelley to Jesse H. Jones, Federal Loan Administrator, November 19, 1940, all in Box 13, RG 69, NARA.

42. See Fred S. Childs, Report Relating to the Proposed Construction of the Newark Airport Hangar, April 1936, and Morton M. Milford, Special Assistant to the Administrator, memo to Mr. C. C. Thompson, October 22, 1936, Box 27, RG 69, NARA; "Newark Asks WPA Aid to Improve Airport," *New York Times*, August 22, 1935, 27; "Airport in Newark Gets Big WPA Fund," *New York Times*, September 22, 1935, 23; "Newark Mayor Honored," *New York Times*, October 20, 1935, 15; Engineering Review, Newark Airport WPA Project, James W. Costello, Chief Engineer, Department of Public Affairs, A. H. Armstrong, Principal Assistant Engineer, Newark Airport, May 10, 1938, Box 27, RG 69, NARA.

43. Otto Kein memorandum Re: Inspection Report of the St. Louis, Missouri Airport Project, December 15, 1938, Box 23, RG 69, NARA; "$200,000 Airport Projects Planned," *Saint Louis Globe-Democrat*, June 24, 1937.

44. J. W. Gentry, District Director, WPA Report of Completed or Discontinued Project, June 6, 1937, Box 4, RG 69, NARA; "WPA Plans Air Markers," *San Diego Evening Tribune*, November 17, 1936; WPA Weather Data Will Aid Aviation, *New York Times*, July 30, 1940, 37.

45. A. B. McMullen, Chief, WPA Airport Section Safety and Planning Division, to Earl C. Popp, Regional Supervisor, Bureau of Air Commerce, December 25, 1937, Box 5, and WPA Engineering Division memo to the Project Control Division, November 29, 1937, Box 13, RG 69, NARA.

46. Harry Goldberg to L. L. Odell, October 18, 1935, Box 13, RG 69, NARA.

47. W. M. Aldous to John S. Wynne, December 18, 1936, Box 23, and B. M. Harloe to Matthew S. Murray, April 6, 1939, Box 23, RG 69, NARA.

48. John S. Wynne to F. C. Harrington, November 17, 1936, Box 27, RG 69, NARA.

49. Childs, Report Relating to the Proposed Construction.

50. "Airport Plan Hits New Snag: WPA Cannot Move Tracks," *Chicago Daily News*, April 23, 1937, and "Airport Compromise Is Near," *Chicago Herald and Examiner*, July 23, 1937, copies in Box 13, RG 69, NARA.

51. "Offers Airport Repairs," *Knoxville News Sentinel*, November 30, 1933, 3; "Re: Filling Station for McGhee Tyson Airport," June 3, 1930, Knoxville, Tennessee, City Council Records (Microfilm), Book 13, 324–25; "Longer Airport Needed," *Knoxville News Sentinel*, August 5, 1930, 6; "Airport Gets Improvements," *Knoxville News Sentinel*, June 24, 1930, 4; "Delay Airport Station," *Knoxville News Sentinel*, September 24, 1930, 8; "Airport Plans Up in Council," *Knoxville News Sentinel*, February 10, 1930, 5; "Air Line Men Visit City," *Knoxville News Sentinel*, October 27, 1930, 2; "Confer on Air Line Tuesday," *Knoxville News Sentinel*, May 4, 1931, 2; "New Airline to Stop Here," *Knoxville News Sentinel*, May 5, 1931, 2; "New Airline Open Thursday," *Knoxville News Sentinel*, May 12, 1931, 2; "Can't Find Promoter," *Knoxville News Sentinel*, May 16, 1931, 2; ; "State Will Ask $104,000 for Relief in Knox County," *Knoxville News Sentinel*, October 12, 1932, 1; "$200,000 Loan Asked by State," *Knoxville News Sentinel*, October 13, 1932, 12; "Knox County Granted $104,736 Relief Loan in R.F.C. Allotment," *Knoxville News Sentinel*, October 15, 1932, 1; "Doe Studies Air Route Through Here," *Knoxville News Sentinel*, November 15, 1932, 1; "Re: Air Route Through Knoxville to Atlanta," November 15, 1932, Knoxville, Tennessee, City Council Records (Microfilm), Book 14, 320; "Air Mail Port Choice Untold," *Knoxville News Sentinel*, June 20, 1934, 7; "Air Lines, P.O. Pass Buck on Port Choice," *Knoxville News Sentinel*, June 16, 1934, 2; "Says Isle Port Has Been Picked," *Knoxville News Sentinel*, June 21, 1934, 1; "Letters Sent by Air Mail Move Fast—If Wind Blows," *Knoxville News Sentinel*, July 12, 1934, 11; "Mail Plane May Stop," *Knoxville News Sentinel*, July 13, 1934, 14; "Eastbound Plane Passes City By," *Knoxville News Sentinel*, July 19, 1934, 18; "Airmail Service Here is Stopped," *Knoxville News Sentinel*, July 20, 1934, 1.

For additional information about airport development in Tennessee and the WPA's role therein, see Jim Fulbright, *Aviation in Tennessee: Tennessee's Aviation History in the Stories of People, Places, and Events*, 36–71; Edwin P. Patton, "Transportation Development," in *Heart of the Valley: A History of Knoxville, Tennessee*, ed. Lucile Deaderick, 178–236; and Carroll Van West, *Tennessee's New Deal Landscape: A Guidebook*, 226–54.

52. "Airport Must Be Improved," *Knoxville News Sentinel*, October 23, 1934, 16; "Hope to Solve Port Problem Once and for All," *Knoxville News Sentinel*, October 31, 1934, 1; "Inspect Sites for Airport," *Knoxville News Sentinel*, November 7, 1934, 1; "Await Reports on Field Check," *Knoxville News Sentinel*, November 8, 1934, 1; "Advise City Not to Spend More on Existing Ports," *Knoxville News Sentinel*, November 20, 1934, 1; "Re: Providing Adequate Airport for City," January 11, 1935, Knoxville, Tennessee, City Council Records (Microfilm), Book 15, 332; "Name Airport Committee," *Knoxville News Sentinel*, January 9, 1935, 11.

53. Benton J. Strong, "Berry Favors Airport Here," *Knoxville News Sentinel*, June

21, 1935, 1; "WPA Asks Airport Survey for City," *Knoxville News Sentinel*, August 7, 1935, 6; "Berry to Press Fund For Airport," *Knoxville News Sentinel*, August 14, 1935, 10; "WPA Chief Says City May Get Airport Fund," *Knoxville News Sentinel*, August 2, 1935, 4; "City Airport Request Ready," *Knoxville News Sentinel*, August 31, 1935, 7; "May Pick Port Site Tonight," *Knoxville News Sentinel*, September 3, 1935, 1; "$491,000 Project Gets WPA O.K. in Nashville," *Knoxville News Sentinel*, September 4, 1935, 1; "Port Project Sent Off," *Knoxville News Sentinel*, September 8, 1935, 1; Harry S. Berry, State Administrator, to L. L. Odell, Chief Technical Officer, WPA Division of Airways and Airports," November 20, 1935, Box 38, RG 69, NARA; "P.O. Official Coming," *Knoxville News Sentinel*, October 13, 1935, B-7; "WPA Receives $470,000 Airport Fund," *Knoxville News Sentinel*, November 8, 1935, 1.

54. "Re: Appropriation of $8,000 from Permanent Improvement Fund for Purchasing Land for New Airport," December 10, 1935, Knoxville, Tennessee, City Council Records (Microfilm), Book 15, 638; "Council Halts Airport Project as American Airlines Announces Passenger Service after Jan. 1," *Knoxville News Sentinel*, December 11, 1935, 1; "The $500,000 Airport Bargain," *Knoxville News Sentinel*, December 11, 1935, 6.

55. "'Don't Muff Chance to Get First Class Airport,' Business Leaders Beg Council; Point to $500,000 for $50,000 Bargain," *Knoxville News Sentinel*, December 12, 1935, 1.

56. "C. C. Will Form Bureau to Get Industries Soon," *Knoxville News Sentinel*, March 28, 1928, 2; "Will Plan Air Tour," *Knoxville News Sentinel*, May 30, 1930, 1; "Plan Schedule for Air Tour," *Knoxville News Sentinel*, May 31, 1930, 10; Dozen Planes Will Start Tour Friday," *Knoxville News Sentinel*, July 24, 1930, 1; "Ten Good Will Airplanes Are on Their Way," *Knoxville News Sentinel*, July 25, 1930, 1; "Air Tourists Welcomed in Middlesboro," *Knoxville News Sentinel*, July 26, 1930, 1; John T. Montoux, "Air Tour Will Bring Throngs to Dedication," *Knoxville News Sentinel*, July 27, 1930, 1; "Thousands Throng to M'Ghee Tyson Airport as Dedication Begins." *Knoxville News Sentinel*, August 1, 1930, 1; "Crowds Swarm around Field; Many Get Through," *Knoxville News Sentinel*, August 1, 1930, 2; "Big Meet Is Climax of Rites at Port," *Knoxville News Sentinel*, August 2, 1930, 1; John T. Montoux, "Airport Fete Goes Beyond Expectations," *Knoxville News Sentinel*, August 3, 1930, 1; "Wanted—An Airport," *Knoxville News Sentinel*, January 5, 1929.

57. "Ordinances; Ordinance No. 710," December 14, 1935, Knoxville, Tennessee, City Council Records (Microfilm), Book 15, 649; "Airport Money Voted; School Bind Hit Snag," *Knoxville News Sentinel*, December 15, 1935, 1 "Knoxville Airport," H. S. Sanders, Regional Engineer, WPA, undated, and "Statement of Project Estimate Detail," March 22, 1938, Box 38, RG 69, NARA.

58. "Three Shifts Soon to Be on Airport Job," *Knoxville News Sentinel*, April 26, 1936, A-6; "WPA Has 3151 at Work on 54 Knox Projects," *Knoxville News Sentinel*, September 6, 1936, A-7; "Many Improvements Result from WPA Work," *Knoxville News Sentinel*, February 28, 1937, Magazine 1; Harry S. Berry, State Administrator, to L. L. Odell, Chief Technical Officer, WPA Division of Airways and Airports, November 20, 1935, Box 38, RG 69, NARA; Al Manola, "The Next Time You Hear One of Those W.P.A. Jokes," *Knoxville News Sentinel*, February 28, 1937, Magazine

1; "Many City Improvements Result from WPA Work," *Knoxville News Sentinel*, February 28, 1937, Magazine 1; "Work Starts on New Half-Million-Dollar Airport," *Knoxville News Sentinel*, March 13, 1936, A-2; "Cameraman Gets 'Aviator-Eye View' of New Airport," *Knoxville News Sentinel*, April 18, 1936, 6; "Making the Grade—And Making It Level—On Alcoa Airport Job," *Knoxville News Sentinel*, August 16, 1936, A-8; "Stately Structure Rising at New Airport," *Knoxville News Sentinel*, October 11, 1936, A-2; "Airport Begins to Look Like It's Supposed To," *Knoxville News Sentinel*, March 22, 1937, 9; "Crack Fliers Will Stage 'Aerobatics' at Dedication of New Airport July 11," *Knoxville News Sentinel*, June 13, 1937, 1; "New Port Takes Over Air Business," *Knoxville News Sentinel*, July 30, 1937, 24; Hodges Briscoe to Mr. McDaniel August 25, 1937, Hodges Briscoe Collection (1 Box), Calvin M. McClung Historical Collection, East Tennessee History Center, Knoxville Tennessee.

59. Knoxville Airport, H. S. Sanders, Regional Engineer, WPA, undated, Box 38, RG 69, NARA; "New Port Here to Give State 'Air Highway,'" *Knoxville News-Sentinel*, July 11, 1937, A-8; "Airline Is Using New Airport Now," *Knoxville News Sentinel*, July 29, 1937, 2; "New Port Takes Over Air Business," *Knoxville News Sentinel*, July 30, 1937, 24; E. H. Briscoe untitled letter, July 18, 1990, Hodges Briscoe Collection (1 Box), Calvin M. McClung Historical Collection, East Tennessee History Center, Knoxville Tennessee; "Airline Service to be Improved," *Knoxville News Sentinel*, August 29, 1937, 12; "Air Travel Is Soaring," *Knoxville News Sentinel*, September 27, 1937, 5.

Chapter 7

1. See Bailey, "Aviation Policy: Past and Present," Southern Economic Journal 69, no. 1 (July 2002): 12–20; Mark Rose, Bruce Seely, and Paul Barrett, *The Best Transportation System in the World: Railroads, Trucks, Airlines, and American Public Policy in the Twentieth Century*, 228–39, and T. A. Heppenheimer, *Turbulent Skies: The History of Commercial Aviation*, 314–50.

2. Roger Bilstein, *Flight in America: From the Wrights to the Astronauts*, 161. For more information, see Dominick Pisano, *To Fill the Skies with Pilots: The Civilian Pilot Training Program, 1939–1946*.

3. Heppenheimer, *Turbulent Skies*, 120; *Final Report of the WPA Program, 1935–43*, 51, 84; "Defense Projects Get WPA's Priority," *New York Times*, June 7, 1940, 14; "WPA to Increase Work on Defense," *New York Times*, June 15, 1940, 8; "WPA Construction As a Defense Aid," *New York Times*, July 7, 1940, 4; "Defense Projects Expanded by WPA," *New York Times*, November 11, 1940, 19; "Large WPA Fund Spent on Defense," *New York Times*, July 15, 1941, 15; "Pre-Crisis WPA Aid in Defense Hailed," *New York Times*, October 19, 1941, 25. For more information on postwar airport construction, see Janet R. Bednarek, *Airports, Cities, and the Jet Age: U.S. Airports Since 1945*, 61–79.

4. Carl Solberg, *Conquest of the Skies: A History of Commercial Aviation in America*, 262; Bernard C. Nalty, ed., *Winged Shield, Winged Sword: A History of the United States Air Force*, 251.

5. Heppenheimer, *Turbulent Skies*, 75–169; Bilstein, *Flight in America*, 169–78.

6. R. E. G. Davies, *A History of the World's Airlines*, 243.

7. Heppenheimer, *Turbulent Skies*, 124–25; Davies, *History of the World's Airlines*, 243; Bilstein, *Flight in America*, 178.

8. See Davies, *History of the World's Airlines*, 243–70; Richard H. K. Vietor, "Contrived Competition: Airline Regulation and Deregulation, 1925–1988," *Business History Review* 64, no. 1 (Spring 1990): 61–108; and Harold J. King, "The Rate-Making Function of the Civil Aeronautics Board," *American Journal of Economics and Sociology* 1, no. 2 (January 1942): 167–90.

9. Davies, *History of the World's Airlines*, 432. Prior to the development of these aircraft, earlier planes like the Douglas DC-4 and DC-6 could cross the country nonstop from west to east, but prevailing winds prevented them from doing so in the other direction. These same aircraft could cross the Atlantic, but only with a refueling stop in Newfoundland—a time-consuming and annoying inconvenience for passengers.

10. For more information on the expanding global influence of US aviation, see Jenifer Van Vleck, *Empire of the Air: Aviation and the American Ascendency*.

11. See Bilstein, *Flight in America*, 178–95; Heppenheimer, *Turbulent Skies*, 137–69; and David Courtwright, *Sky As Frontier: Adventure, Aviation, and Empire*, 110–40.

12. See Solberg, *Conquest of the Skies*, 331–32, 361–67, and Heppenheimer, *Turbulent Skies*, 70–183, 261–91, 314–43.

13. Introduced into commercial service in early 1952, the Comet immediately demonstrated the massive gains in speed and altitude that jets could offer. Unfortunately, the British aircraft proved to be fragile, and two Comets were lost to crashes in early 1954 as a result of metal fatigue leading to explosive depressurization. In the wake of these tragedies the British were forced to go back to the drawing board and totally redesign the aircraft, in the process losing the technological advantage to their American cousins. For more information, see Davies, *History of the World's Airlines*, 451–55, 479–83.

14. It should be noted that the airlines were not blameless in creating this situation. Juan Trippe—the head of Pan Am—almost singlehandedly pushed the entire US airline industry to embrace jet aircraft with his initial purchase. Trippe moved aggressively to secure the new planes in order to maintain Pan Am's world leadership in technology and prestige. As a result, other carriers rushed to follow his lead, lest their reliance on outdated, propeller-driven aircraft cost them customers. See ibid., 479, 482–85.

15. Quote from Heppenheimer, *Turbulent Skies*, 170. Jet aircraft need significantly longer runways than do their piston-engined counterparts. For instance, a fully loaded Douglas DC-7, one of the largest propeller-driven airliners, needed roughly 7,000 feet of runway, whereas a Boeing 707 needed at least 11,500. For more information, see ibid., 185.

16. See ibid., 175–83. In 1972 the FAA—renamed the Federal Aviation Administration—was placed under the control of the newly created Department of Transportation. The same year witnessed the creation of the National Transportation Safety Board, which took control of the CAB's role in investigating air crashes. Simultane-

ously, the CAB merged with the Department of Transportation, maintaining its control over airline rates and routes until deregulation in 1978. See Solberg, *Conquest of the Skies*, 365.

17. Heppenheimer, *Turbulent Skies*, 209–11.

18. Bilstein, *Flight in America*, 265–66. Interestingly, Charles Lindbergh played a leading role in promoting environment-based opposition to the SST program. See Heppenheimer, *Turbulent Skies*, 246.

19. Heppenheimer, *Turbulent Skies*, 247.

20. Ibid., 314–21.

21. Ibid., 314.

22. Vietor, "Contrived Competition," 102; Bilstein, *Flight in America*, 285–92; Heppenheimer, *Turbulent Skies*, 314–44; Rose, Seely, and Barrett, *Best Transportation System*, 228–39.

23. See "Practical Traveler: Passengers Speak Up: The Views from the Back of the Plane," *New York Times*, December 16, 2007; Matthew Wald, "E.P.A. Is Prodded to Require Cuts in Airline Emissions," *New York Times*, December 6, 2007; Randall Stross, "Theater of the Absurd at the TSA," *New York Times*, December 17, 2006; Matthew Wald, "Tougher Security, More Delays: Many Foreign Visitors Face Increased Scrutiny at Airports, and Flight Cancellations Because of Threats are the Latest Headache," *New York Times*, January 18, 2004; and Matthew Wald, "Aviation Experts Bemoan Delays in the Sky: Air Traffic System Is Scorned as Badly in Need of Modernization," *New York Times*, September 29, 1999.

24. "Smithsonian Institution Has Record Year in 2009, With 30 Million Visits," *Washington Post*, January 7, 2010; "National Air and Space Museum Press Kit," Smithsonian Air and Space Museum, accessed July 12, 2010, http://www.nasm.si.edu/events/pressroom/presskits/museumkit/facts_uhc.cfm.

25. Peggy McGlone, "Air and Space Museum's Makeover Estimated at $1 Billion," *Washington Post*, June 22, 2016.

Bibliography

Archival Collections

American Heritage Center, University of Wyoming, Laramie, Wyoming.

Manufacturers Aircraft Association Records
Roscoe Turner Papers

Calvin M. McClung Historical Collection, East Tennessee History Center, Knoxville, Tennessee.

Hodges Briscoe Collection

Columbia University Special Collections, New York, New York.

Oral History Collection, Aviation Section

Herbert C. Hoover Presidential Library, West Branch, Iowa.

Herbert Hoover Papers as Secretary of Commerce
Presidential Campaign General Correspondence
Herbert Hoover Presidential Papers
William MacCracken Jr. Papers
Clarence M. Young Oral History

Franklin D. Roosevelt Presidential Library, Hyde Park, New York.

Franklin D. Roosevelt Papers Relating to Family, Business, and Personal Affairs
Franklin D. Roosevelt Papers as Assistant Secretary of the Navy
Franklin D. Roosevelt Papers as Governor of New York
Franklin D. Roosevelt Papers as President
Harry Hopkins Papers
James Farley Papers
James Roosevelt Papers
James Rowe Papers
Eleanor Roosevelt Papers

Knox County Archives, East Tennessee History Center, Knoxville, Tennessee.
Knoxville City Council Records (microfilm)

Manuscript Division, Library of Congress, Washington, DC.
Hugo Black Collection

National Air and Space Museum, Smithsonian Institution, National Air and Space Archives, Suitland, Maryland.
National Aeronautic Association Archives

National Archives and Records Administration, Washington, DC.
Record Group 28—Records of the Post Office Department
Record Group 46—Records of the Senate Special Committee to Investigate Ocean Mail and Air Mail Contracts

National Archives and Records Administration, College Park, Maryland.
Record Group 69—Records of the Works Progress Administration
Record Group 135—Records of the Public Works Administration
Record Group 197—Records of the Civil Aeronautics Board
Record Group 237—Records of the Federal Aviation Administration and Preceding Agencies
Record Group 255—Records of the National Aeronautics and Space Administration

Smithsonian Institution Archives, Washington, DC.
Accession 00-008—National Air and Space Museum, Aeronautics Department, Chairman Records, 1990–94
Accession 07-141—National Air and Space Museum, Department of Aeronautics, Exhibition Records, 1971–88
Accession 07-184—National Air and Space Museum, Department of Aeronautics, Exhibition Records, 1972–85
Accession 099-081—National Air and Space Museum, Department of Aeronautics, Records, 1965, 1970–89
Accession 99-127—National Air and Space Museum, Aeronautics Department, Exhibition Records, 1971–74

University of Miami Special Collections, Miami, Florida.
Pan American Airways Papers

Books and Articles

Bailey, Elizabeth E. "Aviation Policy, Past and Present." *Southern Economic Journal* 69, no. 1 (July 2002): 12–20.

Ball, Howard. *Hugo L. Black: Cold Steel Warrior*. New York: Oxford University Press, 1996.

Banner, Stuart. *Who Owns the Sky? The Struggle to Control Airspace from the Wright Brothers On*. Cambridge, MA: Harvard University Press, 2008.

Barber, William J. *From New Era to New Deal: Herbert Hoover, the Economists, and American Economic Policy, 1921–1933*. New York: Cambridge University Press, 1985.

Barnes, Catherine A. *Journey from Jim Crow: The Desegregation of Southern Transit*. New York: Columbia University Press, 1983.

Bednarek, Janet R. Daly. *Airports, Cities, and the Jet Age: U.S. Airports since 1945*. New York: Palgrave Macmillan, 2016.

———. *America's Airports: Airfield Development, 1918–1947*. College Station: Texas A&M University Press, 2001.

———, and Michael H. Bednarek. *Dreams of Flight: General Aviation in the United States*. College Station: Texas A&M University Press, 2003.

Berg, A. Scott. *Lindbergh*. New York: G. P. Putnam's Sons, 1998.

Bernstein, Barton J. "The New Deal: The Conservative Achievements of Liberal Reform." In *Towards a New Past: Dissenting Essays in American History*. New York: Vintage Books, 1967.

Biddle, Wayne. *Barons of the Sky: From Early Flight to Strategic Warfare: The Story of the American Aerospace Industry*. Baltimore: The Johns Hopkins University Press, 2001.

Bilstein, Roger E. *Flight in America: From the Wrights to the Astronauts*. Baltimore: Johns Hopkins University Press, 2001.

———. *Flight Patterns: Trends in Aeronautical Development in the United States, 1918–1929*. Athens: University of Georgia Press, 1983.

Bloom, Nicholas Dagen. *The Metropolitan Airport: JFK International and Modern New York*. Philadelphia: University of Pennsylvania Press, 2015.

Boyne, Walter J. *Beyond the Wild Blue: A History of the United States Air Force*. New York: St. Martin's Press, 1997.

Brinkley, Alan. *The End of Reform: New Deal Liberalism in Recession and War*. New York: Alfred A. Knopf, 1995.

———. *Voices of Protest: Huey Long, Father Coughlin, and the Great Depression*. New York: Vintage Books, 1983.

Brooks, Peter W. "The Development of Air Transport." *Journal of Transport Economics and Policy* 1, no. 2 (May 1967): 164–83.

Brown, Anthony E. *The Politics of Airline Deregulation*. Knoxville: University of Tennessee Press, 1987.

Bunke, Harvey C. "Commercial Aviation and the Civil Aeronautics Act of 1938." *Southern Economic Journal* 20, no. 4 (April 1954): 356–68.

Burner, David. *Herbert Hoover: A Public Life*. New York: Atheneum, 1984.

Burns, James MacGregor. *The Lion and the Fox: The First Political Biography of Franklin Delano Roosevelt*. New York: Harcourt, Brace & World, 1956.

Butler, Susan. *East to the Dawn: The Life of Amelia Earhart*. Reading, MA: Addison-Wesley, 1997.

Button, Kenneth, ed. *Airline Deregulation: International Experiences*. London: David Fulton Publishers, 1991.

Caidin, Martin. *Barnstorming*. New York: Bantam, 1965.

Chambers, John Whitclay, II. *The Tyranny of Change: America in the Progressive Era, 1900–1917*. New York: St. Martins Press, 1980.

Cochran, Jacqueline, *The Stars at Noon*. Boston: Little Brown and Company, 1954.

Conkin, Paul K. *The New Deal*. 3rd ed. Wheeling, IL: Harlan Davidson, 1992.

Cook, James, J. *Billy Mitchell*. Boulder, CO: Lynne Reinner, 2002.

Corn, Joseph J. *The Winged Gospel: America's Romance with Aviation, 1900–1950*. New York: Oxford University Press, 1983.

Courtwright, David. *Sky As Frontier: Adventure, Aviation, and Empire*. College Station: Texas A&M University Press, 2004.

Crouch, Tom D. *A Dream of Wings: Americans and the Airplane, 1887–1905*. New York: W. W. Norton and Company, 2002.

——, ed. *Charles A. Lindbergh: An American Life*. Washington, DC: Smithsonian Institution Press, 1977.

Daniels, Roger. *Franklin D. Roosevelt: Road to the New Deal, 1882–1939*. Urbana: University of Illinois Press, 2015.

Daley, Robert. *An American Saga: Juan Trippe and his Pan American Empire*. New York: Random House, 1980.

David, Paul T. *The Economics of Air Mail Transportation*. Washington, DC: The Brookings Institution, 1934.

Davies, R. E. G. *Airlines of the United States since 1914*. Washington, DC: Smithsonian Institution Press, 1998.

——. *A History of the World's Airlines*. London: Oxford University Press, 1964.

——. *Rebels and Reformers of the Airways*. Washington, DC: Smithsonian Institution Press, 1987.

Davis, Kenneth S. *F.D.R.: The New Deal Years, 1933–1937, A History*. New York: Random House, 1979.

Degler, Carl. *Out of Our Past: The Forces That Shaped Modern America*. New York: Harper and Row, 1984.

Dennenberg, Barry. *An American Hero: The True Story of Charles A. Lindbergh*. New York: Scholastic, 1996.

Dierikx, Marc. *Clipping the Clouds: How Air Travel Changed the World*. Westport, CT: Praeger Publishers, 2008.

Dilger, Robert J. *American Transportation Policy*. Westport, CT: Praeger Publishers, 2003.

Dobson, Alan P. *FDR and Civil Aviation: Flying Strong, Flying Free*. New York: Palgrave Macmillan, 2011.

Final Report of the WPA Program, 1935–43. Washington, DC: Government Printing Office, 1947.

Foulois, Benjamin D., and C. V. Glines. *From the Wright Brothers to the Astronauts: The Memoirs of Major General Benjamin D. Foulois*. New York: McGraw-Hill, 1968.

Fraser, Chelsea. *Heroes of the Air*. New York: Thomas Crowell Company, 1942.

———. *The Story of Aircraft*. New York: Thomas Crowell Company, 1939.

Freidel, Frank. *Franklin Roosevelt: A Rendezvous with Destiny*. Boston: Little, Brown and Company, 1990.

Frederick, John H. *Commercial Air Transportation*. Homewood, IL: Richard D. Irwin, 1961.

Freyer, Tony Allan. *Justice Hugo Black and Modern America*. Tuscaloosa: University of Alabama Press, 1990.

Fritzsche, Peter. *A Nation of Fliers: German Aviation in the Popular Imagination*. Cambridge: Harvard University Press, 1992.

Fulbright, Jim. *Aviation in Tennessee: Tennessee's Aviation History in the Stories of People, Places, and Events*. Goodlettesville, TN: Mid-South Publications, 1998.

Gaudry, Marc, and Robert Mayes, eds. *Taking Stock of Air Liberalization*. Boston: Kluwer Academic Publishers, 1999.

Gibbs-Smith, Charles Harvard. *Aviation: A Historical Survey from Its Origins to the End of World War II*. London: Her Majesty's Stationery Office, 1970.

Gilbert, Glen. *Air Traffic Control: The Uncrowded Sky*. Washington, DC: Smithsonian Institution Press, 1973.

Glines, Carrol V. *The Saga of Air Mail*. Princeton, NJ: Van Nostrand, 1968.

Goldstein, Lawrence. *The Flying Machine and Modern Literature*. Bloomington: Indiana University Press, 1986.

Hamilton, James. *The Power to Probe: A Study of Congressional Investigations*. New York: Random House, 1976.

Hawley, Ellis W. *The New Deal and the Problem of Monopoly: A Study in Economic Ambivalence*. 2nd ed. New York: Fordham University Press, 1995.

———, ed. *Herbert Hoover as Secretary of Commerce: Studies in New Era Thought and Practice*. Iowa City: University of Iowa Press, 1981.

———, Murry N. Rothbard, Robert F. Himmerburg, and Gary D. Nash. *Herbert Hoover and the Crisis of American Capitalism*. Cambridge: Schenkman Publishing Company, 1973.

Haynesworth, Leslie, and David Toomey. *Amelia Earhart's Daughters: The Wild and Glorious Story of American Women Aviators from World War II to the Dawn of the Space Age*. New York: William Morrow and Co., 1998.

Heppenheimer, T. A. *Turbulent Skies: The History of Commercial Aviation*. New York: John Wiley and Sons, 1986.

Hofstadter, Richard. *The Age of Reform: From Bryan to F.D.R.* New York: Vintage Books, 1955.

Hopkins, Harry L. *Spending to Save: The Complete Story of Relief*. New York: W. W. Norton, 1936.

Hudson, James J. *Hostile Skies: A Combat History of the American Air Service in World War I*. Syracuse, NY: Syracuse University Press, 1968.

Huthmacher, J. Joseph, and Warren I. Susman, eds. *Herbert Hoover and the Crisis of American Capitalism*. Cambridge, MA: Schenkman Publishing Company, 1973.

Josephson, Mathew. *Empire of the Air: Juan Trippe and the Struggle for World Airways*. New York: Harcourt, Brace and Company, 1944.

King, Harold J. "The Rate-Making Function of the Civil Aeronautics Board." *American Journal of Economics and Sociology* 1, no. 2 (January 1942): 167–90.

Kolko, Gabriel. *Railroads and Regulation, 1877–1916*. Princeton, NJ: Princeton University Press, 1965.

——. *The Triumph of Conservatism: A Reinterpretation of American History, 1900–1916*. New York: The Free Press, 1963.

Komons, Nick A. *Bonfires to Beacons: Federal Civil Aviation Policy under the Air Commerce Act, 1926–1938*. Washington, DC: Smithsonian Institution Press, 1989.

Krog, Carl E., and William R. Tanner. *Herbert Hoover and the Republican Era: A Reconsideration*. Lanham, MD: University Press of America, 1984.

Launius, Roger D., and Janet R. Daly Bednarek, eds. *Reconsidering a Century of Flight*. Chapel Hill: University of North Carolina Press, 2002.

Lawson, Alan. *A Commonwealth of Hope: The New Deal Response to Crisis*. Baltimore, MD: The Johns Hopkins University Press, 2006.

Leary, William M., Jr. *Aerial Pioneers: The U.S. Airmail Service, 1918–1927*. Washington, DC: Smithsonian Institution Press, 1985.

——. "At the Dawn of Commercial Aviation: Inglis M. Uppercru and Aeromarine Airways." *Business History Review* 53, no. 2 (Summer 1979): 180–93.

Lee, David D. "Herbert Hoover and the Development of Commercial Aviation, 1921–1926." *Business History Review* 58, no. 1 (Spring 1984): 78–102.

——. "Senator Black's Investigation of the Airmail, 1933–1934." *The Historian* 53, no. 3 (Spring 1991): 423–42.

Lehrer, Henry R. *Flying the Beam: Navigating the Early U.S. Airmail Airways, 1917—1941*. West Lafayette, IN: Purdue University Press, 2014.

Leighninger, Robert D., Jr. *Long-Range Public Investment: The Forgotten Legacy of the New Deal*. Columbia: University of South Carolina Press, 2007.

Lerner, Michael A. *Dry Manhattan: Prohibition in New York City*. Cambridge, MA: Harvard University Press, 2007.

Leuchtenburg, William E. *Franklin D. Roosevelt and the New Deal: 1932–1940*. New York: Harper, 1963.

——. *Herbert Hoover*. New York: Times Books, 2009.

——. *The Perils of Prosperity, 1914–1932*. Chicago: University of Chicago Press, 1993.

Levine, Michael E. "Regulating Airmail Transportation." *Journal of Law and Economics* 18, no. 2 (October 1975): 317–59.

Lewis, David W., ed. *Airline Executives and Federal Regulation: Case Studies in American Enterprise from the Airmail Era to the Dawn of the Jet Age*. Columbus: Ohio State University Press, 2000.

——, and Wesley Phillips Newton. *Delta: History of an Airline*. Athens: University of Georgia Press, 1979.

——, and William F. Trimble. *The Airway to Everywhere: A History of All American Aviation, 1937–1953*. Pittsburgh: University of Pittsburgh Press, 1988.

Lipsner, Benjamin B. *The Airmail: From Jennies to Jets*. New York: Wilcox & Follett Company, 1951.

Lyons, Eugene. *Herbert Hoover: A Biography*. Garden City, NY: Doubleday & Company, 1948.

MacDonald, Austin F. "Airport Problems of American Cities." *Annals of the American Academy of Political and Social Science*, Vol. 151, *Postwar Progress in Child Welfare* (September 1930).

Manchester, William. *The Glory and the Dream: A Narrative History of America, 1932–1972*. New York: Bantam Books, 1974.

Maynard, Crosby. *Flight Plan for Tomorrow: The Douglas Story*. Santa Monica, CA: Douglas Aircraft Company, 1962.

McGraw, Thomas K., ed. *Regulation in Perspective: Historical Essays*. Cambridge, MA: Harvard University Press, 1981.

McManus, John C. *Deadly Sky: The American Combat Airman in World War II*. Novato, CA: Presidio, 2002.

Meyer, John R., and Clinton V. Oster, eds. *Airline Deregulation: The Early Experience*. Boston: Auburn House Publishing Company, 1981.

Mosley, Leonard. *Lindbergh: A Biography*. New York: Doubleday & Company, 1976.

Nalty, Bernard C., ed. *Winged Shield, Winged Sword: A History of the United States Air Force*. Washington, DC: United States Air Force, 1997.

Nash, Gerald D. *The Great Depression and World War II: Organizing America, 1933–1945*. New York: Bedford/St. Martins, 1979.

Nash, Lee, ed. *Understanding Herbert Hoover: Ten Perspectives*. Stanford, CA: Hoover Institution Press, 1987.

Nye, David E. *American Technological Sublime*. Cambridge: Massachusetts Institute of Technology Press, 1994.

Olsen, James Stuart. *Herbert Hoover and the Reconstruction Finance Corporation*. Ames: Iowa State University Press, 1977.

Overy, Richard J. *The Air War, 1939–1945*. Washington, DC: Potomac Books, 2005.

Patton, Edwin P. "Transportation Development." In *Heart of the Valley: A History of Knoxville, Tennessee*, edited by Lucile Deaderick, 178–236. Knoxville: East Tennessee Historical Society, 1976.

Pedigree of Champions: Boeing since 1916. Seattle, WA: Boeing, 1985.

Phillips-Fein, Kim. *Invisible Hands: The Businessmen's Crusade against the New Deal*. New York: W. W. Norton, 2009.

Pisano, Dominick. *To Fill the Skies with Pilots: The Civilian Pilot Training Program, 1939–1946*. Champaign: University of Illinois Press, 1993.

——, ed. *The Airplane in American Culture*. Ann Arbor: University of Michigan Press, 2003.

Pisano, Dominick, and F. Robert van der Linden. *Charles Lindbergh and the Spirit of St. Louis*. Washington, DC: Smithsonian Institution Press, 2002.

Pisano, Dominick, and Cathleen S. Lewis, eds. *Air and Space Historiography: An Annotated Bibliography*. New York: Garland Publishing, 1988.

Provenzo, Eugene F., Jr. "The St. Petersburg–Tampa Airboat Line." *Florida Historical Quarterly* 58, no. 1 (July 1979): 72–77.

Public Works Administration. *America Builds: The Record of the PWA*. Washington, DC: Government Printing Office, 1939.

Rae, John B. "Financial Problems of the American Aircraft Industry, 1906–1940." *Business History Review* 39, no. 1 (Spring 1965): 99–114.

Rich, Doris L. *Amelia Earhart: A Biography*. Washington, DC: Smithsonian Institution Press, 1989.

———. *Jackie Cochran: Pilot in the Fastest Lane*. Gainesville: University Press of Florida, 2007.

Rickenbacker, Edward V. *Rickenbacker*. Englewood Cliffs, NJ: Prentice-Hall, 1967.

Rose, Mark, Bruce Seely, and Paul Barrett. *The Best Transportation System in the World: Railroads, Trucks, Airlines, and American Public Policy in the Twentieth Century*. Columbus: Ohio State University Press, 2006.

Rust, Daniel L. *Flying across America: The Airline Passenger Experience*. Norman: University of Oklahoma Press, 2009.

Sampson, Anthony. *Empire of the Sky: The Politics, Contests and Cartels of World Airlines*. New York: Random House, 1984.

Schary, Philip B. "The Civil Aeronautics Board and the All-Cargo Airlines: The Early Years." *Business History Review* 41, no. 3 (Autumn 1967): 272–84.

Schlesinger, Arthur, Jr. *The Age of Roosevelt: The Coming of the New Deal*. Boston: Houghton Mifflin, 1959.

Schwartz, Bonnie Fox. *The Civil Works Administration, 1933–1934: The Business of Emergency Employment in the New Deal*. Princeton, NJ: Princeton University Press, 1984.

Shaw, B. Russell. "What Is an Airport?" *Airports* 1 (December 1928).

Sherry, Michael S. *The Rise of American Airpower: The Creation of Armageddon*. New Haven, CT: Yale University Press, 1987.

Smith, Henry Ladd. *Airways: The History of Commercial Aviation in the United States*. New York: Knopf, 1942.

Smith, Jason Scott. *Building New Deal Liberalism: The Political Economy of Public Works, 1933–1956*. New York: Cambridge University Press, 2006.

Smith, Jean Edward. *FDR*. New York: Random House, 2007.

Solberg, Carl. *Conquest of the Skies: A History of Commercial Aviation in America*. Boston: Little, Brown and Company, 1979.

Taylor, Nick. *American Made: The Enduring Legacy of the WPA: When FDR Put the Nation to Work*. New York: Bantam Books, 2009.

van der Linden, F. Robert. *Airlines and Airmail: The Post Office and the Birth of the Commercial Aviation Industry*. Lexington: University Press of Kentucky, 2002.

Van Vleck, Jenifer. *Empire of the Air: Aviation and the American Ascendency*. Cambridge, MA: Harvard University Press, 2013.

Vietor, Richard H. K. "Contrived Competition: Airline Regulation and Deregulation, 1925–1988." *Business History Review* 64, no. 1 (Spring 1990): 61–108.

Vorderman, Don. *The Great Air Races*. New York: Bantam, 1969.

Ware, Susan. *Beyond Suffrage: Women in the New Deal*. Cambridge, MA: Harvard University Press, 1987.

Weirather, Larry. *The China Clipper, Pan American Airways, and Popular Culture*. Jefferson, NC: McFarland and Company Publishers, 2007.

West, Carroll Van. *Tennessee's New Deal Landscape: A Guidebook*. Knoxville: University of Tennessee Press, 2001.

Williams, J. Kerwin. *Grants-in-Aid under the Public Works Administration: A Study in Federal-State-Local Relations*. New York: Columbia University Press, 1939.

Wilson, Joan Hoff. *Herbert Hoover: Forgotten Progressive*. Prospect Heights, IL: Waveland Press, 1975.

Wohl, Robert. *A Passion for Wings: Aviation and the Western Imagination, 1908–1918*. New Haven, CT: Yale University Press, 1994.

———. *The Spectacle of Flight: Aviation and the Western Imagination, 1920–1950*. New Haven, CT: Yale University Press, 2005.

Zinn, Howard. "The Limits of the New Deal." In *The Politics of History*. Champaign: University of Illinois Press, 1990.

Dissertations and Thesis

Ashcroft, Bruce Alan. "Why We Wanted Wings: American Aviation and Representations of the Air Force in the Years before World War II." PhD diss., University of Texas at Austin, 2003.

Call, Stephen Charles. "A People's Air Force: Air Power and American Popular Culture, 1945–1965." PhD diss., Ohio State University, 1997.

Carlson, Erik Dunton. "The Origins and Development of the Civil Aeronautics Board and the Economic Regulation of Domestic Airlines, 1934–1953." PhD diss., Texas Tech University, 1996.

Colvin, Susan Elaine. "A History of International Commercial Aviation, 1903–1939." PhD diss., University of Arkansas, 1993.

Douglas, Deborah Gwen. "The Invention of Airports: A Political, Economic and Technological History of Airports in the United States, 1919–1939." PhD diss., University of Pennsylvania, 1996.

Johnson, Christopher Derek. "Markets in the Air: The Development of American Aviation Culture, 1918–1934." PhD diss., Northwestern University, 1998.

Johnson, Randall D. "Herbert Hoover and the Aeronautical Telecommunications System: His Influence on its Development and Deployment as Secretary of Commerce, 1921–1927." PhD diss., Ohio University, 2000.

Jones, Howard G. "Entrepreneurial Success and Failure in the Aviation Industry: The History of the Waco Aircraft Company, 1919–1963." PhD diss., Johns Hopkins University, 2000.

Karsner, Douglas George. "'Leaving on a Jet Plane': Commercial Aviation, Airports, and Post-Industrial American Society." PhD diss., Temple University, 1993.

Leonhirth, Janene Gupton. "They Also Flew: Women Aviators in Tennessee, 1922–1950." Master's thesis, Middle Tennessee State University, 1990.

Michaels, Patricia Ann. "The Development of Passenger Service on Commercial Airlines, 1926–1930." PhD diss., University of Kansas, 1980.

Millward, Elizabeth. "Scaling Airspace: Gender in the British Imperial Skies, 1922–1937." PhD diss., York University (Canada), 2003.

Rand, Lawrence A. "The McNary-Watres Air Mail Act of 1930: Herbert Hoover and His Impact upon the Commercial Airline Industry in the United States." PhD diss., New York University, 1998.

Rust, Daniel Lee. "Flying Across America: The Evolving Transcontinental Airline Passenger Experience, 1927–1960." PhD diss., University of Idaho, 2003.

Shaw, Eric J. "Controls on Developing Technology: The United States Commercial Air Transportation System during the Interwar Period, 1919–1939." PhD diss., Salve Regina University, 2000.

Smith, Rhonda Lynn. "Jacqueline Cochran: An American Aviator in Peace and War." PhD diss., University of Kentucky, 1999.

Snider, Jill D. "Flying to Freedom: African-American Visions of Aviation, 1910–1927." PhD diss., University of North Carolina at Chapel Hill, 1995.

Stratton, Scott David. "The End of Aviation's Honeymoon and 'The World's Greatest Air Race': The New Age of Airmindedness and the 1934 MacRobertson Air Competition." PhD diss., Arizona State University, 2007.

van der Linden, Frank Robert. "Progressives and the Post Office: Air Mail and the Creation of United States Air Transportation." PhD diss., George Washington University, 1997.

Van Vleck, Jennifer. "No Distant Places: Commercial Aviation and American Globalism, 1915–1968." PhD diss., Yale University, 2008.

Index

CPSIA information can be obtained
at www.ICGtesting.com
Printed in the USA
BVHW070539291218
536643BV00002B/2/P

9 781623 497217